The Philosophy of William James
An Introduction

This is an accessible introduction to the full range of the philosophy of William James. It portrays that philosophy as containing a deep division between a promethean type of pragmatism and a passive mysticism. The pragmatist James conceives of truth and meaning as a means to control nature and make it do our bidding. The mystic James eschews the use of concepts in order to penetrate to the inner conscious core of all being, including nature at large. Richard Gale attempts to harmonize these pragmatic and mystical perspectives.

This introduction is drawn from and complements the author's much more comprehensive and systematic study, *The Divided Self of William James*, a volume that has received the highest critical praise. With its briefer compass and nontechnical style this new introduction should help to disseminate the key elements of one of the great modern philosophers to an even wider readership.

Richard M. Gale is Professor Emeritus at the University of Pittsburgh and Adjunct Professor at the University of Tennessee, Knoxville.

The Philosophy of William James

An Introduction

RICHARD M. GALE

University of Pittsburgh, Professor Emeritus
University of Tennessee, Knoxville

PUBLISHED BY THE PRESS SYNDICATE OF THE UNIVERSITY OF CAMBRIDGE
The Pitt Building, Trumpington Street, Cambridge, United Kingdom

CAMBRIDGE UNIVERSITY PRESS
The Edinburgh Building, Cambridge CB2 2RU, UK
40 West 20th Street, New York, NY 10011-4211, USA
477 Williamstown Road, Port Melbourne, VIC 3207, Australia
Ruiz de Alarcón 13, 28014 Madrid, Spain
Dock House, The Waterfront, Cape Town 8001, South Africa

http://www.cambridge.org

First published 2005

Printed in the United States of America

Typeface ITC New Baskerville 10/13.5 pt.   *System* LATEX 2_ε [TB]

A catalog record for this book is available from the British Library.

Library of Congress Cataloging in Publication Data
Gale, Richard M., 1932–
The Philosophy of William James : an introduction / Richard M. Gale.
p. cm.
Rev. ed. of: The divided self of William James. 1999.
Includes bibliographical references and index.
ISBN 0-521-84028-7 – ISBN 0-521-54955-8 (pb.)
1. James, William, 1842–1910. I. Gale, Richard M., 1932– Divided self of
William James. II. Title.
B915.J24G35   2004
191–dc22   20040456000

ISBN 0 521 84028 7 hardback
ISBN 0 521 54955 8 paperback

For Mari Mori
Mother-in-Law Extraordinaire

Contents

Preface

This book is a shorter and more popular version of my 1999 book, *The Divided Self of William James*. To achieve this I had to cut out all references to the vast secondary source literature and greatly simplify my discussion by omitting most of the technical parts of the book, such as would be accessible only to professional philosophers. I thank Terence Moore for initially suggesting this project and helping me as I proceeded, especially for checking my natural proclivity to be overly technical and rigorous, that is, boring.

The William James that I present is *my* William James. Any interpretation of James that purports to be *the* correct one thereby shows itself not to be. For James sought a maximally rich and suggestive philosophy, one in which everyone could see themselves reflected, being like a vast ocean out of which each could haul whatever is wanted, provided the right-sized net is used. But there isn't any one net that is *the* right-sized one. When a philosopher aims for maximum richness and suggestiveness it will result in numerous surface tensions and inconsistencies in the text. This gives great leeway to interpreters, which is just what James wanted, because it forces them to philosophize on their own. Too often sympathetic interpreters attempt to protect a great philosopher against his hostile critics by watering down his philosophy so that it winds up agreeing with our common-sense beliefs. They unwittingly trivialize the history of philosophy by rendering both the philosopher and his critics muddleheads, he for not being able clearly to say what he meant and they for failing to see that he was just

telling us what we already believed. *My* William James, in contrast, will
be the bold and original James, the one who rightly triggered a storm
of passionate criticism, both positive and negative. *Pace* Wittgenstein's
perverse slogan that philosophy should leave everything just as it is, I
think a philosophy should present a new vision that shakes things up by
challenging many of our common beliefs. My motto as an interpreter
is, "Don't trivialize the history of philosophy." When in doubt, go with
the exciting version of the philosopher.

Introduction

William James (1842–1910) had a peripatetic childhood in which his father, the theologian Henry James, Sr., hustled him and his four younger siblings, among whom was the novelist Henry James, Jr., from one European nation to another in search of an adequate education. After a brief stint as a painting student of William Morris Hunt he entered the Lawrence Scientific School at Harvard in 1861. Upon graduation in 1864 he enrolled in the Harvard Medical School, completing the M.D. degree in 1869, with a year off to participate in Louis Agassiz's research expedition to Brazil. After suffering serious ill health and depression from 1869 to 1872, he became an instructor in physiology at Harvard, where he spent his entire career until his retirement in 1907. He rapidly moved up the academic ladder, becoming instructor in anatomy and physiology in 1873, assistant professor of physiology in 1876, assistant professor of philosophy in 1880, full professor in 1885, and professor of psychology in 1889.

The best way to characterize James's philosophy is that it is a passionate quest to have it all, to grab with all the gusto he can, which, for James, means achieving the maximum richness of experience. This requires having each of his many selves, which includes the scientist, moralist, and mystic, fully realize itself. Unfortunately, this grand quest is thwarted by the apparent tensions and conflicts between the perspectives of these different selves. The scientist accepts determinism and epiphenomenalism in a world that is stripped of everything that would give it human value and purpose. But for the moralist there are undetermined acts of spiritual causation in a nonbifurcated world. The mystic, in opposition to both of these perspectives, eschews concepts completely so that it can achieve at least a partial unity with the conscious interiors of not only other persons, including supernatural ones, but nature at large. The clash between his mystical self and these other selves will turn out to be the deeper and more intractable division within James. For whereas his pragmatism could serve as a reconciler but not as a unifier between his scientific and moralistic selves by showing that they both employed concepts to gain a promethean power to control their environment, with truth being based on how successfully they did this, it is of no avail in resolving this clash. For the mystical stance requires overcoming this promethean self.

In giving dramatic voice to this clash James became the representative philosopher of New England culture in the nineteenth century. On the one hand, it is inspired by the Darwinian view of man as engaged in a never ending struggle to survive and, on the other, by the pioneer ideal of conquering a hostile environment so that it will bend to our purposes. It has unbridled optimism that science will be able to supply us with the needed technology to achieve this promethean goal of becoming the masters of nature. But coupled with this quest is a deep mystical strain that finds expression in Concord transcendentalism and the nature mysticism of writers like Emerson, Wordsworth, and Longfellow. Herein it is our active, promethean self that must be overcome so that we can enter into I–Thou type relations with reality through acts of conceptless sympathetic intuition. What follows is a brief overview of my book whose purpose is to supply the reader with a synoptic vision of how the different chapters hang together.

Chapter 1 shows how James's Darwinian-based prometheanism gives rise to a type of utilitarian ethical theory that holds us to be morally obligated always to act so as to maximize desire–satisfaction over desire–dissatisfaction, that is, to act in a way that enables us, if not to have it all, to have as much of it as we can under the given circumstances. Because we are determined by our very biological nature to be always intent on satisfying some felt need or desire, it seems reasonable to make the attainment of this our moral ideal. The challenge of the deontologist, who holds there to be intrinsically valuable states, such as justice, will figure prominently in the discussion, the outcome of which will be that James must find some way to accommodate these deontological moral intuitions within his desire-maximizing ethical theory.

Chapter 2 shows that belief is an *action* for James in the sense that we can either believe at will (intentionally, voluntarily, on purpose) or at will do things, such as acting as if we believe, that shall self-induce belief. When this is combined with our moral obligation always to *act* so as to maximize desire–satisfaction, it follows that we are always morally obligated to believe in a manner that maximizes desire–satisfaction. This yields the following syllogism.

1. We are always morally obligated to act so as to maximize desire–satisfaction over desire–dissatisfaction.
2. Belief is an action.
3. Therefore, we are always morally obligated to believe in a manner that maximizes desire–satisfaction over desire–dissatisfaction.

Thus, from the moral duty to act so as to have it all, or as much of it as the circumstances permit, the moral duty to believe in a way that accomplishes this follows when it is added that belief is an action.

James, however, would not accept this syllogism unless it is added to premise 2 that belief is a *free* action, for James held that *ought* implies *can* in the full-blooded sense of *freely* can. If we have a moral duty to believe in a certain manner we must be free to do so. Chapter 3 presents James's libertarian theory of free will and shows how he applied it to belief itself. Chapter 4 explores his famous doctrine of the will to believe that justifies our believing without adequate evidence when doing so will help to maximize desire–satisfaction. The evidentially nonwarranted proposition that we are free to believe becomes a prime candidate for a will-to-believe type option that justifies our believing that we can freely believe at will, thereby making our beliefs subject to the duty prescribed in premise 1 in the preceding syllogism.

Because the true is what we ought to believe, it follows that a proposition is true when believing it maximizes desire–satisfaction. This attempt to base epistemology on the moral duty to try to have it all is James's boldest and most original contribution to philosophy and is the topic of Chapter 5, wherein it is shown how James's highly revisionary analysis of truth and belief acceptance is motivated and justified by his promethean quest to have it all. James's analysis of truth in terms of what maximizes desire–satisfaction for believers will be found to incorporate guiding principles or instrumental rules enjoining us to have beliefs that are both consistent and epistemically warranted, and to follow a conservative strategy when it becomes necessary to revise our web of belief; however, we are permitted to violate these rules when doing so on some occasion will maximize desire–satisfaction.

Chapter 6 explores his future-oriented pragmatic theory of meaning and reference, which also is fueled by his promethean quest to gain power to control our environment so as to realize our goals, and the theory of "truth" that falls out of it on the assumption that a theory of meaning gives truth conditions for the proposition expressed by a sentence. This theory is at odds with the one in Chapter 5 based on maximizing desire–satisfaction. The clash will be neutralized by having James reject this assumption, thereby interpreting the pragmatic theory of meaning as giving conditions for a proposition to be epistemically warranted, rather than true, thus the reason for the scare quotation marks around "truth" in the title of Chapter 6, "The Semantics of 'Truth.'"

James appeals to his promethean ethical theory of belief formation and acceptance to legitimate letting each of his many selves take its turn at seeking self-realization, thereby enabling him to have it all. For whether we take the stance to the world of the scientist, moral agent, melioristic theist, or mystic we employ the same promethean pragmatic theory for determining the meaning, reference, and truth of whatever we might say from these different perspectives. Unfortunately, the magical elixir of methodological univocalism does not go far enough in enabling each of his many selves to see the light of day and flourish, for there are clashes between the claims and assumptions made by these different selves from their different perspectives – and the one thing that James personally could not abide was a contradiction.

The scientific self accepts universal determinism, epiphenomenalism, and the bifurcation between man and nature, while the moral agent self believes that there are undetermined acts of spiritual causation in a world that has human meaning. Furthermore, whereas both use concepts as teleological instruments for gaining power to control the world of changing objects, the mystical self eschews concepts altogether in order to penetrate to the inner conscious core of a cotton-candyish reality through an act of sympathetic intuition. How are the clashes between the claims made from these different perspectives, each of which supposedly is a requirement for "having it all," to be reconciled?

Chapter 7 examines a strategy that James had for neutralizing these seeming clashes. Let each of his many selves be directed to its own world with no world qualifying as *the* real world absolutely or *simpliciter*. The predicate "is real" or "is the actual world" is not the monadic predicate it grammatically appears to be, but instead is the disguised three place predicate "___ is real for self ___ at time ___." When used by a person on some occasion this predicate gets filled out as "A certain world *W* is real for me now." This doctrine, which aptly could be called *ontological relativism*, allows us, as our interests and purposes change, successively to take different worlds to be the real or actual world without inconsistency.

The seeming inconsistencies between the claims made by our different selves are neutralized by restricting them to a certain perspective or world. *Qua* the tough-minded scientist, James affirms determinism and that there is no psychosis without neurosis, but *qua* the tender-minded moral agent, he rejects both and instead accepts the reality of undetermined acts of spiritual causation. *Qua* promethean man of action, he carves reality up into a plurality of discrete individuals in terms of pragmatically based classificatory systems, but *qua* mystic, he eschews concepts altogether so as to achieve a deep unification between himself and a surrounding mother sea of consciousness. And so on, and so on. What is real depends upon the purposes and interests that are freely selected by a self. The doctrine of ontological relativism turns out to be an instrument forged by James's promethean self that aids his endeavor to have it all.

James's highly influential theory of Pure Experience, often called "neutral monism," held that no individual is intrinsically physical or mental but becomes one or the other when we *take* it in a certain way by placing it in some temporal sequence of events. Whether a sequence is physical or mental depends on the manner in which its members function in relation to each other, in particular whether or not they stand in nomically based causal relations with each other in the manner described by Kant in his Second Analogy of Experience. I will argue that the theory of pure experience was implicitly restricted to the world of sensible realities and had the reconciling function of neutralizing clashes that arose between the claims of realists and idealists as to the true nature of these realities and the manner in which "inner" states of consciousness are hooked up with "outer" physical states. Through the dissolution of this pseudoproblem our intelligence is freed from the coils of traditional epistemology so that it can more effectively perform its promethean function.

The Antipromethean Mystic

Prometheanism, however, is not the whole story about James's philosophy, as many commentators would have it. For coexisting with his promethean self was a mystical self, and ultimately it was the mystical self that had its way, or at least the final word, quite literally since mysticism is the dominant theme of his final two books, *A Pluralistic Universe* and *Some Problems of Philosophy*. Whereas his promethean self wants to ride herd on objects so as to control them for his own ends, his mystical self wants to become intimate with them by entering into their inner conscious life so as to become unified with them, though not in a way that involves complete numerical identity, for James always favored pluralistic mysticism, such as is found within the Western theistic tradition, over its monistic Eastern version. But what James most craved was not unification with others but unification among his many selves that continually threatened to render him schizophrenic through disintegration into the sort of split personality that so fascinated him in the research of Janet.

This quest for intimacy, and ultimately union, between himself and others, as well as among his many selves, begins with his giving pride of place to introspection over objective causal analyses.

Chapter 8 shows how James's analysis of personal identity over time is based exclusively on what is introspectively vouchsafed to each individual.

Chapter 9 explores James's attempt to "I–Thou" other persons by projecting onto them what he finds when he introspects his own mind. By an act of empathetic intuition he enters into the inner conscious life of these Thous. By discovering this inner life, which is what bestows significance on their lives, they cease to be an *It* to be used by his promethean self and become something to be cherished and respected because each has its own special way of experiencing the world and finding some meaning in it. Whereas his promethean self accepts the ethical rule of maximizing desire–satisfaction, his mystical self enriches this with a democratic deontological principle that persons must, in virtue of their possessing a unique inner life that renders their life significant, be left free to flourish in the manner that they deem best, provided that they don't interfere with the right of others to do likewise. This entails that they cannot be used as mere means to realize the maximization of desire–satisfaction. Thus, there is a clash between the maximizing ethics of prometheanism and the mystically based deontological ethics of reverence and respect for the autonomy of others. The I–Thou experiences between man and man get extended to I–Thou experiences between man and nature at large and, finally, to supernatural spirits, including God, also called the *More* and the *surrounding mother-sea-of-consciousness*.

But James's quest for intimacy and union does not stop with I–Thou-ing other *persons*, both natural and supernatural. He wants to accomplish this for reality at large. To accomplish this, as Chapter 10 demonstrates, he must learn how to jettison all concepts so that he can have a pure intuition of the inner life of all these others. He is aided in this endeavor by a string of a priori arguments that show the impossibility of concepts being true of reality. These arguments play the same role in James's quest for intimacy and union as do koans in Zen Buddhism: In both cases the subject is shocked into a new form of consciousness through the dialectical activity of immersing herself in the paradoxes, or koans. The mystical James must dispense with all concepts because they are the agents of his active, promethean self through their presenting this self with recipes for using objects.

To discover the true nature or essence of things he must begin by introspecting what goes on in his own consciousness and then project what he finds onto the world at large, as was the case with I–Thou-ing other persons. What he finds through introspection of what goes on when he endures over time and acts intentionally so as to bring something about is a fusing or melting together of neighboring conscious stages; he then assumes that there is a similar sort of mushing together between all spatial and temporal neighbors, the result of which is panpsychism because only in consciousness can such mushing together occur. James's quest for intimacy with the universe through projecting what is introspectively vouchsafed onto external reality, thus, is also a quest for unification between both the subject and objects, as well as between the objects themselves. Thus, the quest for intimacy and unification that begins with the sort of I–Thou experiences depicted in Chapter 9 reaches its full zenith in the mystical experiences of unification between man and nature that are the subject of Chapter 10. It is not only the full-blooded mystical experiences of absorption into a surrounding mother-sea-of-consciousness that are salvific but also the conceptless Bergsonian intuitions of the flowing into each other of spatial and temporal neighbors.

At the root of the clash between his promethean and mystical self is his ambiguous attitude toward evil, his both wanting and not wanting to believe that we have absolute assurance that we are safe because all evils are only illusory or ultimately conquered. When James was in his healthy promethean frame of mind he tingled all over at the thought that we are engaged in a Texas Death Match with evil, without any assurance of eventual victory, only the possibility of victory. This possibility forms the basis of his religion of meliorism. But there is a morbid side to James's nature, a *really* morbid side, that "can't get no satisfaction" in the sort of religion that his promethean pragmatism legitimates. In order to "help him make it through the night" he needs a mystically based religion that gives him a sense of absolute safety and peace that comes through union with an encompassing spiritual reality. The assurance that all is well comes not from philosophical theodicies, for James always charged them with being intellectually dishonest, but from what is vouchsafed by mystical experiences of unification.

The best way to bring out his ambivalent attitude toward evil is through an account of the two different attitudes he took toward his famous experience of existential angst in 1868, when he came upon a hideous epileptic youth in an insane asylum. He gave the following description of this experience.

That shape am I, I felt, potentially. Nothing that I possess can defend me against that fate, if the hour for it should strike for me as it struck for him. There was such a horror of him, and such a perception of my own merely momentary discrepancy from him, that it was as if something hitherto solid within my breast gave way entirely, and I became a mass of quivering fear. (*VRE* 134)

The sight of the idiot made James aware of the radical contingency of existence, that everything hangs by a very delicate thread that can snap at any moment, no matter what we might do, freely or otherwise.

In his 1884 introduction to *The Literary Remains of the Late Henry James*, James alludes impersonally to the existential angst experience when he says: "we are all potentially sick men. The sanest and best of us are of one clay with the lunatics and prison inmates" (*ERM* 62). Unlike his father, who must escape the existential angst that evil occasions by postulating some absolute being or God who gives assurance of salvation and safety, James's response is to "turn a deaf ear to the thought of being" and instead to suck it up and courageously follow the melioristic route of living the morally strenuous life without any assurance of success. He concludes his Introduction with one of the most tender and diplomatic, yet cutting, sentences ever written in which he contrasts himself with his beloved father.

Meanwhile, the battle is about us, and we are its combatants, steadfast or vacillating, as the case may be. It will be a hot fight indeed if the friends of philosophic moralism should bring to the service of their ideal, so different from that of my father, a spirit even remotely resembling the life-long devotion of his faithful heart. (*ERM* 63)

But, surprise of surprises, eighteen years later in *The Varieties of Religious Experience* (45–6), immediately upon his anonymous description of his experience of existential angst, he draws an opposite conclusion from it. The message now is that our salvation must be found not in living the morally strenuous life but rather in finding an abiding sense of safety and peace through absorption into a higher surrounding spiritual reality. It is as if he is treading the same path as his former promethean self but now goes in a diametrically opposed direction when he gets to the crucial fork in the road at which sits the epileptic youth.

The theme of the insufficiency of meliorism and the healthy-minded outlook in general is repeated over and over again in this book. We are told that "the breath of the sepulchre surrounds" our natural happiness (*VRE* 118), that the advice to the morbid-minded person upon whom there falls "the joy-destroying chill" of "Cheer up, old fellow, you'll be all right erelong, if you will only drop your morbidness!" is "the very consecration of forgetfulness and superficiality"

(*VRE* 118–19). What we need is a "life not correlated with death, a health not liable to illness, a kind of good that will not perish, a good in fact that flies beyond the Goods of nature" (*VRE* 119). By experiencing absorption in a supernatural power, the "More" that surrounds our ordinary finite consciousness, we gain "an assurance of safety and a temper of peace, and, in relations to others, a preponderance of loving affection" that cannot "fail to steady the nerves, to cool the fever, and appease the fret, if one be conscious that, no matter what one's difficulties for the moment may appear to be, one's life as a whole is in the keeping of a power whom one can absolutely trust" (*VRE* 230, 383). Armed with such mystically-based assurance, James might now be able to view the epileptic youth without having one of his father's Swedenborgian vastation experiences, but I wouldn't bet on it because he never completely shook off his morbid-minded self. The clashes between James's promethean and mystical selves are synchronic rather than diachronic, for he never succeeded in becoming a unified self.

So far it has been seen that James's mystical self, unlike his promethean pragmatic self, dispenses with all concepts so that it can assume a passive stance for the purpose of becoming unified, at least partially, with the inner consciousness of whatever it experiences. As a consequence of these unifying experiences the mystical self adopts a deontological ethical stance toward others, in contrast to the desire–satisfaction maximizing project of the active self, and furthermore views evils as only illusory or sure to be overcome, assurance of which is denied to his promethean melioristic self. There are, however, even deeper clashes between these two selves over meaning and truth.

Whereas the promethean self, in virtue of always running ahead of itself into the future for the purpose of satisfying desires, adopts an exclusively future-oriented theory of meaning that identifies a concept with a set of conditionalized predictions, the mystical self interprets the meaning of mystical claims in terms of the present content of mystical experiences. The pragmatic James reduced the whole meaning of claims about God and the absolute to our being licensed to take a moral holiday or feel safe and secure because all is well, but the mystical James finds their meaning in experiences of a unifying presence; the star performer finally gets into the act. Furthermore, because the meaningful content of the mystic's assertion that there exists a unification is based on the content of the mystical experience itself, the truth of the assertion will depend primarily on whether the experience is objective or cognitive. And among the most important tests for this is the immediate luminosity, the feeling of reality, supplied by the experience.

The most important clash between James's pragmatic and mystical selves, however, does not emerge until Chapter 11. Herein the "Big Aporia" in James's philosophy will be brought out, this consisting in a clash between his pragmatic self's meta-doctrine of ontological relativism – that all reality claims must be relativized to a person at a time – and the absolute, nonrelativized reality claims he based on mystical experiences. An attempt will be made on his behalf to find a one world interpretation that will succeed in neutralizing this clash. If James is to succeed in having it all, some way must be found to unify his many selves so that they all inhabit one and the same world, rather than schizophrenically successively occupying different worlds. Only through a unification of the many worlds will James's many selves get unified, for James's intellectual scruples preclude a *personal* unification of his many selves that is not anchored in a *metaphysical* unification of the many worlds toward which their interests are directed. The latter task requires no less than a synthesizing of the outlooks of the East and the West, the masculine and the feminine, even that of time and eternity. Needless to say, there is a very good chance that this attempt will fail miserably, because things probably have been rigged so that we can't have it all. Chapter 11 has the daunting task of attempting a well-nigh impossible task.

PART I

THE PROMETHEAN PRAGMATIST

1

The Ethics of Prometheanism

In the Introduction it was claimed that this Master Syllogism unifies James's promethean pragmatism.

1. We are always morally obligated to act so as to maximize desire–satisfaction over desire–dissatisfaction.
2. Belief is an action.
3. Therefore, we are always morally obligated to believe in a manner that maximizes desire–satisfaction over desire–dissatisfaction.

Given the quest of James's promethean pragmatism to have it all, or at least as much of it as we mortals can realistically hope to have, it is understandable that he would be committed to premise 1, because having it all requires that all of our many selves have as many of their desires satisfied as is possible. It is the purpose of this chapter to locate this premise in James's text and explore some of the problems that it occasions.

James's only published effort to develop an ethical theory is in his 1891 essay on "The Moral Philosopher and the Moral Life," which was reprinted six years later in *The Will to Believe and Other Essays in Popular Philosophy*. It addresses in turn three different questions concerning the origin of our ethical intuitions, the meaning and status of ethical terms, and the casuistic rule for determining our moral duty in specific cases. His answer to the first question is that our moral intuitions, along with our esthetic ones, are determined by innate structures of our brain that resulted from chance mutations in the distant past that proved beneficial and took hold. This evolutionary account is identical with the one he gave in the final chapter of *The Principles of Psychology* of the origin of our stock of necessary truths. The moral intuitionists, therefore, were right in claiming that moral intuitions and sentiments were innate but wrong, as will be seen, for holding them to be a reading off of objective moral truths in some Platonic heaven.

James gives as an example of a brain-born moral intuition our gut feeling that it is morally wrong to use one person as a mere means to promote the pleasure or happiness of the majority, which intuition underlies the typical counter-examples to utilitarianism in which whatever it is that we want maximized gets maximized through an unjust act.

If the hypothesis were offered to us of a world in which . . . millions [are] kept permanently happy on the one simple condition that a certain lost soul on the far-off edge of things should lead a life of lonely torture, what except a special and independent sort of emotion can it be which would make us immediately feel, even though an impulse arose within us to clutch at the happiness offered, how hideous a thing would be its enjoyment when deliberately accepted as the fruit of such a bargain. (*WB* 144)

This "lost soul" example will come back to haunt James's own ethical theory.

The second question is called the "metaphysical" one because it has to do with the being and meaning of ethical terms. The meaning part of the question seems to fall outside metaphysics, because it concerns what we mean by various ethical predicates, a study that was later to be called "metaethics." James tries to determine the ontological status of ethical states by analyzing the meaning of ethical terms, and this he does through an analysis of our experiential reasons for predicating them. This is in accordance with James's general empirical practice of determining both what we mean by "X," as well as what it is to be X, from a genetic account of the experiences that lead us to say of something that it is X. Later it will be seen how he does this for the concepts of actuality, negation, truth, and self-identity. The outcome of his genetic analysis is that we mean by "good" whatever satisfies a *desire, demand,* or *claim,* for we take something to be good only when it does so. His unannounced shifting around among these three terms will be considered at the end of the chapter, and for the time being I will follow James in sloshing back and forth between them. Given that the good is what satisfies a desire, etc., and that we have an obligation to promote goodness, it follows that we have an obligation to see to it that any desire gets satisfied, unless doing so would result in the denial of a greater quantity of other desires. The obligation is a prima facie one that can be canceled only if the satisfaction of this one desire requires that a greater quantity of other desires go unsatisfied. This is what James means by his remark that "all demands as such are prima facie respectable" (*WB* 153). It is important to note that the obligation-creating power of a desire is completely independent of whose desire it is. When we factor in desires so as to determine what our moral duty is we must do so behind a veil of ignorance in which we do not know, or at least disregard, whose desires they are.

From this definition of "good" he draws the antiplatonic conclusion that prior to the desiring or demanding by sentient beings nothing is good or obligatory. No conscious beings, no normative situations, for "betterness is not a physical relation." There is no "abstract moral 'nature of things' existing antecedently to the concrete thinkers themselves with their ideals" (*WB* 147).

This way of dismissing objective moral truths – moral truths that exist independently of the desires and demands of conscious being – is too quick, for it fails to make the crucial distinction between concrete states of goodness and obligation, on the one hand, and general moral truths, on the other. What James's thought experiment shows is that, at best, there are no *concrete instances* of value and obligation in the world devoid of conscious beings, but this does not establish that there are no *general moral truths* that hold in this world, such as the hypothetical proposition that if there were to exist a conscious being who had a desire, then there would be the prima facie obligation to see to it that it gets satisfied. Plato's metaphorical description of the idea of the good floating about in a non–spatio-temporal realm like a bigger-than-life balloon in a Thanksgiving Day parade really amounts to the claim that there are such objective moral truths.

We know from James's remark that "the moral law [cannot] swing *in vacuo*" that he rejected these sort of abstract moral truths. But why? For there to be such an abstract moral truth there must be something that serves as the bearer or subject of this truth, and traditionally that has been an abstract proposition. But, in this essay, as well as in his writings on truth, James rejects abstract propositions as absurd. An abstract proposition is a nonempirical entity, because it is not locatable in space or time. The reason for this is that it is the denotatum of a noun "that" clause, such as "that Mary is baking pies," and it makes no sense to ask where or when is that Mary is baking pies. Abstract propositions are theoretical entities that are introduced for the purpose of explaining how one can believe falsely, disbelieve what was formerly believed, believe the same as does someone else, as well as how two sentences can mean the same thing. Furthermore, the adage that there are many things better left unsaid seems committed to there being language- and mind-independent propositions to serve as the bearers of truth values. James's nominalistic inclinations prevented him from taking seriously abstract propositions as the meanings of sentences, intentional accusatives, and truth-value bearers. But maybe he should have; for even though they are not themselves empirical entities, they might help to explain these empirical phenomena. James's empiricism, as will be seen in his treatment of the self, was sufficiently liberal as to permit the countenancing of nonempirical entities, provided they played a useful explanatory role.

James's "arguments" against abstract propositions consisted in nothing more than the heaping of rhetorical scorn on them, which is surprising since he knew the works of some able defenders of the theory of abstract propositions, among whom were Bolzano, Brentano (see *PP* 916–17), the early Moore and Russell; however, he was unacquainted with Frege, who was the leading proponent of the theory. In language that prefigured Wittgenstein's mocking account of propositions as queer "shadows of a fact," James says that they are "a sort of spiritual double or ghost of them [the facts]" (*MT* 156). When we believe falsely we believe something, but it cannot be a fact and thus must be a shadow of a fact. Wittgenstein mockingly paraphrases this claim as being like the assertion that it isn't Mr. Smith who hangs in the gallery but only his picture. In each case it is implied that there is a relation between numerically distinct independent entities. These "ghosts" are so *outré* as to be beneath contempt. The problem of propositions figures prominently in the discussion of truth in Chapters 5 and 6.

James makes the surprising claim that there would be concrete values and obligations if there were a single, isolated desirer, which sets him apart from his fellow pragmatists Mead and Dewey, who gave a socialized account of everything that pertained to the normative. This is one among many instances of James's Robinson Crusoe approach to philosophical topics; it will be seen that he thinks an isolated individual can even have her own private concepts and language. That he so committed himself finds partial textual support in his speaking of the world of the single desirer as "a *moral solitude*" and a world containing two desirers as having "twice as much of the ethical qualities in it as our moral solitude" (*WB* 146). The two-desirer world cannot have twice as much of the ethical qualities of the moral solitude world unless the latter has ethical qualities. The following quotation, however, really settles the matter: "Ethical relations . . . exist even in . . . a moral solitude if the thinker had various ideals which took hold of him in turn" (*WB* 159).

Before considering James's answer to the casuistic question, it is necessary to address a question concerning the status of James's claim that "*the essence of good is simply to satisfy demand*" (*WB* 153). Is this intended as a definition of what we ordinarily mean by "good"? If so, it falls victim to G. E. Moore's open question challenge, as do all naturalistic definitions of ethical terms in terms of sensible properties. For it does not seem redundantly pointless to ask, "Yes, action *A* satisfies demand, but is it good?"; and for this reason it is not contradictory to say, "Action *A* satisfies demand but it isn't good." But if "good" *means* satisfies demand, it would be contradictory. Plainly, if James's definition or analysis is intended to be a description of ordinary language, it is a miserable failure.

James is not going to be crushed by this departure from ordinary usage or common sense. In general, James has no compunctions against challenging them when there is good reason to do so. As will emerge in subsequent chapters, he knowingly gives revisionary analyses of truth, reference, the self, and material substances that challenge common sense. Whereas there is good textual evidence that he intended the latter to be revisionary analyses, it is thin in the case of his analysis of good. He never comes out and explicitly says that he is revising ordinary usage, but there are several good reasons for taking him to be doing just this. That many of his analyses are admittedly revisionary gives us some reason to think that he might be doing so here. And if there should be, as will now be shown, good reasons of both a philosophical and internal consistency sort for this analysis to be taken as revisionary, that gives the interpreter good reason to so take it.

The first reason is based on internal consistency. If James's definition of "good" is a description of ordinary usage, he would be committed to holding that a normative proposition is entailed by a purely descriptive one, one that describes only the empirical properties of an act, in this case that it satisfies a desire or demand. He would be required to say that the proposition that act A satisfies a demand or desire *logically entails* that act A is so far morally good. But we know that James would not accept this entailment. In his "Notes for Philosophy 4: Ethics – Recent English Contributions to Theistic Ethics (1888–1889)," he says in effect that no normative proposition is entailed by purely descriptive ones. "Things are either immediately admitted to be good, without discussion, or there is discussion. To prove a thing good, we must conceive it as belonging to a genus already admitted good. Every ethical proof therefore involves as its major premise an ethical proposition; every argument must end in some such proposition, admitted without proof" (*ML* 182). "The scientific and the Ethical judgment are logically distinct in nature" (*MEN* 301). That A satisfies a demand would entail that A is good only if we were to add the additional *normative* premise that whatever satisfies a demand is so far good.

Even though James's definition of "good" is not a description of ordinary usage, it nevertheless recognizes as an ultimate objective moral truth that whatever satisfies a desire or demand is so far good. This clashes with his earlier attack on platonism, for it would seem that there is for him at least this one abstract moral truth. This is the first instance of the making-discovering aporia, which will run throughout his philosophy. Initially, he strikes the promethean-making theme: We make things good by desiring them, yet that it is good that desires get satisfied seems to be something that is not made true by us but instead discovered. I am at a loss to extricate James from this aporia, about which a lot more will be said in later chapters.

Because James's revisionary analysis of "good" is prescriptive rather than descriptive, it does not follow that it cannot be motivated and justified. Various doctrines of James can be marshaled to support its acceptance. All of his admittedly revisionary analyses are motivated, at least in part, by his career-long commitment to empiricism. He will be found to object to our common sense concepts of truth, knowledge, and reference because they involve a mysterious, nonempirical saltatory relation, and he will replace them with concepts based on a genetic analysis of the experiential conditions under which we apply these concepts. By replacing nonempirical concepts with empirically based ones, we put our conceptual house in order so that we can make a more effective use of our intelligence in gaining mastery over our world.

Something similar justifies his revisionary analysis of good. The evils occasioned by these intuitive appeals to what is written down in the platonic heaven are that, in addition to being based on a mistaken view of the ontological status of moral truths and obligations, they lead to pointless, intractable disputes, which are a waste of time. This is the poverty of intuitionism.

This appeal to empiricism, however, hardly is sufficient to justify James's particular empirical account of good over numerous rival empirical accounts, such as utilitarianism. James's chief reason for preferring his particular empirical account over these rivals is based on a Darwinian view of human beings as determined by their biological nature to be always intent on satisfying some felt need or desire, even if the need or desire is not itself directly determined by biological states or processes. Because this is our nature, it seems reasonable to make the attainment of this our moral ideal. For what other end could we have? Given the scientific account, the normative conclusion appears to be the only practically viable alternative open to us human beings. Unlike natural law theorists, James would not claim that the scientific account of man's nature logically entails any normative proposition. Nevertheless, to ask whether it really is good for us to act in accordance with our nature is to raise an idle question.

I believe that there was another motivation for James's revisionary account of good in terms of desire–satisfaction based on his inveterate hipsterism, which was discussed in the Introduction. He was an experience junkie intent on having as many tingles and thrills as possible. This is the object of his quest to have it all. Because we have these tingles and thrills when our desires get satisfied, his absolute normative principle should be to satisfy desire, the more the better. James recognized that there is wide diversity among people in their psychological makeup, for example, in what their sense of rationality is. No doubt, he would acknowledge wide diversity regarding what they take the good life to be. Nevertheless, he assumed that most people were, like himself, out to have it all.

The answer that James will give to the casuistic question should be obvious by now: We are morally obligated "to satisfy at all times *as many demands as we can*. That act must be the best act, accordingly, which makes for the *best whole*, in the sense of awakening the least sum of dissatisfactions" (*WB* 155). It should be noted that James shifts from a maximizing of desire–satisfaction to a minimizing of desire–dissatisfaction formulation. Maybe he thought they came to the same thing. There are, however, possible cases in which they require different acts. Imagine a deity who has a choice between creating desirers who will have some but not all of their desires satisfied or creating no desirers at all. The former choice is required by the desire–satisfaction maximizing rule and the latter by the desire–dissatisfaction minimizing rule. Probably what James had in mind was a net principle like that of the utilitarians to the effect that we are always morally obligated to act in a manner that maximizes desire–satisfaction over desire–dissatisfaction among the actions available to us. For the sake of brevity, in the future the "over desire–dissatisfaction" qualification will be dropped, but it must be understood as applying. In the 1881 "Reflex Action and Theism," he wrote that "The only possible duty there can be in the matter is the duty of getting the richest results that the material given will allow" – hints of his hipsterism (*WB* 103). The "richest result" would seem to be one in which the maximum number of desires get satisfied. It is an empirical question, and a very difficult one at that, as to what course of action will maximize desire–satisfaction in any given situation. The sciences, especially the social sciences, will have to serve as our guide in determining which action, among those open to us, will best maximize desire–satisfaction. This aspect of James's theory was praised by Dewey, since it fit his own attempt to wed science and ethics.

There are a number of questions about James's maximizing casuistic rule that must be addressed. How similar is it to the different versions of utilitarianism? To begin with, there is the distinction between act and rule utilitarianism, the former holding that on every occasion we should act so as to maximize utility, the latter that we should choose general rules of conduct on the basis of maximizing utility but that once the rules are in place we must follow them, even if doing so on some occasion does not maximize utility.

James clearly recognizes the value of having general rules of conduct when there is good inductive evidence that following them for the most part maximizes desire–satisfaction, a matter about which science must guide us. "The presumption in cases of conflict must always be in favor of the conventionally recognized good. The philosopher must be a conservative, and in the construction of his casuistic scale must put the things most in accordance with the customs of the community on top" (*WB* 156). Supposedly, "the customs of the community" are to be accorded this pride of place because of their established track record in maximizing desire–satisfaction in the past. But in spite of this conservative endorsement of following conventional rules of conduct, James is not a rule desire–satisfaction maximizer, because he permits us to make exceptions to an established rule when we have good evidence that doing so on some occasion will maximize desire–satisfaction, which was another ground of Dewey's lavish praise. Quoting T. H. Green's claim that "Rules are made for man, not man for rules," he urges us to experiment with new rules and procedures for maximizing good (*WB* 156–7). Because James accords such an important instrumental role to conventional rules, but does not give them the exceptional status that modern day rule utilitarians do, his theory of desire–satisfaction maximization is of the *rule instrumental* sort; rules have only an instrumental status as guiding principles and are subject to exceptions. It will be seen in Chapter 5 that James's criterion for belief acceptance based on maximizing desire–satisfaction also is complemented with a type of rule instrumentalism; past experience teaches us that we are well advised, for the most part, to give pride of place to the conventional rule of basing one's beliefs upon the best available empirical evidence.

Obviously, James's maximizing rule differs from Bentham's in regard to what is to be maximized, it being pleasure over pain for Bentham and desire–satisfaction over desire–dissatisfaction for James. This is important because James thought that we desired things other than pleasure and the avoidance of pain, such as to heroically struggle for our ideals. Some desires are manifestations of instinct and emotional expression that have absolutely nothing to do with pleasure and pain. "Who smiles for the pleasure of the smiling, or frowns for the pleasure of the frown?" (*PP* 1156). In an incredibly funny footnote he takes Bain to task for his attempt to explain our sociability and parental love by the desire for pleasure, in particular that of touch. He concludes that for most of us it cannot possibly "be that all our social virtue springs from an appetite for the sensual pleasure of having our hand shaken, or being slapped on the back" (*PP* 1158). Bain is unable to explain why we would not derive just as much pleasure from touching "a satin cushion kept at about 98 degrees F" as we do from touching a baby's face. As Ellen Suckiel has stressed to me in correspondence, "desire–satisfaction," for James, must not be understood as it typically is in terms of the satisfaction of the individual's physical and psychological wants and needs.

The most striking counter-examples to the principle that the only things we desire are pleasure and the avoidance of pain are found in James's own deontological desires to do his moral duty as a free agent. It was the worry that he was not a free, morally responsible agent that triggered his emotional crisis of 1870. James did not desire just that certain desirable states of affairs be realized but that they be realized as a result of his own free agency. Herein James recognizes an intrinsic, deontological value to being a free agent who causes in the right way the realization of desirable ends. There is a serious problem whether James can be committed consistently to both his casuistic rule and his deontological values. This is exactly the same problem faced by the utilitarian who says both that we always must choose that alternative that maximizes utility and that we always must act from considerations of virtue. This gives us inconsistent motivations, since the latter recognizes an intrinsic, deontological value to acting from considerations of virtue that the former does not. If James is to follow his casuistic rule consistently, he must factor in deontological desires on all fours with every other sort of desire.

Although James's casuistic rule differs from classical utilitarianism in regard to what we are to maximize, does it resemble the latter in being purely quantitative? The text speaks unambiguously in favor of the quantitative interpretation. His formulation of the rule clearly is quantitative: "There is but one unconditional commandment, which is that we should seek incessantly...so to vote and to act as to bring about the very *largest total* universe of good which we can see" (*WB* 158; my italics). The 1888–9 "Notes for Philosophy 4..." formulates a precursor to the casuistic rule of the 1891 essay that clearly is quantitative. "Consider *every* good as a real good, and *keep as many as we can.* That act is the best act, which makes for the best whole, the best whole being that which prevails at least cost, in which vanquished goods are least completely annulled" (*ML* 185). Some commentators claim that James incorporated qualitative considerations into his casuistic rule because he occasionally spoke of the desirability of equilibrium and inclusivity, but these concepts admit of a purely qualitative analysis.

Saying that James's casuistic rule is quantitative does not go far enough, for there are three different ways in which it can be quantitative. Our duty could be to satisfy the desires of the greatest *number of people*, the greatest *number of desires*, or the greatest *quantity of desires* in which the amount or intensity of a desire is factored in (*WJ* 81). The text seems to support the latter interpretation: "Any desire is imperative to the extent of its *amount*" (*WB* 149; my italics). What really nails down the case for this interpretation is the manner in which he brings in God's desires and demands. God's demands "carry the most obligation simply because they are the *greatest in amount*" (*WB* 149; my italics). God is the biggest kid on the block, and although he is not infinite for James, his desires and demands are of such a magnitude as to outweigh the collective desires of men, and thus should be obeyed. Thus, although all people count equally, not all desires do. In other writings, James conceives of God as a supremely good being and thus the one person whose judgment of us we should care about most, but in "The Moral Philosopher and the Moral Life" he does not make use of the deontological goodness of God but only the immensity of his desires.

Herein James runs smack into the question of Plato's *Euthyphro*: is an act pious (morally obligatory) because it is loved (demanded) by the gods or is it loved (demanded by) the gods because it is pious (morally obligatory)? Suppose that not God but Descartes' evil demon exists. Would James still hold that the demands of the de facto biggest kid on the block are to carry the day? Obviously James, being one of the nicest human beings of all time, would not continue to adhere to his greatest-in-amount version of the casuistic rule, but then he would be smuggling in deontological considerations to the effect that the reason why we should obey God but not the evil demon is because God is morally good and the demon is not.

We do not have to bring in infinite or near infinite beings to find counter-examples to the greatest-in-amount version. Suppose there are available six units of food and that an incredibly huge man desires, *really desires*, to eat six units of food and there are five other persons who have mild desires to eat one unit of food. If the fat man's desire outweighs the sum of the latter five mild desires, it follows that we have a moral obligation to see to it that the former desire is satisfied to the exclusion of the latter five desires. But this violates our democratic sensitivities. It is not fair that one should get to eat and five be denied. One should not get more than one's fair share because they are unusually lustful. Horniness should not serve as a mark of distinction. This result would not follow if the casuistic rule was interpreted as requiring that we act so as to minimize desire–dissatisfaction.

The other two interpretations – the greatest *number of people* or the greatest *number of desires* are vulnerable to the same objection. A good counter-example to both versions is James's own example of the "lost soul" who is endlessly tortured so that millions can have all of their desires satisfied. Here it is both the greatest number of people and the greatest number of desires that get satisfied. James, of course, thought that we would not allow the torture of one person so as to satisfy the desires of the multitude because he thought we had brain-born moral intuitions of a Kantian sort. But if we were not to have such deontological desires, then we would be required to use the lost soul as a mere means to promote the maximization of desire–satisfaction over desire–dissatisfaction.

How might James meet this counter-example and a slew of similar ones? His initial response was that we have a brain-born moral intuition that would not allow us to use one person as a mere means to promote the happiness of others. In other words, we have a Kantian-type desire that one person not be used as a mere means for promoting the interests of others. But this intuition or desire is a deontological one that is incompatible, for the reason just given, with maximizing ethical theories, whether of a utilitarian or desire–satisfaction maximizing sort.

Maybe James should bite the bullet, as would an ardent act utilitarian, and say that the lost soul counter-example is not a counter-example because we should accept the offer to have millions be happy at the cost of one lost soul who gets tortured endlessly. The manner in which

James defends vivisection in an 1875 article in the *Nation* seems to commit him to this response.

A dog strapped on a board and howling at his executioners, or, still worse, poisoned by curare, which leaves him paralyzed but sentient, is, to his own consciousness, literally in a sort of hell. He sees no redeeming ray in the whole business. Nevertheless, in a world beyond the ken of his poor, benighted brain, his sufferings are having their effect–truth, and perhaps future human ease, are being brought by them. He is performing a function infinitely superior to any which prosperous canine life admits of, and, if his dark mind could be enlightened, and if he were a heroic dog, he would religiously acquiesce in his own sacrifice. (*ECR* 11–12)

Why shouldn't what is true for this dog also be true for the lost soul? Plainly, James cannot say that we are not morally permitted to do to the lost soul what we are permitted to a dog, because the former is a *person*, due to its being a free rational agent, and thus the subject of certain rights, such as the Kantian one never to be used as a mere means, and the dog is not. For this appeals to deontological considerations that are incompatible with his exclusively maximizing of desire–satisfaction ethical theory. That a dog's pain might not be as intense as a human's pain does not justify using it as a mere means to promote human interests. James says that the dog would willingly sacrifice itself "if he were a heroic dog," and thus could say that the lost soul also would willingly sacrifice himself if were a heroic individual. This way out faces the objection that not all dogs or individuals are in fact willing to be heroic martyrs, and that in cases in which they do not voluntarily step forward to sacrifice themselves we have a moral duty to see to it that they are sacrificed so as to maximize desire–satisfaction, be it in any one of the three senses of quantity. James's maximizing ethical theory, like utilitarianism, requires us to heroically martyr ourselves when this will maximize desire–satisfaction or utility, but we *ordinarily* take such an act to be supererogatory, not morally obligatory. Although James, as has just been argued, is not a slave to our ordinary or common-sense moral intuitions, he does accept our ordinary intuition that it would be wrong to use one individual as a means and in fact says that it is brain-born.

Does James have some way around this and a host of similar counterexamples? One option is for him to appeal to his rule instrumentalism. He could say that we would do a better job in the long run of maximizing desire–satisfaction if we adopted the rule, subject to exceptions of course, that each of us be willing to sacrifice ourselves for the benefit of others, provided that the selection process is random. (Think of an organ lottery in which all of us are voluntary participants, agreeing to give up our life if our number comes up so that our organs can be used for transplants.) The problem is that if someone does not voluntarily accept this rule, she still is fair game for being the sacrificial lost soul. One is going to be a heroic martyr, like it or not. And this seems wrong, not only to the vast majority of people but to James as well, at least at those times when he was not intent on developing an ethical theory.

Another strategy that is open to James is to say that his revisionary analysis of good and obligation, like all of his other revisionary analyses, is not intended to hold for every possible world but only the actual world, and thus counter-examples based on merely possible cases cut no ice. James criticized absolute idealism's attempt to give an analysis of truth that would hold in all conceivable worlds, worlds of an empirical constitution entirely different from ours, for being "too thin, as if the actual peculiarities of the world . . . were entirely irrelevant. But they cannot be irrelevant" (*PU* 149). No doubt, he would want to say the same about analyses of other concepts.

Supposedly, lost soul type counter-examples are too counterfactual. James, no doubt, would have found the challenge posed by the immoralist, based on how we would act if we were to be rendered retribution-proof, say through possessing the ring of Gyges that enables the wearer to become invisible, to be too counter-factual to be taken seriously. James, along with many of his contemporaries, believed in the essential goodness of men, that if the circumstances required, they would dutifully accept being the lost soul.

The problem with this response is that James's revisionary analysis does not hold even for the actual world. That it does not is dramatically brought out by the doctor who says to his patient, "Mister Jones, I have good new and bad news for you. The bad news is that you will die within a month from an untreatable cancer. And the good news is that I won one million dollars in the lottery." If James were right in his estimation of human nature, it should not occasion a laugh. But it does.

James's contrast between "the easy-going and the strenuous mood" concerns the difference between the cognitive and existential dimensions of the ethical life. It is one thing to accept an ethical rule and quite another to get oneself to follow or live up to it. In the easy-going mood we do not sufficiently exert ourselves in following the casuistic rule, often because we fail to adopt the required disinterested perspective. A person lazily follows the course of least resistance because she considers only her present desires and not the ones that she and others will have in the future. "When in the easy-going mood the shrinking from present ill is our ruling consideration. The strenuous mood, on the contrary, makes us quite indifferent to present ill, if only the greater ideal be attained" (*WB* 159–60).

The cognitive-existential distinction enters into his "faith-ladder" formulation of his will-to-believe doctrine at the very close of each of his final two books, *A Pluralistic Universe* and *Some Problems of Philosophy*. The following steps may be called the "faith-ladder":

1. There is nothing absurd in a certain view of the world being true, nothing self-contradictory.
2. It *might* have been true under certain conditions;
3. It *may* be true, even now;
4. It is *fit* to be true;
5. It *ought* to be true;
6. It *must* be true;
7. It *shall* be true, at any rate true for *me* (*SPP* 113 and *PU* 148).

Each of the steps up until 7 is cognitive in that it involves *believing* of some proposition either that it is possible or that it is desirable. It is at step 7 that the existential or conative dimension enters in, for in saying that this proposition, which one's intellect has already assessed as both possible and desirable, *shall* be true one is forming the effective intention or will to act so as to help make it true. This is of a piece with the distinction between our believing or accepting the casuistic rule and our psyching ourselves up so that we can form an effective intention to act in accordance with what it requires.

James attempts to stimulate us to lead the morally strenuous life by invoking God, first in the capacity of someone who knows the answer to the casuistic question, and second as our ideal social self whom we should do our best to please. A person's social self, for James, is the recognition she receives from others. "*A man has as many social selves as there are individuals who recognize him* and carry an image of him in their mind" (*PP* 281). But a person does not care equally about each person's opinion of her. She gives greater weight to the opinions of her peers and those whom she respects and loves. For most people, God would be their ideal social self, since he is the person they most respect and admire.

It has been pointed out that it is very difficult for us to determine the answer to the casuistic question, since our ability to predict the future is so radically limited. The dauntingness of the task of determining which course of action among those open to us will best maximize desire–satisfaction in the long run can easily demoralize us so that we take the easy way out and do what is in the line of least resistance. Given God's omniscience, or near omniscience for James, if God were to exist, the right answer to the casuistic question would exist in his mind, even though we are not able to access his mind. By postulating the existence of God and thus the existence of the right answer to the casuistic question, we gain inspiration faithfully to pursue finding the right answer. Thus, the idea of God and his knowledge is an inspiring ideal of reason that energizes us to find the answer to the casuistic question.

The invocation of God as an ideal of reason that benevolently energizes us is of a piece with his occasional Peircean postulation of a future scientific millennium in which some theory is accepted by all competent scientists. "The 'absolutely' true, meaning what no farther experience will ever alter, is that ideal vanishing-point toward which we imagine that all our temporary truths will some day converge. It runs on all fours with the perfectly wise man, and with the absolutely complete experience" (*P* 106–7 and *MT* 143–4). Herein God is brought in not as the *biggest* but the *knowingest* kid on the block. We have seen that James waffles on the question of moral realism, initially denying the existence of timeless moral truths and then seemingly committing himself to the existence of at least one such truth – that it is good that a desire be satisfied and therefore we have a moral obligation to maximize desire-satisfaction. The postulation of a God in whose mind there exists the answer to the ultimate casuistic question seems to be a version of scholastic conceptualism that finds a middle ground between James's nominalism and realism. Thus, James winds up coming down on all three sides of the nominalism-conceptualism-realism issue as it pertains to moral truths. At the end of this chapter an attempt is made to extricate James from this apparent inconsistency and also to find some way for him to accommodate the deontological moral intuitions that underlie lost soul type counter-examples.

It is now time to tackle the thorny problem as to why James used "desire," "demand," and "claim" interchangeably, using "desire" and "demand" each eleven times and "claim" five; he even speaks occasionally of "likes," "preferences," and what "feels good." It is surprising that none of the many commentators have been disturbed by this, because it is obvious that, although "demand" and "claim" are roughly synonymous, "desire," being a psychological term, differs significantly from each of these quasilegalistic terms. Because "demand" and "claim" are roughly synonymous, I will not consider "claim" in what follows.

Certainly, we are more inclined to lend someone ten dollars who *desires* that we do than someone who *demands* that we do, assuming no threat is being made. Furthermore, there are many things that we desire that we never would demand. Every person has many desires that they would be ashamed to demand be satisfied nor would they even want to see them satisfied. It might be thought that an easy solution to James's sloshing back and forth between "desire" and "demand" is to have him use "desire" for what goes on in his moral solitude and restrict "demand" to the "ethical republic." The text does not permit this interpretation, since James holds that demands occur in the moral solitude world if the lone person's present self makes demands on her future self or vice versa. The text does not give us any easy way to explain James's apparent confounding of desires with demands, and it is up to the commentator to follow through on his behalf, which is just what I now will do.

The first step in my reconstruction of James is to point out that, although desire and demand are quite different, there still is an important connection between them, consisting in the fact that what a person demands usually is something that she also desires. The converse, as just indicated, is not true. The next step is to argue that we would do a better job of maximizing desire–satisfaction if we adopted as an instrumental rule that we should always act so as to maximize *demand*–satisfaction.

Why is this the case? First, there are many desires that people have that ought not to be satisfied because doing so would deny satisfaction to many other desires that they and others have. By adopting the instrumental rule always to act so as to maximize demand–satisfaction, we are requiring that people in effect play rational critic to their own desires, as is argued by Dewey in "Theory of Valuation." The immediately given urges, drives, propensities, and inclinations get reconstructed by an inquiry into their causes and consequences that converts what is desired into what is desirable. And it is what each person deems desirable after this inquiry that gets fed into the casuistic equation as a demand. A demand is what a person publicly requests after such an inquiry. Thus, by adopting as an instrumental rule that we should always act so as to maximize demand–satisfaction, *subject to deontological exceptions*, we do a better job in the long run of realizing the *summum bonum* of maximizing desire–satisfaction.

What are the exceptions? There seem to be at least two – desirers who are either not around to make demands or are too weak to do so. The text makes clear that James wanted us to factor into the casuistic equation the desires of yet-to-be-born persons, as well as our future selves, even though they are not around now to make demands. "There can be," he says, "no final truth in ethics any more than in physics, until the last man has had experience and said his say" (*WB* 141). In the strenuous mood we are "awakened . . . by those claims of *remote posterity* which constitute the last appeal of the religion of humanity" (*WB* 160; my italics).

There also are people who are not around to make demands because they are spatially remote and cannot get to the "polls." If they will be affected by our decisions, then their desires also must be factored in. We shall have to speak up on their behalf.

All of this clearly agrees with the letter and spirit of the text. However, it is less clear what James would want to say about those desirers who fail to make demands because of weakness and timidity, or even an inability to communicate. Many, maybe even most, persons would say that their desires should be factored equally into the casuistic equation, especially when they are had by those who have not yet come of age or are infirm. James, however, says that "Some desires, truly enough, are small desires; they are put forward by *insignificant persons*, and we customarily make light of the obligation which they bring" (*WB* 149; my italics). These desires get factored in all right, but in a significantly discounted manner. There is an elitist ring to this. People are deserving of having their desires taken seriously, only when they have the courage to demand that they be accorded this status. Only "significant" persons count, and to achieve significant personhood a person must pass the courage test by demanding that others accord her this status. An exception to this might have to be made for those who have not yet come of age, as well as sentient animals, a topic that never enters into James's discussion. It is not clear from the text just what James meant by "insignificant persons."

Even if the desire–demand aporia has been neutralized by these considerations, there remain outstanding aporias concerning the ontological status of moral truths and the maximizing-deontological tension. Again, it is up to the commentator to follow through and do the best she can on James's behalf.

James's waffling on the realism-nominalism question as it pertains to moral truths is only a special instance of his general waffling about the ontological status of platonic abstracta, as will be seen when an exposition is given in Chapter 11 of his account of percepts and concepts. It will emerge that his account of the latter seems to face the same aporia due to its apparent commitment to both realism and nominalism. Immediately after giving his nominalistic, concept-empiricist analysis, which holds that concepts are both abstracted from and dependent upon percepts, he goes on to balance the books by adding that "physical realities are constituted by the various concept-stuffs of which they 'partake'" (*SPP* 58). That James was happy to accept the realist commitment of this talk about participation in the forms is clear from his claim that the

absolute determinability of our mind by abstractions is one of the cardinal facts in our human constitution. Polarizing and magnetizing us as they do, we turn towards them and from them, we seek them, hold them, hate them, bless them, just as if they were so many concrete beings. *And beings they are, beings as real in the realm which they inhabit as the changing things of sense are in the realm of space.* (*VRE* 54; my italics)

James gives us a hint as to how to resolve the aporia when he says that

The map which the mind frames out of them [concepts] is an object which possesses, *when once it has been framed,* an independent existence. It suffices all by itself for purposes of study. The "eternal" truths it contains would have to be acknowledged even were the world of sense annihilated. (*SPP* 43; my italics)

At first glance it looks like this passage commits James to a platonic realism about concepts that clashes with his nominalism; however, the qualification "when once it has been framed" gives him a way of reconciling the two. His nominalism denies that concepts actually exist independently of empirical particulars, such as our acts of conceiving them. But, if we are to have thoughts about concepts, we must think of them as having a world-independent existence and standing in certain eternal relations to each other. In the specific case of moral truths, they do not have an eternal existence independent of our desirings but once we frame thoughts of them we must conceive of them as having such an existence. Another way of putting this is that it is a rule of the moral language game that moral truths be accorded a platonic status by the players, but there are no actual moral truths or laws that obtain or are in effect until we choose to play the game.

James's oft-used potentiality-actuality distinction can be utilized here. There is the possibility of there being platonic moral truths (or concepts) before we actually play the moral language game (or conceive of them), but these possibilities become actualized only when we actually play the game (or conceive of them). This way of finding a compromise between nominalism and realism, as will be seen in later chapters, accords with the manner in which he deployed the potentiality-actuality distinction to truth and self-identity over time. Before a person actually judges or remembers that she is identical with some past self, she is only possibly identical with this self, and before a proposition is actually verified it is only possibly true. The categorical version of the law of bivalence, which holds that every proposition is true or false, accordingly is conditionalized by James so that it holds instead that every proposition is possibly true or possibly false. Once the proper verification or judgment of self-identity has occurred, the potentiality in question is actualized and we say retrospectively that the proposition was true all along and the person was identical with this past self. Present truth casts its shadow backward, but without the present truth there is no shadow to be cast over the past. Similarly, the things that we are required to say about the prior existence of moral truths by our present playing of the moral language game or making obligation-creating demands casts its shadow backward. Thus, the platonic heaven resembles a cheap boarding house in which there is a lot of coming and going.

This way of deploying the potentiality-actuality distinction is highly promethean. It gives us the promethean role of being the creators of *actual* truth, moral or otherwise, as well as concepts and our own self-identity over time, through our different actions. Our verificatory and judgmental acts, however, do not create the potentialities for there being these actualities. Thus, it isn't promethean all the way down. The realist is right, therefore, to insist on the need for some sort of a given, which James often compared with the block of marble that is given to the sculptor. A critical evaluation of this doctrine will come later when detailed expositions are given of James's analyses of truth and self-identity over time.

The maximizing-deontological aporia is the more difficul: of the two to neutralize. I know of no way to reconcile James's deontological intuitions, such as those that he appealed to in condemning using the lost soul (but not the dog) as a means for maximizing desire–dissatisfaction, with his casuistic rule that we are always to act so as to maximize desire–satisfaction. His writings abound in deontological sermonettes that extol the intrinsic value of freely leading the morally strenuous life, of being the right sort of cause of the realization of one's desires. He often writes like a good Kantian who sees our highest moral duty to be that of obeying objective moral truths or duties. Echoing Carlyle, he says that we must have

the vision of certain works to be done, of certain outward changes to be wrought or resisted.... No matter how we succeed in doing these outward duties, whether gladly and spontaneously, or heavily and unwillingly, do them we somehow must; for the leaving of them undone is perdition. No matter how we feel; if we are only faithful in the outward act and refuse to do wrong, the world will in so far be safe, and we quit of our debt towards it.... be willing to live and die in its service – and, at a stroke, we have passed from the subjective into the objective philosophy of things. (*WB* 134)

He also believed that there are desires, such as sadistic ones, that ought not to be satisfied, even if doing so maximizes desire–satisfaction.

We have already considered the attempt to reconcile the casuistic rule with these deontological intuitions by recognizing that among the desires people actually have, and which therefore must enter into the casuistic equation, are to see that justice is done and that people are never used as mere means. In addition to the consistency problem, this places too much weight on the contingent desires of people. If, as seems actually to be the case, the deontological desires of persons are outweighed by their purely self-interested ones, then we would be morally obligated to see to it that the latter desires are the ones that get fulfilled, to the disadvantage of the "lost souls" of the world. Furthermore, this attempted reconciliation gives the wrong answer to a variant on the question of the *Euthyphro*: Are we prima facie obligated to see to it that a desire for what is deontologically good gets satisfied because it is desired or because what is desired is good? James's casuistic rule requires us to give the former answer but the latter is required by our and James's deontological intuitions.

I believe that the only viable way for James to resolve this aporia is to reject his claim that "*the essence of good is simply to satisfy demand*," along with the desire–satisfaction maximizing casuistic rule based on it. He should recognize that there are a plurality of goods, of which desire–satisfaction is only one along with various deontological goods. A consequence of this is that the defeaters or overriders of our prima facie obligation to see to it that a desire gets satisfied will no longer be just an outweighing set of conflicting desires but deontological principles that get violated as well.

This expanded concept of the good requires that his casuistic rule,

1. We are always morally obligated to act so as to maximize desire–satisfaction over desire–dissatisfaction,

be replaced by

1′. We are always morally obligated to act so as to maximize *good*.

This rule is too general to supply guidance in making real-life nitty-gritty ethical choices when there is a conflict between what is deontologically right and what will maximize desire–satisfaction (pleasure, happiness). Unfortunately, there is no more specific version of it that ensures that there will not be undecidable cases. For rule 1, undecidability always results from incomplete knowledge, due to not all of the ballots being in or our not being able to predict the future consequences of different courses of action, but for 1′ the undecidability is due to the rule not being specific enough. It is a sad, even tragic, feature of our moral life that there is no acceptable casuistic rule that provides us with a clear-cut decision procedure for weighting different goods, and thus we must muddle along with great trepidation when making moral choices.

In the remainder of the book, I have, for the sake of simplicity and closeness to James's text, worked with version 1 of the casuistic rule. It is my contention that *almost* everything that James accomplished by appeal to 1 could be accomplished equally well by the use of 1' instead. The reason for the "almost" qualification is that by incorporating deontological values into his casuistic rule he might somewhat undercut the promethean force of his philosophy, because each self now is subject to deontological constraints that might cramp her quest for full self-realization. Whether my contention is merited will have to be decided in the light of the full range of James's philosophy, and therefore I must, at this time, issue a promissory note.

2

The Willfulness of Belief

The previous chapter dealt with premise 1 of James's Master Syllogism.

1. We are always morally obligated to act so as to maximize desire–satisfaction over desire–dissatisfaction.
2. Belief is an action.
3. Therefore, we are always morally obligated to believe in a manner that maximizes desire–satisfaction over desire dissatisfaction.

Premise 2 is the concern of this chapter. For the argument to work, however, premise 2 must be beefed up to assert that

2′. Belief is a free action,

the reason being that 3 morally obligates us to believe in a certain manner but we can have a moral obligation to act in a certain way only if we are free to do so. This chapter concentrates only on whether belief is an action for James, leaving its freedom for Chapter 3 and our justification for believing in its freedom to Chapter 4.

James's overall argument for belief being an action is based on his identification of belief with the will, and the will, at least in one of its senses, with effortful attention to an idea. Because effortful attention is something that we can do intentionally or voluntarily, it follows by Leibniz's law of the indiscernibility of identicals that

All references in this chapter are to *The Principles of Psychology*, unless otherwise indicated.

belief also is an intentional action, and thereby, provided it is free, subject to the casuistic rule:

1. We are always morally obligated to act so as to maximize desire–satisfaction over desire–dissatisfaction.

It is via our acts of effortful attention that we are able to play the promethean role of *co*-creators of actuality, truth, value, meaning, and personal identity, as well as the course taken by future history. The "co" qualification is inserted because James always recognized the demand of the realist for some kind of a given. But to be truly promethean beings, our acts of attending, willing, and believing also must be free in the radical libertarian sense that involves a creation ex nihilo; but again, as Chapter 3 will bring out, there is a concession to realism, since they are limited by a given situation, thereby failing to be a total causa sui.

That James identified attention, will, and belief, taken in a purely psychological sense, with each other is clear from the following quotations. He begins by claiming that "volition [will] is nothing but attention" and then completes the trilogy of identifications by stating that *"Will and Belief, in short, meaning a certain relation between objects and the Self, are two names for one and the same* PSYCHOLOGICAL *phenomenon"* (424, 948). Although "attention," "will," and "belief" are coreferential, they have different senses or meanings and thus require separate treatments. That they are coreferential is a very bold and original thesis and will be found to be subject to many serious challenges. For the purpose of James's Master Syllogism the thesis need not be true. All that is needed is that belief can be induced, either directly or indirectly, by willful attention, not that belief is identical with attention and the will.

James's psychology employs two different ways of understanding a psychic state. "First, the way of analysis: What does it consist in? What is its inner nature? Of what sort of mind-stuff is it composed? Second, the way of history: What are its conditions of production, and its connection with other facts?" (913). The way of "analysis" involves introspecting our own mind so as to discover what goes on when we are conscious in the concerned manner. This will be called the method of "phenomenological or introspective analysis." The "way of history" is an objective inquiry into the causes and consequences of the psychic state and thus will be called a "causal analysis." Throughout *The*

Principles of Psychology James tries to strike a proper balance between the two, but, as is seen in the part of this book on the anti-promethean mystic, ultimately gives pride of place to the method of phenomenological analysis or introspection.

Although each of us can know what attention, will, and belief are from introspecting our own minds, we cannot define them in terms of any more basic conscious states. Each is a simple, sui generis state, similar to a sensation of green in this respect. For each of them we can phenomenologically distinguish between a simple and complex case. In the simple case our consciousness is filled with an idea of an act sans any other competing idea. By some preestablished neurological mechanism, this state of consciousness triggers the envisioned act. In the complex case, we are aware of conflicting ideas competing for the sole occupation of our consciousness, and herein there is room for an intentional action of making an effort to attend or consent to one of these ideas to the exclusion of the others. This effort or fiat also is phenomenologically vouchsafed. Thus, in both the simple and complex cases, the final conscious state is the same, some idea filling the mind without any competition; but in the complex case there is an initial competition between conflicting ideas that gets resolved by an effort to attend or consent. Another way to say this is that in the complex but not the simple case the final state of consciousness is brought about by an intentional action.

The reader is urged always to bear in mind James's distinction between the simple and complex cases of attention, will, and belief; for he sometimes makes seemingly general claims that he carelessly fails to restrict to one of the two cases. For example, he says that attention is "reactive spontaneity" and a "taking possession by the mind," which makes attention look like it is intentionally brought about in every case (380, 381). Similarly, he says without any restriction that will involves a "consent to the idea's undivided presence" and that belief is an "acquiescence" or "consent" to an idea's presence in the mind, both of which again speak for the final state of consciousness being brought about intentionally (1169, 913). His claim that "*Effort of attention is thus the essential phenomenon of will*" also is misleading (1167). Probably what he means by "essential" is that effortful attention is the *important* kind of attention.

I. Attention

James begins with the newborn baby's awareness of the big, blooming, buzzing confusion, charmingly called "baby's first sensation," as if it were a toy by Mattel. This is a sheer chaos, a cotton-candyish mush, because the subject does not apply concepts or categories that relate one part of it to another. "All of the 'categories of the understanding' are contained," however, in this pure sensation, but there is not yet any attending activity on the part of the babe and thus no part of the sensory field stands out from its background (657). There are not yet, for example, any perspectival accents of now and then, here and there, this and that, and I and you (381). No *perception* has yet occurred, since, for James, a *sensation* becomes a perception only when there is an application of a concept to its sensory content. The babe *sees* all of the sensory contents and the relations between them but does not see that these contents stand in relations, because no concepts are applied. Because the application of a concept involves judgment or belief, the babe does not yet have any beliefs about what is sensorily given. James is not consistent on this point, for he says that if a baby's first sensation is "of a lighted candle against a dark background, and nothing else," the existence of the candle will "be believed in," will be "known to the mind in question" (917). Because one cannot believe or know without using concepts, this imputes to the babe the possession of concepts. This is yet another example of his proclivity to engage in Robinson Crusoe mythologizing, of a piece with his notion of a "moral solitude" in Chapter 1.

The babe cannot attend to any part of the originally given chaos until it has acquired concepts and the ability to wield them in judgments. "*The only things which we commonly see [perceive] are those which we preperceive*, and the only things which we preperceive are those which have been labeled for us, and the labels stamped into our mind. If we lost our stock of labels we should be intellectually lost in the midst of the world" (420). A preperception is "nothing but the anticipatory imagination of what the impressions or the reactions are to be" (415). For James, concepts are acquired through abstraction from past sensations, which is a topic for Chapter 11. The babe has not yet had a sufficiently rich fund of past sensations from which to derive the concepts that are needed to label things.

It is unclear whether a baby's first sensation counts as an *experience* at all. James first makes the Kantian claim that "Millions of items of the outward order are present to my senses which never properly enter into my *experience*" because "My *experience* is what I agree to attend to" (380; my italics). This has the consequence that a baby's first sensation is not an experience at all. But James immediately adds that "without selective interest, *experience* is an utter chaos," which seems to allow for an inattentive experience of the baby's first-sensation sort (381). The best way for James to resolve this terminological confusion is to reserve "experience" for attended consciousness and call a baby's first sensation a mere case of consciousness. This squares with James's claim that without attention "the *consciousness* of every creature would be a gray chaotic indiscriminateness, impossible for us even to conceive" (381; my italics).

Again, it is important to stress that James recognized a distinction between simple and complex cases of attention. In the simple case, "Attention to an object is what takes place whenever that object most completely occupies the mind," (*TT* 69), there being no need for the subject to be an active agent in bringing about this state of consciousness. You could just find yourself attending to one part of the sensorily given to the exclusion of others; your idea of it just happens to stand out from the pack. Similar remarks are made about will and belief. "Volition . . . is absolutely completed when the stable state of the idea is there," and "Belief means only a peculiar sort of occupancy of the mind" (*PP* 1165, 1166). But he also says that attention is "reactive spontaneity" (380), a "taking possession by the mind" (381), which points to it being an intentional action. Again, the reader must make the suitable restriction to complex cases on James's behalf.

It might be urged that *all* cases of attention involve an intentional action on the grounds that since attention requires the application of a concept it involves the intentional action of *making* a judgment or *forming* a belief. The problem with this is that although we can at will join concepts together in our imagination into a propositional complex we cannot in most cases believe at will. James asks rhetorically, "If belief consists in an emotional reaction of the entire man on an object, how *can* we believe at will? We cannot control our emotions" (948). How James deals with the problem of self-inducing beliefs is to figure prominently in his account of the will to believe and thus is considered in Chapter 4.

So far we have been considering only James's phenomenological analysis of attention. His causal analysis of attention in terms of interest contains an apparent inconsistency. He says, on the one hand, "The things to which we attend are said to *interest* us. Our interest in them is supposed to be the *cause* of our attending" (393). Yet he also says that "what-we-attend-to and what-interests-us are synonymous terms" (1164). But because the terms designating respectively a cause and effect are not synonymous, it follows that interest is not the cause of our attending, *pace* what James has just said on page 393. I believe that the account that makes interest the cause of attention squares better overall with the text and thus is the one that will be employed. No doubt, whatever we attend to is of interest to us, either directly or through its association with things that have direct interest (you attend to a relative in whom you have no direct interest because you are interested in obeying the maxim that one should take care of one's relatives); however, this is not because attention and interest are one and the same but rather because attention, whether simple or complex, always is caused by interest, and thus they go together.

That attention always is caused by interest raises an active-passive, creating-discovering aporia, which will be found to run throughout James's promethean philosophy. In Chapter 1 it involved a clash between our *creating* value and obligation through our desirings or demandings and our *discovering* an objective moral truth, the casuistic rule, by appeal to our brain-born moral intuitions. In the simple case we do not intentionally bring it about that we are in the attending state, since we make no previous effort to be in this state. It is only in regard to the complex cases that James speaks of our choosing to attend as we do. "Each of us literally *chooses*, by his ways of attending to things, what sort of a universe he shall appear to himself to inhabit" (401). This is the height of his prometheanism, according to which each of us chooses which one of the many possible worlds is to be the actual world, thereby usurping the Deity's prerogative of doing this.

The problem is that our choice to attend to one universe or object over its competitors is caused by our interest, but our interest, in turn, being an emotional state, is not subject to our wills. We can no more control at will what interests us than we can what we love. James seems to agree: "The accommodation and the resultant feeling *are* the attention. We don't bestow it, the object draws it from us. The object has the initiative, not the mind" (425). This clashes with his activistic claim that attending in the complex case involves a "taking possession by the mind," a "reactive spontaneity." The best expression of the aporia comes from James's own pen. In both the simple and complex cases the mind "turns to it [the object that is to be attended to] . . . in the *interested active emotional way*" (948; my italics). The agent discovers rather than creates its emotionally based interest. An attempt is made on James's behalf to resolve this aporia in the next chapter.

II. Will

Everything that has been said about attention has a parallel with respect to the will, since "attention" and "will" refer to one and the same psychological phenomenon for James, although they differ in sense. As he did in his account of attention, James will again distinguish between active and passive cases, though at times he writes carelessly as if all cases of will involved an intentional effort or fiat. His exposition begins with the simple or passive case of willing, called "ideo-motor action," which has no fiat or effort to attend. He then goes on to consider the complex case of a conflict between ideas that requires for its resolution a fiat or effort.

All human behavior initially is involuntary. Incoming sensations are followed by bodily behavior either through instinct, reflex, or accident. That sensations will lead to a motor discharge is due to the fact "that consciousness is *in its very nature impulsive. . . . Movement is the natural immediate effect of feeling, irrespective of what the quality of the feeling may be*" (1134–35). The organic material of the human brain is highly plastic, permitting new neural pathways to be dug in it. "An acquired habit, from the physiological point of view, is nothing but a new pathway of discharge formed in the brain, by which certain incoming currents ever after tend to escape" (9). When there is a constant conjunction between a sensory input and a motor discharge, this causes a new habit to be formed, consisting in a new pathway from the part of the brain in which the incoming sensory input is registered to some motor response (11).

The bodily behavior, say the moving of your arm, caused by the incoming sensation has experiential accompaniments consisting in kinesthetic and visual sensations of your arm moving and some of its effects. Thus, there will result another constant conjunction, this one between your sensory ideas of your arm moving and its moving. By a complex physiological law, which I will not formulate here (see 1183–8 for the details), your having the idea of your arm moving can take the place of the original incoming sensation as the triggering event of your arm's moving. Thus a new habit is formed that enables your having kinesthetic and visual ideas of your arm moving and its effects to discharge into the motor organs that move your arm. Notice that there is no mysterious sort of backward causation going on here. Initially, these ideas came after or while your arm moved, but now, after the formation of this secondary habit, they come before the movement and thus cause it in an ordinary forward-directed manner.

Once the secondary habit has been formed, the subject can voluntarily or willfully move his arm. He does so by activating his memories of what it felt like when his arm moved, thereby consciously ideating in a my-arm-is-moving manner. If there is no conflicting idea in his mind to that of his arm moving, such as the thought that he must not move his arm because it is broken, his arm will move in virtue of the secondary habit. "*A supply of ideas of the various movements that are possible, left in the memory by experiences of their involuntary performance, is thus the first prerequisite of the voluntary life,*" the other prerequisite, in the simple case of ideomotor action, being the lack of any competing idea (1099–1100).

James holds that it is a brute contingent fact that our will is efficacious over only our own body, that we can cause our arm but not the table to move by thinking of it as moving (947–8, 1165). As an avid psychical investigator, he took seriously the possibility of telekinesis, though he didn't find the evidence for it very strong. James adds the rather startling claim that he is able to will or exert a volition that a table should move, and is surprised that others report themselves unable to do so. He speculates that the reason why they think they cannot do so is that they know it is not in their power to move the table and this "sense of impotence inhibits the volition" (1165). If they were to have a desire for the table to move, it would be a mere wish, not a want, since the desire is a conflicted one.

I very much doubt that this is the right account of why these people, and James ought to be among them, are unable to will that the table move. The crucial idea of a movement in the case of ideomotor action is of the resident kinesthetic sensations that accompany the movement, rather than just the idea of the visual sensations occasioned by the movement or its effects, such as one could have of the table moving. Obviously, we have no idea of the kinesthetic sensations that are resident in a table's moving and thus have no idea of what it is like for a table to move voluntarily. And as a result we have no idea of the manner in which we should ideate so as to cause the table to move. We don't know, in general, what it is like to be a table and do tablely things, like stoically remaining immobile when someone thumps on us to emphasize the point that it is this very table that he refers to when he makes counterfactual claims about it.

In a complex case of will there is a competition between warring ideas to be the sole, steadfast occupant of the mind and thereby to get satisfied. In such a case our idea of each action is inhibited from discharging into the appropriate motor response by its competitor. This produces in us a state of indecision. James wrongly says that "As long as it lasts, with the various objects before the attention, we are said to deliberate," for to deliberate requires that in addition to being conflicted we examine each of the conflicting ideas in regard to its suitability for realization (1136). While deliberating we oscillate between the different futures portrayed by the ideas. We are in a state of tense unrest and thus desire to get the issue decided so that we can take repose in action. But this desire is countered by the "dread of the irrevocable" (1137).

James outlines five ways in which a decision finally is made. First, there is the "reasonable type" of decision that comes after rational deliberation in which one of the alternatives emerges as the one best supported by the facts. In the next two types of decision, the final fiat occurs before the completion of a rational inquiry. We let ourselves indifferently drift in one of the directions on the basis of either an external or internal accident. In the fourth some outward experience causes us suddenly to undergo a radical change of mood, say, from the easygoing to the strenuous mood. It is in the fifth type that an express volition or effort decides the matter. We feel a "heave of the will" that succeeds in inclining the beam in one of the directions. Even after we have settled on one of the possible courses of action, the thought of the denied possibilities tortures us. Herein we motivelessly make one of the competing motives emerge as the decisive one through our effort to attend to it. What this portends for the freedom of the will is the topic of Chapter 3.

It has been objected to James's claim that "*the terminus of the psychological process in volition . . . is always an idea*" (1171) that in many cases it is easier to just intentionally perform an action than it is to first form an idea of it. This "just-do-it" objection is a powerful one, but all is not lost for James. Although his theory is not true in general, it does apply to some cases that are among the most important ones in our lives, because we in effect decide what kind of persons we will become. These are complex cases in which we are not able to "just do it" but instead first must work on our own minds so that we become vividly conscious in a certain manner. In the important character-determining cases we need to dramatically envision our performing the competing alternative actions and the consequences of doing so. Not only can this be the key factor in determining us to pursue one of the alternatives, it also can greatly increase the chances of our successfully pursuing it.

We are like an actor to whom many scripts are presented from which we must choose one in which to star. Some scripts are immediately rejected because we cannot seriously entertain playing that role. Getting ourselves eventually to accept one of the scripts over its serious competitors consists in vividly playing over one of the roles in our imagination until it dominates, this amounting to the that's-me feeling and thereby the decision to play that role.

The same sort of aesthetic ideating is crucial, at least for many persons, in picking the character they will play in real life. Consider James's marvelous case of the reformed alcoholic who is offered a drink by his host.

His moral triumph or failure literally consists in his finding the right *name* for the case. If he says that it is a case of not wasting good liquor already poured out, or a case of not being churlish and unsociable when in the midst of friends, or a case of learning something at last about a brand of whiskey which he never met before, or a case of celebrating a public holiday, or a case of stimulating himself to a more energetic resolve in favor of abstinence than any he has ever yet made, then he is lost; his choice of the wrong name seals his doom. But if in spite of all the plausible good names with which his thirsty fancy so copiously furnishes him, he unwaveringly clings to the truer bad name, and apperceives the case as that of 'being a drunkard, being a drunkard, being a drunkard,' his feet are planted on the road to salvation; he saves himself by thinking rightly. (*TT* 110)

More than just finding the right name is involved. There also is the dramatic envisionment of his future as a sober man and as a drunkard. On the one hand, he can form comforting pictures of himself being the carefree, hard-drinking bon vivant or even the sullen, self-destructive alcoholic who is so irresistible to women and novelists, maybe even one of the delightful characters in O'Neill's *The Iceman Cometh* who says, "What have you done to the booze, Hickey? It's lost its life." On the other hand, he could vividly ideate about his future life as a drunkard in a way that would deter him from electing to play this role. He imagines the deleterious physical effects of drinking, being an object of derision and contempt, letting down his loved ones. Or, even better for James, he could form positive images of his future sober life in which he experiences "the blessings of having an organism kept in lifelong possession of its full youthful elasticity by a sweet, sound, blood, to which stimulants and narcotics are unknown, and to which the morning sun and air and dew daily come as sufficiently powerful intoxicants" (*TT* 114). It is clear that the man does not reject the offer of a drink in this case by "just doing it," but rather by the complicated, circuitous process of dramatic projection into alternative future roles that will be determinative of what sort of a person he will become.

Many of our important moral decisions are made through aesthetic ideational projection into different roles. This could be called the theory of "Hollywood ethics." A person might not steal, for example, not because he feels constrained by the moral law, but rather because he can't see himself playing the role of someone who cares that much about material possessions. Unlike other ethical theories, Hollywood ethics does not purport to tell us what is the ethically good or right thing to do, but when practiced seriously and honestly, it can help us to find our authentic self and a way of life that is right for us. According to the "ideal observer theory" of ethics, the morally right or good thing to do is what the ideal observer, who is completely rational and possessed of all the relevant facts, would choose to do. The fully dedicated and honest performer of the thought experiment required by my Hollywood ethics, is not the "ideal observer," but he is the closest that we mortals can come to achieving this status. That James's theory of complex cases of will neatly fit in with Hollywood ethics is, I take it, a point in its favor.

III. Belief

Finally, we come to the major concern of this chapter, belief, and in particular whether it is inducible at will, thereby making it subject to James's casuistic rule, provided it also is free. Belief, like will, is nothing but the attending to an idea sans competitors and admits of the same distinction between simple and complex cases, depending on whether or not the attending state results from an effort. There is, of course, a difference between belief and will in that we can have beliefs about things, such as a table moving, that we don't or, some would say, can't will, due to our will directly controlling only our own body. This, however, is only a physiological, not a psychological, difference. The reader of the chapter "The Perception of Reality" in *The Principles of Psychology* must be especially alert to the distinction between the two senses in which James uses "belief": (i) the stable occupancy of an idea in consciousness sans competitors; and (ii) a propositional attitude of consent or acceptance taken to an idea, resulting in a state of type (i). Whereas it is made clear that every case of belief must involve a type (i) state, he fluctuated on whether *every* act of believing also requires a type (ii) consensual act. If it does, belief hardly is the same as will, since, as several quotations have attested, there can be a case of will that is only of type (i).

The following quotation brings to a head James's waffling on whether there can be a belief state without an act of consent that brings this state about.

In its inner nature belief, or the sense of reality, is a sort of feeling more allied to the emotions than to anything else. Mr. Bagehot distinctly calls it the 'emotion' of conviction. Consent is recognized by all to be a manifestation of our active nature. I just now spoke of it as acquiescence. It would naturally be described by such terms as 'willingness' or the 'turning of our disposition.' What characterizes both consent and belief is the cessation of theoretic agitation through the advent of an idea which is inwardly stable, and fills the mind solidly to the exclusion of contradictory ideas. (*PP* 913)

The first two sentences clearly speak for the possibility of there being a type (i) belief state without any type (ii) act of consent. Notice that he uses "conviction" to characterize the belief state. A conviction or being convinced, unlike acquiescence and consent, is not an action, it being absurd to say that you became convinced, as opposed to consented or acquiesced, intentionally, on purpose, voluntarily, carefully, and so on for all the other intentional action modifiers. The charitable way to interpret this passage is to say that when he switches in the third and fourth sentences to speaking respectively about acquiescence and consent, he shifts from talking about the passive type (i) beliefs to the active type (ii) beliefs. Unfortunately for this interpretation, the third sentence, "I just now spoke of it as acquiescence," through its use of the anaphoric "it," refers back to the type (i) beliefs of the previous two sentences. James certainly did not mean to require that every belief state result from an act of consent. Other passages of similar ilk could be quoted.

There *are* passages, however, in which James clearly allows for an exclusively type (i) belief, for example his highly mythologized "baby's first sensation" of the lighted candle that is believed (!) by the babe to be existent because "*Any object which remains uncontradicted is ipso facto believed and posited as absolute reality*" (918). James's attempt to make this sound plausible appeals to a false dichotomy between believing and disbelieving – because the babe doesn't disbelieve the reality of the candle, it must believe in its reality – which overlooks the third possibility of having no belief at all. James might have been misled into accepting this false disjunction because he confounded it with his other thesis that "The sense that anything we think of is unreal can only come, then, when that thing is contradicted by some other thing of which we think" and "We never disbelieve anything except for the reason that we believe something else which contradicts the first thing" (914, 918).

James asks us to "compare this psychological fact with the corresponding logical truth that all negation rests on covert assertion of something else than the thing denied" (*PP*914). Herein we see James's penchant to semanticize and ontologize a genetic analysis of the psychological cause of our taking something to be the case, just as he did in Chapter 1 with his genetic analysis of the conditions under which we take something to be good or obligatory. Because we are led to deny the existence of something when we discover or believe that there is some positive reality that logically excludes it, what we mean by, for example, "The table is not red" is "There is some positive property of the table, *F*-ness, that is incompatible with redness," and, furthermore, the very being of a negative state of affairs – a lack, absence, want, or privation – is logically dependent upon there being some positive reality whose properties are incompatible with its properties.

Not only does the incompatibility theory seem false in general, since I might believe that some man lacks an odor without believing that he has some positive property that logically excludes his having an odor, and even be right about this, it also is inconsistent with James's prized and oft-repeated doctrine of the mystery of existence. James was intent on showing that, *pace* absolute idealism, there must be some fact that defies explanation, namely that there is something rather than nothing. (See primarily *EP* 58–64 and *WB* 107–8, as well as *PP* 1269, *SPP* 27, and *ML* 412.) As Bergson showed in his *Creative Evolution*, the incompatibility theory of negation, when interpreted ontologically, entails, *pace* the doctrine of the mystery of existence, that it is necessary that there exist some positive reality, and thus that there is something rather than nothing, since something can fail to exist only if there exists in its place some positive reality that logically excludes it. This constitutes an ontological argument for the existence of positive entities. James read this book in 1907 and heaped lavish praise upon it, but he still adhered to the mystery of existence in *Some Problems of Philosophy*, which he began to write two years later. I believe that the best way for James to resolve this inconsistency between the mystery of existence and the incompatibility theory of negation is to give up the latter, for, not only does it seem false, it goes too far in the direction of rationalism, being only a stone's throw from the principle of sufficient reason in demanding an explanation for every negative fact in terms of positive facts alone.

With respect to type (ii) beliefs, there are various propositional attitudes, called "psychic attitudes" by James, that the mind can adopt to a proposition, understood as a "combination of 'ideas' by a 'copula'" (917, 916). There is that completely neutral attitude of merely entertaining or thinking of the proposition, which can then give way to a believing, denying, willing, or questioning of the proposition. James seems to equate the belief and will psychic attitudes when he writes that "All that the mind does is in both cases [will and belief] the same; it looks at the object and consents to its existence, espouses it, says 'it shall be my reality'" (948).

It is crucial that a proposition can retain its identity from one manner of being attended to by a psychic act to another, for otherwise certain valid argument forms would not be valid. Consider the valid argument form of *modus ponens*: If *p*, then *q*. *p*. Therefore, *q*. The proposition *p* is not asserted or consented to in the hypothetical premise, but it is in the second premise. Unless *p* is the very same proposition in both of its appearances, the argument fails to be valid through equivocation.

James is quite explicit that his theory of psychic attitudes applies only to complex cases of type (ii). "Often we first suppose and then believe ... But these cases are none of them *primitive* [simple] cases. They only occur in minds long schooled to doubt by the contradictions of experience" (946). It is when there is a conflict between two or more ideas competing for sole occupancy of our mind that there is a need for a psychic attitude or act of belief, in the form of a consent, acceptance, or acquiescence to one of the competing ideas.

Once the act of consent has succeeded in bringing about a type (i) state of consciousness, neurophysiology will take over and lead to a motor response. When the state consists in thinking of one of our own actions, the action will follow in just the same way as if we had willed it, but if it consists instead in a thought of some object other than our own body behaving in a certain way, the behavior will not follow.

That action is the normal outgrowth of belief can help to explain James's startling remark that "We would believe everything if we only could" (*PP* 928). This preference cannot be explained in terms of the belief state's peace of mind vis-à-vis that of indecision – our "proneness to act or decide merely because action and decision are, as such, agreeable, and relieve the tension of doubt and hesitancy" (1137). This explains only why we want to be in a belief state, not why we want to believe *everything*. Nor is the explanation to be had in terms of our having a *National Enquirer* type mentality that delights in believing "everything" about everybody. I believe an explanation can be found in terms of James's promethean quest to actualize all of his many selves. To actualize all these selves, an incredible diversity of acts must be performed. Because belief leads to action, the more beliefs we have, the more actions we perform and thus the more headway we make on this grand promethean quest. There also is an appeal to James's hipsterism, because each action occasions its own special tingle or thrill.

One gets the feeling that James's reasons for insisting that a belief lead to action were not based exclusively on neurophysiological facts, which were exceedingly sparse at that time, but on normative considerations as well. At the heart of the pragmatism of both Peirce and James is Bain's claim that a belief is what a man is willing to act on. For James this was not a purely descriptive claim based on conceptual analysis or neurophysiology but in part normative. A man *ought* to act on his beliefs.

James had an intense disdain for the idle dreamer and aesthete. "There is no more contemptible type of human character than that of the nerveless sentimentalist and dreamer, who spends his life in a weltering sea of sensibility and emotion, but who never does a manly concrete deed" (129).

The habit of excessive novel-reading and theatre-going will produce true monsters in the line. The weeping of a Russian lady over the fictitious personages in the play, while her coachman is freezing to death on his seat outside, is the sort of thing that everywhere happens on a less glaring scale. Even the habit of excessive indulgence in music, for those who are neither performers themselves nor musically gifted enough to take it in a purely intellectual way, has probably a relaxing effect upon the character. One becomes filled with emotions which habitually pass without prompting to any deed, and so the inertly sentimental condition is kept up. The remedy would be, never to suffer one's self to have an emotion at a concert, without expressing it afterwards in some active way. (129)

By identifying the type (i) belief state, which is an emotional state, with the will state, James assured that belief would find its proper hookup with "concrete manly deeds."

James's causal analysis of belief deals with its causes as well as its effects, which are or, better, ought to be overt actions of a "manly" sort. His analysis of the causes of belief also parallels that of the causes of the will. Any uncontested thought constitutes a belief, as well as a will. There are two different ways, one active and the other inactive, in which one can have an uncontested thought, whether or not it is preceded by a conflict between rival thoughts. It can be caused in a nonactive way by the thought having emotional sting based on its "coerciveness over attention, or the mere power to possess consciousness," "liveliness, or sensible pungency," "stimulating effect upon the will," "emotional interest, as object of love, dread, admiration, desire," "congruity with certain favorite forms of contemplation," or "independence of other causes" (*PP* 928–9). Plainly, none of these causes involve intentional agency. The believer does not control them at will. James's claim that "the more a conceived object *excites* us, the more reality it has [for us]" also makes the cause a nonaction, since we cannot control at will what excites us (935).This is the first leg of the creating-discovering aporia.

There is, however, an active way in which a belief state can be caused and that is through the effort to attend to an idea. The *act* of consent, acceptance, or acquiescence are things that an agent does intentionally. In the conflicted cases the act of consent often comes as a result of effort, and this raises the question of what causes this effort. This will be discussed in the next chapter, since it gets to the root of James's theory of freedom.

In some cases, try as we will to attend to an idea, we are unable to establish its steadfast, uncontested presence in our mind. As James puts it, "a man cannot believe at will abruptly" (948). Fortunately, there is an indirect way of willfully inducing such recalcitrant beliefs, namely by *acting as if* we believed, which is just what Pascal enjoined nonbelievers to do who want to acquire real faith. "*We need only in cold blood* ACT *as if the thing in question were real, and it will infallibly end by growing into such a connection with our life that it will become real*" (949). This acting-as-if-you-believe recipe for self-inducing a belief is given in a letter James wrote eighteen years earlier, in 1872, to his brother Bob: "Have faith and wait, and resolve whatever happens to be faithful 'in the outward act' (as a philosopher says) that is *do* as if the good were the law of being, even if one can't for the moment really believe it. The belief will come in its time" (*CWJ* 4:432). In "The Gospel of Relaxation" James says that "Action seems to follow feeling, but really action and feeling go together and by regulating the action, which is under the more direct control of the will, we can indirectly regulate the feeling, which is not" (*TT* 118). Given that belief is a feeling of conviction for James, this recipe applies also to belief. For this chapter's purpose of establishing that James held belief to be an action, this is all that is needed. Although belief is not always a "basic action" in the sense of something that we just do without first intentionally doing anything else, it is self-inducible by basic actions and thereby becomes subject to our will. Accordingly, the second premise of James's Master Syllogism must be understood as asserting that belief is a free action or inducible by free actions, but for the sake of brevity the final disjunct shall be omitted. The conclusion, in turn, will have to be changed to read that we are always morally obligated to believe or get ourselves to believe in a manner that maximizes desire–satisfaction over desire–dissatisfaction.

Conclusion

James has made out a strong case that belief is an intentional action or indirectly inducible by intentional actions, which is all that is needed for the purpose of supporting premise 2 in his Master Syllogism. But it is highly dubious that he has made good on his strong thesis that from a psychological point of view there is an identity between attention, will, and belief. At best, he has shown that in all three cases there is an idea occupying consciousness sans competitors. But that hardly shows that they are one and the same, for there is a difference between the case in which I believe but do not will that some proposition be true and the one in which I will but do not believe that this proposition will be true: In the former I adopt a believing but not a willing attitude toward the proposition, whereas in the case in which I will but do not believe this proposition the reverse is the case. For example, I might believe but not will that Jones will succumb to cancer.

James himself, at times, seemed to recognize a difference between the believing and willing psychic attitudes.

We stand here [in the case of the will] exactly where we did in the case of belief. When an idea *stings* us in a certain way, makes as it were a certain electric connection with our Self, we believe that it *is* a reality. When it stings us in another way, makes another connection with our Self, we say, *let it be* a reality. To the word 'is' and to the words 'let it be' there correspond peculiar attitudes of consciousness which it is vain to seek to explain. The indicative and the imperative moods are as much ultimate categories of thinking as they are of grammar. (*PP* 1172–3)

This seems, by its use of the plural "attitudes of consciousness," to make the believing attitude different from the willing or "let it be" attitude, even when directed toward one and the same proposition.

James's theory needs to be reconstructed into a three-tiered affair. On the first level is the entertaining of a proposition in a manner that is neutral between different psychic or propositional attitudes. The second tier involves a psychic or propositional attitude toward this proposition of believing, willing, questioning, doubting, hoping, and the like, each of which is unique. On the third level is the effort to adopt one of these psychic attitudes toward the proposition, which might consist in an effort to attend in a certain manner, as for example to ideate in the manner required by my Hollywood ethics. It will be shown in the next chapter that for James freedom enters on the third level, it being the amount of effort that is expended that is subject to the free will of the person. As a result of this third-tier freedom, a person has the freedom to control what he believes, sometimes by just making an extra effort either to attend to an idea to the exclusion of its competitors or to adopt a believing psychic attitude toward it, and, at other times, by making an extra effort to will to do things that will indirectly induce belief.

3

The Freedom of Belief

The previous chapter presented James's reasons for thinking that belief is an intentional action or inducible by intentional actions. The purpose of this chapter is to explore James's reasons for claiming that belief also is a free action; for if it is not free, we cannot have, as the conclusion of his Master Syllogism asserts, a moral obligation to believe in a way that maximizes desire–satisfaction, given that ought implies can. This chapter is subdivided into four parts. The first presents James's theory of freedom. The second gives his reasons why it cannot be decided on epistemic or evidential grounds that we are or that we are not free in this sense. The third expounds his reasons for thinking that it is desirable in terms of maximizing desire–satisfaction to believe that we are free. The fourth presents some objections to his theory of freedom and how James could respond to them. It will be found in Chapter 4 that among the several necessary conditions for having a will-to-believe option are that the proposition to be believed cannot have its truth or falsity determined on epistemic or evidential grounds and that believing it has desirable consequences. Thus, if one or more of the objections to James's theory should prove fatal, his theory would not qualify as a candidate for a will-to-believe option, since its *falsity* can be epistemically determined.

Throughout his adult life, James ardently believed in the libertarian doctrine of free will, replete with its contra-causal spiritual acts of will. His near life-ending emotional crisis of 1870 was occasioned by his doubt that he was free in this sense and therefore that he was able to function as a morally responsible agent. Through a promethean act of will he self-induced this belief by following his formula of acting as if he believed, part of which involved publicly declaring that he was free, thus the point of his claim that "our first act of freedom, if we are free, ought in all inward propriety to be to affirm that we are free" (*WB* 115. see also *PP* 1177). Through this public avowal he commits himself in the eyes of his fellow persons to acting as if he is free and thereby assuming full moral responsibility for his actions. Because this belief in free will was foundational to his existence as a man he was unable to resist his own strictures in *The Principles of Psychology* against metaphysical digressions when he got to the subject of freedom in the chapters on "Attention" and "Will." He not only waxed metaphysical but did so in the manner of an itinerant New England preacher out to save our souls, which is what he really was. It is quite amazing in the midst of a psychology textbook suddenly to be given a half-time locker room pep talk by the author.

James, for reasons that shortly will be considered, was a committed incompatibilist, believing that a free act must, among other things, not have a prior sufficient cause. A free act must be at least a *chance* occurrence in that it is not determined in any way by prior states of the universe. For James, no free acts are to be found on the first tier in my reconstructed version of James's theory of will and belief at the end of the last chapter, since it is causally determined by the workings of the brain where ideas enter consciousness and thus get entertained in the neutral sense. It also is causally determined whether an effort is made on tier three to bring about a willing or believing on tier two of one of these ideas from tier one. The only place that free will can get into the act is in regard to the amount of effort that is made to will or believe one of these ideas via attending to certain ideas, such as in my Hollywood ethics. It is only "the *effort to attend,* not to the mere attending, that we are seriously tempted to ascribe spontaneous power. We think we can make more of it *if we will*; and the amount which we make does not seem a fixed function of the ideas themselves, as it would necessarily have to be if our effort were an effect and not a spiritual force" (*PP* 426–7).

James characterizes this spiritual force as an "original force" and the "star performer" (*PP* 428). Its free efforts "originate ex nihilo, or come from a fourth dimension" (*PP* 1178). To be an original force, for James, it must be an irreducibly conscious event that is not causally determined. After giving a very fair and forceful exposition of the epiphenomenalistic "effect theory" of the amount of the effort to attend, according to which it is only a causally determined effect of physiological events, he expresses his personal preference for the "cause-theory." "The reader will please observe that I am saying all that can *possibly* be said in favor of the effect-theory, since, inclining as I do myself to the cause-theory, I do not want to undervalue the enemy" (*PP* 424–5).

This cause-theory gives James a way of dissolving the creating-discovering aporia. We do not "create" in his prime mover or ex nihilo first cause sense the fact that we are conscious of or attend to certain ideas nor that we make an effort to adopt a certain psychic attitude toward them: All of these facts are causally determined by our interests, which, in turn, are causally explained in terms of physiological facts pertaining to the activity of the brain. Thus we merely discover but do not create these facts. We are the free cause and sole creator only of the *amount* of effort that we make to adopt a certain psychic attitude toward one of these ideas. It will be seen that although the area within which our free will operates is very constricted, the long range effects of this radically limited use of free will can be very extensive.

That the amount of these efforts to attend against the course of least resistance, such as in a case of moral temptation, do not have a prior sufficient cause in the physiological workings of the brain cannot be epistemically determined, since we cannot make sufficiently fine-grained measurements of brain events so as to discover whether the effect-theory is true. "The feeling of effort certainly *may* be an inert accompaniment and not the active element which it seems. No measurements are as yet performed (it is safe to say none ever will be performed) which can show that it contributes energy to the result" (*PP* 428). Thus, "The last word of psychology here is ignorance, for the 'forces' engaged are certainly too delicate and numerous to be followed in detail" (*PP* 429). This gets repeated in the later chapter on "Will," when he says that such measurements "will surely be forever beyond human reach" (*PP* 1176).

James makes clear that his reasons for believing that the amount of effort we make to attend is contra-causal are "ethical." His so believing has great benefits for him, enabling him to satisfy his most important desire, namely to function as a morally responsible agent. "The whole feeling of reality, the whole sting and excitement of our voluntary life, depends on our sense that in it things are *really being decided* from one moment to another, and that it is not the dull rattling off of a chain that was forged innumerable ages ago"(*PP* 429).

Our very sense of our own self-worth as persons depends on this belief, since "the effort seems to belong to an altogether different realm, as if it were the substantive thing which we *are*, and those ["our strength and our intelligence, our wealth and even our good luck"] were but externals which we *carry*" (*PP* 1181). James extols the stoical hero who, regardless of external deterrents, can still find life meaningful "by pure inward willingness to take the world with those deterrent objects there" (*PP* 1181). "The world thus finds in the heroic man its worthy match and mate; and the effort which he is able to put forth to hold himself erect and keep his heart unshaken is the direct measure of his worth and function in the game of human life" (*PP* 1181). This sets the stage for the eloquent concluding paragraph of the section on free will.

Thus not only our morality but our religion, so far as the latter is deliberate, depend on the effort which we can make. *"Will you or won't you have it so?"* is the most probing question we are ever asked; we are asked it every hour of the day, and about the largest as well as the smallest, the most theoretical as well as the most practical, things. We answer by *consents or non-consents* and not by words. What wonder that these dumb responses should seem our deepest organ of communication with the nature of things! What wonder if the effort demanded by them be the measure of our worth as men! What wonder if the amount which we accord of it be the one strictly underived and original contribution which we make to the world! (*PP* 1182)

We are essentially a "spiritual force," for that is the "substantive thing which we *are*" (*PP* 1181). A lot more will be said in Chapters 8 and 9 about the nature of this immaterial, nonnatural self, which is not denizen of the natural spatio-temporal order that science describes and explains, but instead a transcendental being or force from James's "fourth dimension" that brings about effects in this order.

It is in his famous article on "The Dilemma of Determinism" that James gives his fullest and most compelling reasons for thinking that it is desirable for most people to believe that they are one of these immaterial selves possessed of his sort of contra-causal free will. We have already seen that James assumes that most other people are like him in this respect: Their whole sense of their own self-worth and the meaningfulness of life depends on their believing that they have such freedom, for without it they could not function as morally responsible agents. He now develops an ingenious argument to show the disastrous consequences for the believer in determinism, consequences that are avoided by the believer in his contra-causal free will. This is the dilemma of determinism argument, from which the article gets its title.

The key assumption that underlies the argument is that determinism is incompatible with free will, because it entails fatalism, namely that whatever happens is the only thing that could have happened, that possibilities are not in excess of actualities, that nothing that happens could have been avoided or prevented. In order to show that determinism entails fatalism, an acceptable definition of *determinism* must first be given. James is well aware of the danger of begging the question at the outset by giving an emotively charged definition. Whereas the words *freedom* and *chance* have associations that are respectively eulogistic and opprobrious, fortunately "no ambiguities hang about this word [*determinism*] or about its opposite, *indeterminism*. Both designate an outward way in which things may happen, and their cold and mathematical sound has no sentimental associations that can bribe our partiality either way in advance" (*WB* 117; my italics).

James, however, immediately forgets his admonition against using emotive and rhetorical language, for in the very next paragraph he gives about as question-begging a rhetorical definition of *determinism* as one could imagine. Determinism, we are told, "professes that those parts of the universe already laid down absolutely appoint and decree what the other parts shall be" (*WB* 117). This gets repeated in *The Principles of Psychology* when he writes that if determinism is true then whatever efforts of will we make were "*required* and *exacted*," that "whatever object at any time fills our consciousness was from eternity bound to fill it then and there, and *compel* from us the exact effort, neither more nor less, which we bestow upon it" (*PP* 1175; my italics). Plainly, James's use of legalistic language confounds positive with scientific laws because it makes the unnoticed slide from an event happening in accordance with a scientific law to its being coerced or compelled to occur by some positive law of the state or decree of a sovereign. It is as if the law of $f = ma$ were to threaten all the material particles in the world that they sure as hell better obey it or else.

But this is not the end of James's question-begging rhetorical definition of *determinism*. He also avails himself of ball-and-chain type metaphors in his description of causation. Determinism holds that "The whole is in each and every part, and *welds it* with the rest into an absolute unity, an *iron block*, in which there can be no equivocation or shadow of turning" (*WB* 118; my italics). This is followed by talk about "one unbending unit of fact" if determinism is true. And, again, if determinism is true then the whole of our voluntary life is "the dull rattling off of a *chain* that was forged innumerable ages ago," and "the world must be one *unbroken* fact" (*PP* 429, 1177; my italics). Plainly, it is unfair to burden the determinist with accepting a view of causation that makes an effect a link in a chain or inexorably welded to its cause in one big iron block, for this makes the effect look like an unfortunate member of a chain gang, completely destitute of any freedom.

Yet another rhetorical device that James employs to make determinism appear to have fatalistic consequences is the use of metaphors that spatialize the time of a deterministic universe so that future events are always there, our mind coming upon them one after the other in its journey up its world-line, to paraphrase the accounts given by Weyl and Eddington of the Minkowskian world of relativity theory. For determinism, "There is nothing inchoate . . . about this universe of ours, all that was or is or shall be actual in it having been from eternity virtually there," and "The future has no ambiguous possibilities hidden in its womb" (*WB* 118, 117). Indeterminism, on the other hand, holds that "actualities . . . float in a wider sea of possibilities from out of which they are chosen; and, *somewhere*, indeterminism says, such possibilities exist, and form a part of truth" (*WB* 118). This spatialization of time in the deterministic universe suggests that as our minds "travel" up their world-lines into the future they come upon preexistent events and thereby play no active or creative role in bringing them about, and, furthermore, when they make a choice there is only one choosable object hanging from the rafters in the Hall of Future Possibilities, as Paul Edwards pointed out to me. Time presents them with no branching tributaries that they might choose to journey along.

While James's "arguments" for determinism entailing fatalism amount to nothing but a skein of question-begging rhetorical definitions, his incompatibilist intuitions still might be right. If determinism is true, then whatever we do is the only thing that it was causally possible for us to do. But if we causally couldn't have done otherwise, then could we have done otherwise? Could we have avoided or prevented doing what we did? My intuitions, along with those of many other philosophers, not to mention the vast majority of laypersons, require a negative answer to these questions. If James were alive today, he would look with favor on some recent arguments to prove that determinism entails fatalism, such as the unpreventability argument. If determinism is true, there is a deductive-nomological explanation for every event. Take any future event E that we think we are able to prevent. There is a deductive nomological explanation of E in terms of a conjunction of a set of causal laws and a description of the state of the universe before we were even born. Since we can prevent neither the universe from having been in this state nor these causal laws from holding true, we cannot prevent anything that is entailed by their conjunction, such as the future occurrence of E.

Having explored James's reasons, or lack thereof, for believing in incompatibilism, we are in a position to consider his dilemma of determinism argument, which, it must be emphasized, is directed against not the truth of determinism but only the desirability of believing it to be true. Because the determinism issue is not epistemically decidable, he thinks that we are justified in choosing what to believe in this matter on the basis of the consequences for good and ill of believing one way or the other.

The argument begins with the fact that we express judgments of regret about some evil or ought-not-to-be, of which the world abounds. Assuming both determinism and incompatibilism, it follows that these evils could not have been prevented or avoided. And this is pessimism. But "our deterministic pessimism may become a deterministic optimism at the price of extinguishing judgments of regret" (*WB* 127). This requires saying that our judgments of regret are false. A false judgment, however, is itself an evil or an ought-not-to-be, and thus we still face the same pessimistic consequence. In fact, one can't believe falsely that there is evil, for if their belief is true there is evil, and if it is false there again is evil, namely, their own false belief.

For the purpose of critically evaluating this dilemma argument it is necessary that it be given an explicit mounting. The argument is formulated in the form of a conditional proof, in which pessimism is deduced from the assumption that determinism is true, along with certain other truths.

1. Determinism is true. assumption for conditional proof
2. If determinism is true, then whatever happens could not have been avoided or prevented. the incompatibilist premise
3. There is a judgment of regret, J, that there are events that ought not to be. an empirical premise
4. J is either true or false. an instance of the law of bivalence
5. If J is true, then there are events that ought not to be but could not have been avoided or prevented. first horn of the dilemma and follows from 1, 2, and 3
6. That there are events that ought not to be but could not have been avoided or prevented is pessimism. true by definition
7. If J is true, pessimism is true. from 5 and 6
8. A false judgment is an ought-not-to-be. premise
9. If J is false, there are events (namely, false judgments) that ought not to be but could not have been avoided or prevented. second horn of dilemma and follows from 1, 2, and 8
10. If J is false, then pessimism is true. from 6 and 9
11. Pessimism is true. from 4–10 by dilemma argument
12. If determinism is true, then pessimism is true. from 1–11 by conditional proof

Supposedly, it is quite undesirable to believe in pessimism, for then we would have no reason to take life seriously and try to make the world a better place (you know, by putting our shoulder to the wheel). But pessimism is a logical consequence of determinism. Does this argument show that anyone who believes in determinism will also believe in pessimism? Of course not: Belief is not closed under deduction, a person not having to believe everything that is entailed by what she believes. It only shows that someone who is rational enough to be aware of the deductive consequences of her belief in determinism, coupled with the controversial assumption of incompatibilism, will believe that pessimism is true. The irrational types are beyond redemption by this argument. Thus, James's argument must be restricted to those who are sufficiently rational as to be among the saving remnant. This is not much of a concession on James's part, since he supposes that his readers want to think logically and thus would welcome help in doing so. Nor does the argument even show that every sufficiently rational person who accepts determinism will take a seat on the sideline in life's struggles against evil, for the psychology of some persons would allow them both to accept pessimism and lead the morally strenuous life. James just happens not to be among them.

There is a way out of the dilemma that consists in challenging its second horn,

9. If J is false, there are events (namely, false judgments) that ought not to be but could not have been avoided or prevented.

by denying the premise

8. A false judgment is an ought-not-to-be.

The gnostic or subjectivist denies that false judgment is an evil and is prepared to give a theodicy of sorts for false beliefs based on their promoting the outweighing good of deepening our awareness and understanding of evil. James gives a most eloquent and convincing presentation of this view that is due not only to his passion for fairness but also, I suspect, to his philosophical nymphomania; however, he soon thereafter pulls the plug on it. To find our highest good in our subjective appreciation of the world's evils belittles the morally strenuous life, sapping our incentive to take seriously our moral duties to perform certain overt actions. James tells us that it "violates my sense of moral reality through and through" (*WB* 136). Subjectivism, at least in those whose psychology resembles James's, thereby engenders an undesirable passivism and ethical indifference.

Once consecrate the . . . notion that our performances and our violations of duty are for a common purpose, the attainment of subjective knowledge and feeling, and that the deepening of these is the chief end of our lives – and at what point on the downward slope are we to stop? . . . And in practical life it is either a nerveless sentimentality or a sensualism without bounds. Everywhere it fosters the fatalistic mood of mind. It makes those who are already too inert more passive still; it renders wholly reckless those whose energy is already in excess. All through history we find how subjectivism, as soon as it has a free career, exhausts itself in every sort of spiritual, moral, and practical license. (*WB* 132)

Indeterminism alone makes of the world a suitable arena for our deepest moral concerns and aspirations. "It says conduct, and not sensibility, is the ultimate fact for our recognition. With the vision of certain works to be done, of certain outward changes to be wrought or resisted, it says our intellectual horizon terminates" (*WB* 134). One senses James's promethean proclivities lurking in the background, for what matters is changing the world through our overt actions. James admits that not everyone shares his sentiment of rationality in this matter, and he attempts to win them over through his impassioned prose in his halftime pep talks.

James fails to note that subjectivism or gnosticism is not the only basis for justifying or constructing a theodicy for false belief. There is, for example, the free will theodicy for false belief, such as was given by Descartes in his Fourth *Meditation*, according to which false belief results from our misuse of our free will, but that is no reason for indicting the Deity since there is in general such great value to our having free will. This theodicy is not available to the determinist if free will is incompatible with determinism, as James was convinced it was.

The worry is that James's dilemma of determinism argument proves too much, precluding any theodicy for any type of evil. James made a careless remark that had the effect of ruling out the possibility of any theodicy succeeding: "The *ideally* perfect whole is certainly that whole of which the parts also are perfect – if we can depend on logic for anything, we can depend on it for that definition" (*PU* 60). Far from logic requiring this, James's reasoning commits the fallacy of division by assuming that the parts must have the same properties as does the whole. But this is not James's considered opinion, for when he was in a healthy mood he extolled the value of the traditional soul-building theodicy, favored by all the great medieval theists. But take any evil E and any theodicy that attempts to show that E has an overall beneficial consequence in that E is necessary for either the realization of an outweighing good or the prevention of an even greater evil. E, being an evil, is an ought-not-to-be, but, James would go on to argue, if the theodicy works, then *E* is not after all an ought-not-to-be, and thus *E* both is and is not an ought-not-to-be. Because our initial intuition is to take *E* to be an ought-not-to-be, we feel a moral duty to try to prevent and eliminate *E* type events. But when we accept the theodicy for God's allowing *E*, we no longer view *E* as an ought-not-to-be and thereby do not feel morally obligated to try to prevent and eliminate *E* type events.

There is a failure in this argument against the viability of any theodicy to relativize an ought-not-to-be, either to us finite creatures or to God. Thus, when a theodicy shows that some evil, *E*, is justified, it means that God is morally justified in bringing about or permitting *E*, not that we are. *E*, therefore, is not an ought-not-to-be relative to God, the planner and creator of the entire universe, with the possible exception of our free acts and their consequences. This does not entail that *E* is not an ought-not-to-be relative to us finite creatures, for our position and role in the scheme of things is quite different from God's. We are thrown into the world at a later time with the moral duty to prevent and eliminate every evil we can. God, as the planner and creator of the universe, has a different role to play and thereby is not subject to the same duty that we are. Thus, it would be unfair to challenge the soul-building theodicy's attempt to morally exonerate God for creating natural evils, such as physical impediments, as a means for our developing higher character traits, by an analogy with a finite father who purposely breaks his son's legs so that the boy will have an opportunity to engage in soul-building, certainly a wicked thing to do. For this overlooks the radical difference in the perspective and role of God and finite creatures. A broken limb is an ought-not-to-be relative to us but not to God.

Some Objections

If there is a telling objection to James's theory of free will, it will stand epistemically discredited and thus not be a suitable target for a will-to-believe option. The standard objections to libertarian theories will be considered. First, there is the perennial objection that a libertarian type freedom, in virtue of postulating a nonphysical cause, be it a Cartesian soul substance or some type of spiritual act of effort or will, of some change in the physical world, violates the law of the conservation of angular momentum. Herein some spiritual event that is not itself possessed of any physical energy, and thus cannot get plugged in for the f in the $f = ma$ law, causes an acceleration of a physical object, thereby violating the law of the conservation of angular momentum.

James never explicitly addressed this objection, but the manner in which he developed and defended his theory indicates that he was concerned with finding a way around this objection. James's version of libertarianism is far superior to that of others, from Aristotle down through Sartre and Chisholm, in giving hope of escaping this objection. For in his version a free act of effort operates directly on consciousness, having as its immediate effect the sustaining of attention to some idea or the adoption of a psychic attitude, rather than a bodily movement, as is the case with other versions of libertarianism. For example, in Aristotle's famous example of the stick moves the stone, the hand moves the stick, and the man moves his hand, something that is not an event in the physical world, the man, directly causes an acceleration. By making the immediate effect of an effort of will the strengthening of an idea in consciousness, rather than the acceleration of a physical object, James's theory does not seem to violate the conservation law.

James gives some hints that he was worried about his theory violating a conservation law, for he wrote that "The world . . . is just as *continuous with itself* for the believers in free will as for the rigorous determinists, only the latter are unable to believe in points of bifurcation as spots of really indifferent equilibrium or as containing shunts which there . . . *direct existing motions without altering their amount*" (*MT* 303; my italics; see also *PP* 144 and *ERM* 87). This is a variant on Descartes' pineal gland theory, and, unfortunately, involves the same violation of the conservation of angular momentum. The shunts – acts of free will – do alter, *pace* James, the *amount* of existing motions, not by changing the speed of any object but instead by changing its direction and thereby its velocity, resulting in a change in the angular momentum of the entire system. Obviously, a lot more work would have to be done to rework James theory so that it does not violate this conservation law, but James would not be in agony if it did since he believed that this law was only an empirical generalization that permitted occasional exceptions. Moreover, as seen in Chapter 7, he thought that we are free to adopt the perspective of the moral agent rather than that of the scientist and thus reject the law of the conservation of angular momentum in its universal form. "Science . . . must be constantly reminded that her purposes are not the only purposes, and that the uniform causation which she has use for, and is therefore right in postulating, may be enveloped in a wider order, on which she has no claims at all" (*PP* 1179). "When we make theories about the world and discuss them with one another, we do so in order to attain a conception of things which shall give us subjective satisfactions" (*WB* 115). This involves an application of his casuistic rule from Chapter 1 to the formation of theoretical beliefs.

An even more prevalent objection than the conservation law one is the charge that the libertarian's concept of a causally undetermined free act is conceptually absurd. There are two versions of this objection. The first, and less formidable, version is that an undetermined action is a purely random or chance occurrence and therefore not attributable to a person in a way that makes her morally responsible for it. The second version holds that the absurdity is due to the fact that the undetermined free acts are without reason or motive and therefore not intentional actions at all.

James opens himself up to the first version of the objection by his popularizing penchant for giving nutshell definitions of complex ideas, not realizing that the only thing that should be put in a nutshell is a nut. He falsely makes it appear as if a free act is *merely* a causally undetermined one when he says that "'free will' . . . is the character of novelty in fresh activity-situations" (*ERE* 93; see also *SPP* 72 and *ML* 412). The same message is sent by his other nutshell definition of *freedom* as "meaning a better promise as to this world's outcome" (*P* 63. See also *MT* 6). There could be *promise* of a better future independently of what we might freely do. A *novel* action could be a purely capricious or chance occurrence, such as a causally undetermined twitch of a person's nostrils that never occurred before. Furthermore, qualitatively novel states can occur in a deterministic system, such as a collection of billiard balls moving according to Newton's laws, and an action can be free even though it is qualitatively identical to earlier actions. Yet another one of James's nutshell definitions is "'Freedom' means 'no feeling of sensible restraint'" (*SPP* 38). This certainly does not give a sufficient condition, since I could act without feeling any sensible restraint yet be doing so under a posthypnotic suggestion and thereby not be doing so freely.

Fortunately, James has much more to say about freedom than is supplied by these misbegotten nutshell definitions. He has an extended response to the objection of reducing freedom to mere capriciousness in "The Dilemma of Determinism" (*WB* 121–4), the chapters "Attention" and "Will" (*PP* 428–30 and 1175–82), and "Abstractionism and 'Relativismus'" (*MT* 136–8). He charges this objection with vicious abstractionism that consists in taking just one part of what a word means to the exclusion of everything else. Because the indeterminist's past is *causally* disconnected from the future when a free act occurs, it is assumed that the past is *totally* disconnected from the future, thereby overlooking all the other ways in which the past and future are connected in this case. "If any spot of indifference is found upon the broad highway between the past and the future, then no connexion of any sort whatever" is to be found (*MT* 137).

To understand what these other connections are, in virtue of which a free act can rightly be attributed to an agent as something for which she is morally responsible, it is necessary to take the insider's approach by introspecting what goes on when one makes a free choice. Recall that for James there are two ways to investigate a phenomenon, either by an introspective (phenomenological) or causal analysis. A free act, being undetermined, eludes a causal analysis, since it can't be subsumed under a covering law, as it must be in a deductive-nomological explanation. But it would be for James a scientistic prejudice of the worst sort to infer from this that such an act is unintelligible, for there still is the phenomenological way of understanding it through a description of what it is like from the inside to live through the exerting of an effort to attend to an idea in a case of conflict, such as in a case of moral temptation.

James produces brilliant introspectively-based descriptions in the mentioned sources of a free choice. A central theme of Chapters 8, 9, and 10 is that reality in general, in particular change, causation, and the self, can be properly understood for James only through introspective analysis. He makes a far stronger claim than that the insider and outsider approaches are equally valid, each having its own special advantage relative to some human interest and purpose. Rather, he will argue that the externalized approach of the scientist that breaks reality up into a succession of numerically discrete states and coexistent objects renders reality unintelligible, a breeding ground for all of the a priori paradoxes from those of Zeno against change down through those of Bradley against relations.

According to the second version of the objection, the libertarian's free choice is without any motive or reason. The deep objection in the *Euthyphro* to saying that something is good because God chose it to be, rather than vice versa, is that it renders God's choice reasonless. But a choice must have a reason consisting in some good that the chooser thereby hopes to realize. If the choice creates what is good, there is nothing that is good when the choice is being made that could be appealed to as a reason for the choice. And thus God's choice is reasonless and thereby absurd.

The same objection applies to James's free choice. Consider his beloved case of moral conflict or temptation in which two conflicting ideas are racing around in a person's mind, one being the idea of the action in the course of least resistance, the other being the idea of the action that is dictated by conscience or duty. Finally, the chooser makes an effort to attend to one of the ideas to the exclusion of the other so that it will dominate her consciousness and, as a result, lead her to perform the envisioned action. It is causally determined for James that the two ideas are entertained by her, and even that she makes an effort to attend to one of them, but what isn't determined is that she makes the *amount* of effort she does, and it is the amount of the effort that ultimately determines whether the idea in question wins out over its competitor. She can give no reason for exerting the amount of effort that she does other than the unhelpful one of "Because that's the sort of person I want to become, namely someone who chooses from the moral point of view rather than that of self-interest." But she has no reason for that, for wanting to become that sort of person. She is a naked self, devoid of any character that could supply her with reasons for her choice. What she does is to choose her character *ab initio*. But this is absurd, because it requires her to make a reasonless choice.

Although James never explicitly considered this objection, I am quite certain that he would challenge the charge of absurdity, since his truly promethean person must be a causa sui with respect to her own character, and thus she must perform some acts, such as exerting just the amount of effort she does in resolving a moral conflict, that will create her character ex nihilo. Through this ultimate promethean act she makes one of the two competing reasons or motives out to be the dominant one, but she has no reason for doing this. My own intuitions are not clear in this matter, and since I do not know what to do in resolving the issue I will leave the dispute between James and the objector hanging.

Another objection to libertarianism is that it gives us no basis for determining forensic responsibility. A legal system is not pragmatically viable unless there are fairly straightforward ways of empirically determining when a person is responsible for violating one of its laws and thereby fit to be punished in the prescribed manner. James's account of freedom is useless in this regard, since, admittedly, it is not epistemically determinable when the amount of a person's effort to attend is causally undetermined. The great advantage of soft determinism over libertarianism is that it supplies us with empirically workable criteria for a person acting freely, namely that the action was not externally or internally coerced.

James must grant that for pragmatic or utilitarian reasons our forensic criteria for responsibility cannot be based on his criteria for a free act but instead on the verifiable criteria supplied by soft determinism. But it is clear from the overall tenor of James's discussion that he is not concerned with the forensic use of "free" and "responsible" but rather with how we *should* think about our freedom in personal contexts in which we take stock of ourselves and our worth as persons, as well as that of our intimates – our friends and lovers, even our enemies. I advisedly use the word "should" because his analysis, as is typical of his analyses, is in part revisionary, being concerned with how we should conceive of things so as to promote the good life consisting in our full self-realization. It is not an ordinary language analysis that purports to describe how we actually use language. In these personal contexts we are not concerned with the way in which blame, shame, responsibility, and punishment are affixed in the public arena, but how to judge ourselves and thereby our intimates in our heart. James's contention really is that in these moments of solitude we should think of ourselves as original spiritual forces that can mold our own characters ex nihilo. And, James would add, by so thinking of ourselves we get ourselves to make greater efforts to mold our own characters, thereby satisfying the desirable-consequences-for-the-believer necessary condition for having a will-to-believe option to believe.

A closely related objection to the preceding one is that James's libertarianism radically restricts the range of our free actions, confining them to the rather infrequent cases in which we exert a certain amount of effort to attend to a difficult idea in a case of moral conflict, and thereby trivializes our free will. For example, we do say, *pace* James, that people act freely, even in nonconflicted cases, provided there is no coercion. Thus, it is correct to say of the person of charitable character who donates to charity without coercion or conflict that she did it freely, of her own free will.

Again, James's response must be that he is not giving an ordinary language type analysis of such *public* uses of "free," but rather a partially revisionary and normative analysis of the private cases in which we are alone with ourselves and ask who we are, what worth we have, and decide how we want to be judged and in turn to judge our intimates. It is this existential dimension of freedom that James wants to capture.

James also has a good response to the charge of triviality. Although the *number* of our free acts is far less than it ordinarily is taken to be, the *importance* of these acts is anything but trivial, since in them we define our characters and thus how we will behave in the most important matters of life, which, in turn, can have the most important, far-ranging impact on the future history of the world. "Our acts of voluntary attention, brief and fitful as they are, are nevertheless momentous and critical, determining us, as they do, to higher or lower destinies" (*TT* 111). Their remote effects "are too incalculable to be recorded; however, the practical and theoretical life of whole species, as well as of individual beings, results from" them (*PP* 401). The acts they occasion "may seal our doom." Think of James's example of the reformed alcoholic and the "fatal glass of beer." Thus, these sporadic efforts to attend are anything but trivial in their importance.

James is making use of a primitive type of chaos theory, similar to the parable of the war that was lost for the want of a nail that kept one horse from being shod and thus unavailable for the battle that was lost but would have been won had it participated, with this loss eventuating in the loss of the war. The nail part of the story begins with whether or not we freely make enough of an effort to attend to the right idea in a case of moral conflict. The amount of effort we make will determine what action we perform, for good or ill. The impulse to do the ideal or right thing, I, might alone be insufficient to overcome the propensity, P, to do what is in the course of least resistance. It might be, in other terms, that "I *per se* $<$ P"; but when sufficient effort to attend to I, E, is added to the equation, it could result in "$I + E > P$" (*PP* 1155). The next part of James's parable concerns how acting in accordance with I factors into the big equation of history, this being the counterpart to the outcome of the battle and eventually the war. Let M represent the entire world minus the reaction of the thinker upon it, and x be what we contribute by way of action, which results in crucial, character-defining cases, from the amount of effort we freely make to attend. M alone could make for a quite dismal future, whereas $M + x$ makes for a radically different future in which we realize the good life. "Let it not be said that x is too infinitesimal a component to change of the immense whole in which it lies embedded.... The moral definition of the world may depend on" our contributed x factor, miniscule though it is in terms of quantity: "Many a long phrase may have its sense reversed by the addition of three letters, *n-o-t*; many a monstrous mass have its unstable equilibrium discharge one way or the other by a feather weight that falls" (*WB* 81; see also *EP* 333–4).

This is as promethean as it can get. As a result of our relatively few acts of free will, the entire future of the world can be sealed for good or ill. This is anything but a trivializing of free will. In fact, it makes our free will so momentous that some will crack under the strain, wanting assurance that forces beyond our control will assure that the ultimate outcome or denouement of history is a good one, that eventually good wins out over evil. James was among them when in his sick, morbid-minded moods in which he was racked with existential angst at the thought of the hideous epileptic youth, who represented in general the evils that might befall us. James could turn in an instant from the healthy promethean mood, in which every fibre and cell in his body tingled at the thought of engaging in an all-out struggle with evil without any assurance of success, to the morbid one of existential angst.

4

The Will to Believe

The previous three chapters presented a sympathetic exposition of James's Master Syllogism. For it to work, we must not only be able to believe intentionally but do so freely in James's libertarian sense. James argued that we cannot determine on *evidential* grounds whether or not our wills possess such contra-causal freedom to determine the manner in which we are conscious, thus determining what we believe, which in turn will determine how we act. What justification, then, could we have for believing that we are free in this sense? James's answer is that we could have a *pragmatic* justification based on the desirable consequences of so believing. Whereas an evidential or, more generally, epistemic justification presents arguments directed at establishing the truth of the proposition believed, a pragmatic justification is directed at establishing the desirable consequences of believing this proposition. This chapter explores James's attempt to give a pragmatic justification for believing that our wills are free, as well as for believing other propositions that are of great importance to us, such as that God exists.

James's term for a pragmatic justification is a "will-to-believe" justification. The basic idea is that one is justified in believing, or getting oneself to believe, an evidentially undecidable proposition when doing so will have desirable consequences, that is, maximize desire–satisfaction over desire–dissatisfaction. The qualification "or get ourselves to believe" will be dropped hereafter for the sake of brevity. To simplify the discussion we can imagine that each person is able to self-induce a belief in any proposition, p, by ingesting a belief-in-p-inducing pill. This

75

is a surefire way of self-inducing belief, unlike that of acting as if you believe, which can be messy and chancy.

The will-to-believe doctrine is anathema to many philosophers, typical of whom is W. K. Clifford, who issued this universal prohibition: "It is wrong always, everywhere, and for anyone, to believe anything upon insufficient evidence." Given that the title of his essay is "The Ethics of Belief," it is clear that by "wrong" Clifford meant morally wrong. Were he to have meant evidentially wrong, he would have been uttering the empty tautology that it is evidentially wrong to believe anything upon insufficient evidence, that is, that it is evidentially wrong to believe anything that it is evidentially wrong to believe. According to Clifford and his scientistic cohorts there is only one type of justification for a belief, that being an evidential or epistemic one based on evidence unearthed through an empirical inquiry or a proof if the belief is a mathematical one. To believe on any other grounds is the height of immorality.

It is the purpose of James's will-to-believe doctrine to show that there are important exceptions to Clifford's universal prohibition. But before we get down to the details of his account, two different sorts of counter-examples to Clifford's universal prohibition will be presented so that they can be set aside as not relevant to James's concerns. First, there is the trust case in which a person is required to believe certain things about another person in virtue of having a special relation to that person, even when they lack adequate evidence for these beliefs. For example, spouses are morally required to believe in the faithfulness of the other person, even when they lack adequate evidence for this belief. Were they even to inquire into the matter, say by hiring a private detective, it would place them outside the trust relation and thus destroy the relationship. They have a duty not even to inquire into the matter. Of course they might get to a certain point at which they can't help but harbor suspicions; as Big Joe Turner used to sing, "You came home in the wee hours of the morning and your clothes didn't fit you right." It is then that the trust relation ends. James did not discuss the trust case, but there is no doubt that he would agree that it is a counter-example to Clifford; however, it is not a very telling one, because Clifford can easily protect his universal prohibition against it by building in an ad hoc restriction that excludes trust cases. Thus, trust cases are not telling counter-examples, because they are too easily localized.

Much of the recent discussion of the will to believe has concentrated on extreme cases in which there is an overwhelming utilitarian justification for acquiring an epistemically nonwarranted belief, because doing so either prevents a horrendous outcome or brings about some exceedingly beneficial one. For example, an eccentric billionaire might publicly promise to donate a billion dollars to charity if Jones acquires the epistemically nonwarranted belief that Cleopatra weighed 109 pounds when she died, or some overwhelmingly powerful alien invader threatens to destroy the planet unless Jones acquires this belief. Again, James would readily grant that a counter-example has been unearthed but would find it of little interest for his purpose in formulating a will-to-believe doctrine. In the first place, "extreme cases" are, with very rare exceptions, counterfactual, and James in general has little concern with merely possible cases in his analyses, being satisfied if his analyses fit the way things actually are. More important is that in the extreme cases the realization of good consequences or prevention of bad ones is completely external to the believer, being connected with his belief only via the intercession of a third person, the billionaire or alien in the examples. James's version of the will to believe is concerned with the personal or existential dimension of belief, the manner in which it changes a person's character and thereby their readiness to act in certain ways. There is a causal theory of value underlying James's will-to-believe doctrine, according to which the value of an outcome depends, at least in part, on how it is brought about. For this reason, extreme cases can be left out of the discussion of James's doctrine.

James's intent is not just to produce some counter-examples to Clifford's prohibition. If it was, he could have availed himself of the rather obvious trust and extreme case counter-examples and been done with it. Rather, his aim is to spell out the conditions under which in general we are morally permitted to believe upon insufficient evidence. His dislike of doing philosophy in a formalistic, by-the-numbers manner kept him from explicitly listing all these conditions in a neat package of numbered indented sentences, telling us which of them are necessary and which combination of them are sufficient for being morally permitted to believe without epistemic warrant. It will be argued that things go best for James if he is taken as giving a set of sufficient but not necessary conditions, although some individual members of the set are necessary. A lot of work is left to the expositor in extracting these conditions and determining their sufficiency and/or necessity. Thus there is considerable room for alternative interpretations, though there are some conditions that plainly are intended to be necessary.

James begins his essay "The Will to Believe," which is his most complete and forceful exposition of the doctrine, by explicitly listing three conditions that together comprise what he calls a "genuine option" to believe. A person's option to believe a proposition at a certain time is a *genuine option* just in case it is *live, momentous,* and *forced.* Because a genuine option is dependent on variable psychological factors, it must be relativized to a person at a time. What is live and momentous can vary across persons as well across different times in a single person's life.

For a proposition to be *live* for a person at a time, it must then be a real possibility for that person to believe it, as well as to believe its contradictory. His mind must not be made up one way or the other. Thus, the proposition, along with its contradictory, can be seriously entertained even if it cannot win at that time uncontested occupancy of the believer's mind and thereby qualify as a belief for James. To achieve this status will require some work on the part of the believer in the way of making efforts to attend or acting as if he believes (or popping the pill). James parries the capriciousness objection to his account of free will, according to which a person is just as likely to act out of as in character, given that our free choices are undetermined, by pointing out that the range of one's free will is limited to living options. Because a person of benevolent character cannot seriously entertain the thought of doing some sadistic act, it is not a live option for him.

A proposition is *momentous* for a person at a time if the consequences of his believing or not believing it will have very important consequences, relative to his personal scheme of values, supposedly at the time of his decision to believe rather than at some future time. That an option to believe is unique, *pace* what James says, does not alone qualify it as momentous. My one and only chance to see Barry Manilow live is his farewell concert tonight, but that alone hardly makes my option to see it momentous. Again, there can be widespread divergences among persons and for a single person at different times in respect to the momentousness of a given option.

An option to believe is *forced* when the person will not wind up believing the proposition in question unless he decides to believe it. No one, such as a crazed brain surgeon or mad cyberneticist, is going to compel him to have this belief regardless of what he might do. It is completely up to him whether or not he acquires the belief. We might call the alternative in a forced option that the chooser winds up with if no decision is made the "negative alternative." Dated options, such as to accept a proposal of marriage by midnight tomorrow or never see the man again, are good examples of forced options. A forced option, like a unique one, need not be momentous, which would be the case if this proposal were offered to a lesbian.

Several supposedly astute and fair commentators have interpreted James as holding that the three conditions for having a genuine option to believe are together sufficient for having a moral right to believe upon insufficient evidence. This will be shown to be a terrible distortion of the text. Once this perverse straw-man version is given, they have an easy time denigrating it as the will to gullibility or wishful thinking. It licenses me to believe the propositions that I am the Sultan of Wisconsin, the inventor of the sandwich, and the author of *The Critique of Pure Reason*, if my psychology is such that they are live and momentous for me and my option to believe them forced. James would be the last person to agree that the pleasure I derive from believing them justifies my doing so. What is overlooked by these interpretations are the further restrictions that James places upon a will-to-believe option. They not only are stated explicitly but also inform all of his examples, making it hard to understand how any attentive reader could miss them.

Of these additional conditions, the one that is most important for responding to the wishful-thinking objection is the requirement that the chooser cannot determine at the time of his decision the truth value of the proposition in question on epistemic grounds. "Our passional nature not only lawfully may [is morally permitted to], but must decide an option between propositions, whenever it is a genuine option that cannot by its nature be decided on intellectual [epistemic] grounds," and, "*In concreto*, the freedom [moral permission] to believe can only cover living options which the intellect of the individual cannot by itself resolve" (*WB* 20, 32). Sometimes James presents the epistemic requirement in a weaker way that would license believing even in the face of significant evidence against the belief. He speaks of "the right to believe in things for the truth of which *complete objective proof* is yet lacking" and voluntary choice being permitted when "*objective proof* is not to be had" (*MT* 138–9 and *PP* 1177; my italics). Herein the available evidence need not be neutral between the truth or falsity of the proposition. Given that James wants to win over his audience by giving the Cliffordian types as much rope as possible, he ought to go with the stronger version, especially since it is satisfied by his most cherished examples – belief in free will and the good destiny of the world. For these reasons, it is the one that will be operative in what follows. It should be born in mind, however, that James's real position, the one he keeps in the closet when he is trying to win over the Cliffordians, is that if the option is of overwhelming momentousness to the believer, such as Kierkegaard's option to believe in Christianity, the weaker version is operative: One is permitted to believe in the teeth of quite powerful contrary evidence.

When James says that the intellect of the person *cannot* settle the matter, the "cannot" can be of either the *in principle* or weaker *in practice* sort. In practice human neurophysiologists cannot verify that our efforts to attend are not causally determined by brain events due to limits in their powers of mensuration, but it is in principle possible that they do so, for they, along with their instruments, could suddenly make like the incredible shrinking man. It is important to realize that the epistemic undecidability concerns the chooser alone, not other observers. It is conceptually impossible that the chooser, at the time he is deliberating, verify what choice he will make and thereby the occurrence of any event for which his choice is a necessary cause, since he can deliberate only if he is in ignorance of what he shall choose; someone else, however, could verify at that time what his choice will be by appeal to a well-founded inductive argument based on his past track record.

It must be stressed that James's epistemically-undecidable-by-the-chooser-before-the-choice-is-made requirement is not the weak requirement that at the time of the choice the chooser, as a matter of fact, lacks adequate epistemic grounds or evidence for determining the truth value of the proposition, which could be realized if the chooser made a point not to investigate the matter, like Clifford's dishonest ship owner who makes a point not to investigate whether his ship is safe to send to sea. Rather, it is the strong requirement that the chooser lacks adequate evidence one way or the other after discharging his epistemic duty to perform all of the relevant inquiries. Laziness, especially self-interested laziness, will not enable the chooser to satisfy the epistemic-undecidability requirement.

James not only explicitly states the requirement for epistemic undecidability for a will-to-believe option, all of his many examples satisfy it, thus making it all the more amazing that it could have been missed by so many commentators. The stranded mountaineer who must jump across a chasm to get to safety and can increase his chances of succeeding by believing that he has the capacity to do so is not able, *at that time*, to epistemically determine whether he has the capacity, though he can do so after he has attempted the leap, though, if he misses, he'll have to do it very quickly. The person who psyches himself up to lead the morally strenuous life by believing the proposition that good will win out over evil in the long run cannot epistemically determine its truth value, since, in addition to it being beyond our capacity to predict the direction history will take in the long run, the choices that he *shall* make, which is the crucial *x* factor that he contributes to the cosmic equation, are not knowable by him in advance of his choices. In contrast to these Jamesian cases, my epistemically nonwarranted beliefs about being the Sultan of Wisconsin and the like are both in principle and in practice epistemically determinable by me now; and, furthermore, I have violated my epistemic duty by not performing adequate inquiries – to which my response is that since I *am* the Sultan of Wisconsin, I have lackeys to do the drudge work.

There is textual evidence that James required yet another condition for a will-to-believe option, namely that by acquiring the belief the subject can help to make the believed proposition become true: "There are, then, cases where a fact cannot come at all unless a preliminary faith exists in its coming. And where faith in a fact can help create the fact, that would be an insane logic which should say that faith running ahead of scientific evidence is the 'lowest kind of immorality' into which a thinking being can fall," and "In truths dependent on our personal action, the faith based on desire is certainly a lawful and possibly indispensable thing" (*WB* 29). In the 1878 "Some Considerations of the Subjective Method" he wrote that the subjective method, the name he then used for the will-to-believe doctrine, "can only be harmful, one might even say 'immoral' if applied to cases where the facts to be stated do not include the subjective R as a factor," in which R is the contribution that we make through the actions caused by our belief (*EP* 335). Every example that James gave throughout his career of a will-to-believe option involved a belief that played a causal role in helping to make the believed proposition become true or, as will be shortly seen, some other desirable proposition. The Alpine and the good-will-win-out cases clearly satisfy the causal condition, as do all of his confidence-building cases – the Alpine leaper, the ardent but somewhat unconfident suitor, the person who wants to be liked, et al. The reason James became so preachy whenever he discussed free will is that he thought that if we believed we had free will we would make the sort of all-out effort to attend to an idea in difficult cases of conflict that would help to bring it about that we do have free will. "If . . . free acts be possible, a faith in their possibility, by augmenting the moral energy which gives them birth, will increase their frequency in a given individual" (*WB* 84).

It is very much in the spirit of James's promethean pragmatism to have a causal requirement, since the significance and value of belief in general are the worldly deeds to which it leads, a thesis for which, as we saw, James gave both physiological and normative reasons. Remember how he railed against sentimentalists and aesthetes. Merely to be in a pleasurable belief or aesthetic state is not its own justification. There must be some behaviorally rooted reason for choosing to get oneself into such a state. Thus, it would violate the promethean spirit of James's pragmatism to justify an epistemically nonwarranted belief solely in terms of its being a pleasurable belief state. Furthermore, by having a causal requirement James has yet another way, in addition to having the epistemic-undecidability requirement, to protect his doctrine against the wishful thinking objection.

Assuming that James required that causal condition, there are some questions that need to be answered. First, must *P*'s belief be causally sufficient, necessary, or both for making the believed proposition become true? The answer is none of the above. James's examples, especially

the good-will-win-out one, involve only the very weak requirement that
P's belief can help to make p true. The Alpine leaper's belief, obviously, does not have to be either causally sufficient or necessary for his
leaping successfully; for him to be permitted to acquire the belief, it
is enough that his believing increases the probability of success. This
is all that common sense, as well as James, requires. Furthermore, this
weak interpretation dovetails with James's insistence that a very minor
difference in the initial conditions can make the crucial difference in
the final outcome, as in the parable of the nail. For these reasons I will
include the weak version of the causal condition as a fifth requirement
for a will-to-believe option.

Adopting this requirement requires, in turn, adopting yet another
condition, namely that it is desirable that the believed proposition
become true. This requirement is assumed throughout his discussion,
for James's will-to-believe justification is a substitution of this argument
form:

Doing x helps to bring it about that p.
It is desirable that p. Therefore,
It is prima facie morally permissible to do x.

in which "believing p" is substituted for "x" throughout. The reason for
the prima facie qualification is that the permission is subject to potential defeaters or overriders. For example, that p becomes true might
satisfy some desire yet not maximize desire–satisfaction, thereby violating James's casuistic rule. Or its becoming true might violate some
overriding deontological moral principle, as in this case: I promise
to give Jones a revolver but in the interim he turns into a homicidal
maniac and has vowed to kill Smith. My giving Jones a revolver helps
to bring it about that I keep my promise, and that I keep my promise is
desirable. But it violates my prima facie moral permission to give Jones
a revolver, because doing so would result in the death of an innocent
person. This deontological defeater is not overruled if it would maximize desire–satisfaction to give Jones the gun: Smith could be a widely
disliked person whose death would maximize desire–satisfaction over
his continuing to live.

At this point it will help the reader to pause for a recap of the six
conditions that have so far been unearthed from the text for a will-to-
believe option. Person A is morally permitted to believe proposition p

without adequate epistemic warrant at a time *T* if (only a sufficient condition is being given) the option to believe *p* is 1. live, 2. momentous, and 3. forced for *A* at *T*; 4. *A* cannot epistemically determine *p*'s truth-value at *T*; 5. *A*'s believing *p* helps to bring it about that *p*; and 6. it is, all things considered, desirable that *p* become true.

In fairness to those commentators who have not included the causal requirement for any will-to-believe option, it must be pointed out that sometimes James stated his doctrine in a way that didn't justify *believing* an epistemically undecidable proposition but only *adopting it as a working hypothesis*, as we do in science when we select some untested hypothesis as a working hypothesis for the purpose of setting up experiments or in everyday life when we simply act as if the proposition were true. It will be shown that the causal requirement is not applicable to some working hypothesis cases.

The following quotations clearly speak for the working hypothesis version. Some of them simply identify belief or faith with the adoption of a working hypothesis: "Faith is synonymous with working hypothesis," and "To sum up, faith and *working hypothesis* are here one and the same" (*WB* 79 and *EP* 337). Clifford's prohibition is now interpreted as prohibiting adopting as a working hypothesis (acting as if you believed) an epistemically nonwarranted proposition rather than believing it. "Suppose that, having just read the 'Ethics of Belief,' I feel it would be sinful to act upon an assumption unverified by previous experience" (*WB* 80). At the beginning of "The Dilemma of Determinism," James states his intention "to induce some of you to follow my own example in assuming it [the doctrine of libertarian free will] true, and acting as if it were true" (*WB* 115). Among the actions to be performed is publicly declaring that it is true, even though you do not believe what you are saying. His presentation of the "faith ladder" in the 1905 "Reason and Faith," which is the final form taken by his will-to-believe doctrine, says that we are to treat the proposition we desire to be true "as if it *were* true so far as my advocacy and actions are concerned" (*ERM* 125). This very same faith ladder gets repeated at the end of each of his final two books (*PU* 148 and *SPP* 113).

James's examples also reflect his sloshing back and forth between the belief and working hypothesis versions of his doctrine. In "Some Considerations of the Subjective Method" he uses the example of the Alpine climber who must leap a chasm to get to safety (*EP* 332). What is required here, as well as in James's other confidence- and courage-building cases, to increase his chances of success is good old-fashioned sweating-with-conviction belief that he has the capacity to succeed, not just the adoption as a working hypothesis that he does. But in the final paragraph of "The Will to Believe" he has an example of an Alpine climber who is confronted with alternative paths and must pick one of them if he is to save himself from freezing to death and has no reason to prefer one of them over the others. Obviously, he must pick one of them and journey along it, for to make no choice assures his death. The chances of his success are in no way increased by his believing that the chosen path is the right one. He only has to adopt it as a working hypothesis and thereby act as if it is the right one by following it.

The working hypothesis version of the will to believe does not require in general a causal requirement. James himself recognized this when he wrote, "And your acting thus [as if you believed] may *in certain special cases* be a means of making it securely true in the end" (*PU* 148; my italics). The "in certain special cases" qualification implies that in some cases adoption of a proposition as a working hypothesis does not help to make it true. By adopting a proposition as a working hypothesis a scientist does not help to *make* it true but only helps to *discover* that it is true. But "in certain special cases," such as adoption of the hypothesis of libertarian freedom, it does help to make it true, since by acting as if we were free in this sense we help to bring it about that we are. James recognized cases in which believing, in the full-blooded sense, can help in discovering that a proposition is true. By believing that God exists, we increase the chances that we shall have apparent direct nonsensory perceptions of God, such experiences, as Chapter 10 brings out, counting as evidence for God's existence.

Several objections will now be considered. It will turn out that in order to meet them further conditions for a will-to-believe option will have to be added on James's behalf to the previous six. The chooser is supposed to get himself to believe a proposition that he himself takes to be evidentially nonwarranted, but this is impossible according to Dickenson Miller, since you cannot believe and yet in the heart of that very belief be heroically facing the uncertainty of your whole position. Your state of mind would not be belief, which is regarding something as fact, not as uncertain. Miller is right that to believe a proposition is to believe it is a fact, for a fact is a true proposition and one cannot believe a proposition without believing that it is true; but, *pace* Miller, that does not require that it is believed to be certain in the sense of supported by overwhelming evidence. That there are so many anti-rationalistic theists of the Kierkegaardian variety shows Miller's inference from *take to be true* (or a fact) to *take to be certain* to be bogus. Miller is not alone in his mischaracterization of belief. Many contemporary philosophers, such as Richard Swinburne in *Faith and Reason*, wrongly claim that to believe a proposition is to believe that its probability is greater than one-half relative to the available evidence.

There is a close cousin to Miller's objection that might fare better. The point is not that one cannot believe without believing to be certain, but rather that if one believes what he takes to be evidentially unfounded, he will not, *pace* James, have his confidence and courage boosted so that he can act more effectively in making the believed proposition true. The wrong response to this objection is to find some procedure for making the believer forget that he acquired his belief on the basis of a will-to-believe option; there could be a second set of pills such that after one has popped a belief-inducing pill he pops the appropriate one from the second set that makes him forget the non-rational means by which he acquired this belief and instead implants in his mind the false apparent memory of having acquired it after a successful empirical inquiry. The problem with this way around the objection is that the believer must deceive himself, which is bad enough, but in the process destroys his own integral unity and winds up as a divided, schizophrenic self. James's promethean quest to have it all is found in Chapter 11 to have this deleterious consequence and ways will be devised to attempt to escape it. The ideal of an integrated, rational self is a powerful one that deserves more respect than is accorded it by this drastic solution.

A better response is that human psychology is far more variable than this objection envisions. Although it is true that there are some people who are so constituted psychologically that they cannot realize the confidence-building benefits from a belief that they take to be evidentially nonwarranted, there are many people whose psychology permits them to do so, such as our nonrationalist theists. It has already been seen that a will-to-believe option is relative to a person at a time because human psychology is variable in regard to which propositions a person takes to be live and momentous belief options. All this objection shows is that there is another psychological reason for relativizing a will-to-believe option to a person at a time. A seventh condition could be added requiring that

7. *A*'s psychology at *T* is such that he can realize the confidence- and courage-boosting benefits of a belief that *p*, even if he takes *p* to be evidentially nonwarranted.

This next objection comes from James himself. Why, he asks, can't someone act so as to help to make some desirable proposition become true without actually believing it? His response:

Since belief is measured by action, he who forbids us to believe religion to be true, necessarily also forbids us to act as we should if we did believe it to be true. The whole defence of religious faith hinges upon action. If the action required or inspired by the religious hypothesis is in no way different from that dictated by the naturalistic hypothesis, then religious faith is a pure superfluity, better pruned away, and controversy about its legitimacy is a piece of idle trifling, unworthy of serious minds. (*WB* 32)

James even goes so far as to claim that there is no behavioral difference between suspending belief in *R* and actually disbelieving it. "We cannot escape the issue by remaining sceptical and waiting for more light, because, although we do avoid error in that way *if religion be untrue*, we lose the good, *if it be true*, just as certainly as if we positively disbelieve" (*WB* 26). The agnostic must act "meanwhile more or less as if religion were not true" (*WB* 29–30).

This is a disastrous response. By the "religious hypothesis" James here means the proposition *R*. Good will win out over evil in the long run. He claims that because belief is measured by action, a person will act so as to help make *R* become true by leading the morally stren- uous life if and only he first believes that *R* is true. Such benevolent behavior is "dictated," "required," or "inspired" by *R*. As an empirical generalization about human psychology, this is false, because we know of many people who do not believe *R* but nevertheless lead the morally strenuous life.

Underlying James's response is the false assumption that for every proposition *p*, there is a set of actions, *B*, such that a person believes *p* if and only if he performs or is disposed to perform the actions in *B*. James even went so far as to claim that there is no behavioral difference between suspending belief in R and actually disbelieving it. This assumption fails to do justice to the psychological variability among persons in respect to how their beliefs mesh with their actions. Two persons can believe one and the same proposition but act in radically different ways. Both could believe R but only one of them acts so as to help make it true. The person who sits on the sideline might be made overconfident by his belief in R and think that his active participation on the side of the good is not needed or he might have devilist leanings and not want to see R become true. James's assumption of a one-to-one correlation between belief and action is not able to distinguish between believing the factual proposition that R is true and believing the normative proposition that it is good that R is true. The person who acts so as to help make R true could believe the latter but not the former.

There is an easy way around this difficulty that consists in building in yet another epicycle concerning the way in which a will-to-believe option must be relativized to a person's psychological makeup at the time of the choice, namely

8. A knows at T that he will act so as to help make p become true only if he first believes that p is true.

Why must A know this fact about his own psychology? The reason is that the conditions for having a will-to-believe option are supposed to justify A's believing or acquiring the belief that p. But what justifies a belief gives the believer a reason for so believing, something that he could give in response to the challenge to justify his belief. This requires that he be aware of this reason or justification. This seemingly innocent point will be the basis for the next objection.

Imagine that A satisfies conditions 1–7 for having a will-to-believe justification for believing that p is true. Among his reasons for this belief is that only by so believing can he act in a way that will help to make this desirable proposition become true. Thus, if we ask A why he is toiling to help make p become true, among the reasons he will give is that p will in fact become true. But that's an irrational reason for trying to make p true, except in very special circumstances that I will not go into. A relevant reason would be that it is good that p become true. Because you believe that Jones will succumb to his cancer of the liver hardly gives you a reason for acting so as to help bring this about.

Because A has such an irrational reason for acting so as to make p true, he does not do so as a rational, morally responsible agent, and, since rationality is a necessary but not sufficient condition for acting freely, he does not do so freely. This is a very serious matter, especially for the likes of James, who prizes so highly being a free, morally responsible agent. Just recall the emotional breakdown of 1870 that was occasioned by his doubts that he was such an agent. The problem takes an especially virulent form with a will-to-believe based belief in R, given the very extensive nature of the actions and dispositions that are caused by this belief. Whatever good might be realized by A's irrationally acting so as to make R true is outweighed or defeated by his loss of or diminution in his freedom and moral responsibility. At least these are my deontological intuitions and James's as well, I believe.

The irrationality objection, devastating though it is, is easily neutralized. All that is required is to separate the proposition that A must first get himself to believe from the one he thereby helps to make true. Thus, 8 must be revised as

8'. A knows at T that he will act so as to help make q become true only if he first believes that p is true, in which q is not identical with p.

By separating p from q, James can give a will-to-believe justification for believing in good old-time theism, not just his pale moral substitute for it, R. A's psychology at T could be such that he will act in the proper good-making fashion so as to help R become true only if he first believes that the God of traditional Western theism exists. Herein he would have a prudential reason for acting benevolently, since he believes that God will reward him for doing so. This may not be an admirable reason but it nevertheless is a rational one. In the case in which a belief that God exists increases the believer's chance of gaining evidence that God exists for his religious experiences, the believer helps to bring about the desirable proposition that there is evidence for the existence of God by believing that God exists.

There is some textual evidence that James was on to the need to separate the believed proposition from the one that it is desirable to make true, for he often formulated his will-to-believe option in a way that separated them. Sometimes, though not in "The Will to Believe," he separated them in the confidence-building cases. The proposition that the Alpine leaper must believe to increase his chances of leaping

successfully across the chasm is not the *categorical* proposition that he
will successfully make the leap but instead that he has the capacity to
do so, which is the *conditional* proposition that if he were to attempt
the leap, he would succeed. This is the proposition that he first must
believe in order to increase his chances of bringing it about that he
successfully makes the leap. When James says, "I wish to make the
leap, but I am ignorant from lack of experience whether I *have the
strength* for it" or the "*ability* for [this] exploit," he is making use of
this conditional proposition (*EP* 332; my italics). The leaper's belief
that he has the capacity to succeed, unlike the belief that he will in fact
succeed, is a rational reason for attempting to make it true that he leaps
successfully. The you-will-like-me case admits of the same resolution.
He first gets himself to believe the conditional proposition that if he
acts in a friendly manner, people will wind up liking him so that he
can muster the necessary courage and confidence to act in a friendly
manner and thereby help to bring it about that people will wind up
liking him. His conditional belief is a rational reason, though not the
sole reason, for his acting in a friendly manner. Among the other
reasons must be the desirability of being liked by people.

James flip-flops in his manner of stating the common denominator of all religions. In "The Will to Believe" he gives this categorical
formulation: "The best things are the more eternal things, the overlapping things, the things in the universe that throw the last stone, so
to speak, and say the final word," which I paraphrased as:

R. Good will win out over evil in the long run.

This is the proposition that *A* first must believe so as to act in the sort
of good-making manner that will help to make *R* become true. This
interpretation is nailed down by his claiming with respect to propositions like *R* that "There are, then, cases where a fact cannot come at
all unless a preliminary faith exists in its coming" (*WB* 29). Herein the
proposition that first must be believed and the one that is to be made
true *via* the belief are identical.

But in his other writings he gives a conditionalized formulation of
religion to the effect that:

R'. If we collectively exert our best moral effort, then *R* (Good will
win out over evil in the long run).

For instance, he writes, "Suppose that the world's author put the case to you before creation, saying: 'I am going to make a world not certain to be saved, a world the perfection of which shall be *conditional* merely, the condition being that each several agent does its own 'level best'" (*P* 139; my italics). This conditionalized formulation of the religious hypothesis gets repeated at two places in his lecture notes: "Meanwhile I ask whether a world of hypothetical perfection conditional on each part doing its duty be not as much as can fairly be demanded," and pluralism holds that "the world . . . may be saved, on condition that its parts shall do their best" (*ML* 319, 412). What *A* does, accordingly, is to get himself to believe *R'* so that he will act in the morally strenuous way that will help to make *R* become true. Similar considerations apply to a will-to-believe based belief in a metaphysical or world hypothesis. One believes in theism in order to get oneself to live in some desirable way.

Although 8' goes some way to neutralize the irrationality charge, it has to go even further. According to 8', among *A*'s reason for helping to make the desirable proposition *q* become true is that some other proposition, *p*, is true. But his psychological makeup at *T* could be bizarre so that his belief that *p* is true, although a *causal factor* in his acting so as to make *q* true, does not constitute a *rational reason* for so acting. For example, *p* could be the proposition that Verdi wrote *Ernani* and *q* be *R*, and his psychology be such that he will act so as to help make *R* become true only if he first believes *p*. Thus, when he is asked why he is living the morally strenuous life so as to help make *R* true, he will respond that it is because Verdi wrote *Ernani*, thereby rendering his action irrational and thereby not one for which he is morally responsible. Plainly, yet another necessary condition is required, namely,

9. *A*'s belief that *p* is a rational reason for him to act so as to help make *q* become true.

It is now time to pause and give an explicit recap of all the many conditions that together are *sufficient* for being morally permitted to believe upon insufficient evidence. *A* is morally permitted at time *T* to believe an epistemically nonwarranted proposition, *p*, for the purpose of helping to make true another proposition, *q*, IF

A's option at *T* to believe *p* is:

1. live;
2. momentous; and
3. forced.

And furthermore:

4. *A* cannot epistemically determine at *T* the truth-value of *p*;
5. *A*'s believing *p* can help *A* to bring it about that *q*;
6. It is, all things considered, desirable that proposition *q* become true;
7. *A*'s psychology at *T* is such that he can realize the confidence- and courage-boosting benefits of a belief that *p*, even if he takes *p* to be evidentially nonwarranted;
8'. *A* knows at *T* that he will act so as to help make *q* become true only if he first believes that *p*; and
9. *A*'s belief that *p* is a rational reason for him to act so as to help make *q* become true.

I have italicized "sufficient" and put "IF" in block letters to emphasize that conditions 1–9 are together taken to be sufficient but not necessary for a will-to-believe option. The reason for not affirming the necessity of 1–9 is to avoid the following universalizability objection. Imagine that *A* has a brother, *B*, whose psychology exactly resembles his except that *A* alone satisfies condition 8' requiring that the believer knows at *T* that he will act so as to help make *q* become true only if he first believes that *p*. Because *B* is sufficiently strong-willed that he does not need to have the confidence- or courage-building belief in *p* in order to do his best to make *q* become true, he is not morally permitted to believe *p* upon insufficient evidence whereas the weaker-willed *A* is. This violates the principle of universalizability – if *A* is morally permitted (or forbidden) to perform an action in a certain set of circumstances, then everyone in like circumstances is morally permitted (or forbidden) to do the same. It is implausible to respond that *B* is not in the same circumstances as *A*, since he has a stronger will, for someone's being subject to a moral rule should not depend on whether he is weak-willed or cowardly. A similar problem would result if *p* were live (or momentous) for *A* but not *B*.

Because conditions 1–9 purport to give *only* a sufficient condition, there is a ready response to the universalizability objection. That B does not satisfy these conditions does not entail that he is not permitted to believe p; this would follow only if the conditions together were necessary. He can be accorded the same moral right to believe p upon insufficient evidence as is A, only he will not have to exercise this right because of his stronger character.

Given that a major concern of this chapter is to see how James's will to believe can justify an epistemically nonwarranted belief in his doctrine of libertarian free will, it will be instructive to see how conditions 1–9 apply to it. There are many people for whom it is a genuine option to believe the proposition that they possess this sort of freedom. Let this be proposition p. Because of limitations in our powers of mensuration – we're too big and the brain events are too small – it cannot be epistemically determined whether p is true or p is false, thereby satisfying 4. Let q be the proposition that we exert our best moral effort to attend to the idea of the morally good or right alternative in a case of moral temptation. Certainly, it is desirable that q be true, thus satisfying 6. There are persons, William James for example, whose psychological makeup is such that they can believe that p is epistemically undecidable and yet have their confidence and courage raised by their belief in p, as 7 requires. By raising their confidence level they are able to exert themselves in a way that will help to make q become true, thus satisfying 5, and furthermore know this fact about themselves, in accordance with the demands of $8'$. 9's conditions are met because their belief that p is a rational reason for their acting so as to make q become true. A good reason for trying to get yourself to attend to a difficult idea in a moral conflict case is that you have the libertarian sort of free will to do it. Believing that they have free will is both a necessary cause and a rational reason for their attempting to exert themselves to attend to the idea of the morally right alternative in a case of moral conflict.

5

The Ethics of Truth

This chapter will show how James's Master Syllogism entails a theory of truth that makes the true a species of the good. This moralization of truth is James's most bold and original doctrine and will be found to be well deserving of our admiration if not our total acceptance.

To begin with, it can be shown that the conclusion of James's Master Syllogism

   3. We are always morally obligated to believe in a way that maximizes desire–satisfaction.

in conjunction with other of his doctrines, entails that a proposition is true when believing it maximizes desire–satisfaction. Here's how the deduction goes. James defines truth as "what we ought to believe" and then asks rhetorically, "Ought we ever not to believe what it is better for us to believe?" (*P* 42). When the implicit claim that

   4. The true is what we ought to believe.

is conjoined with 3 it makes for another valid syllogism, whose conclusion is

   5. A proposition is true when believing it maximizes desire–satisfaction.

This could be called James's "Truth Syllogism."

Another way of deriving 5 from 3 is to conjoin James's slogan that

   6. "The reasons why we call things true is the reason why they *are* true" (*P* 37).

with his claim that

7. The reasons why we call something true is that our belief in it has proven satisfactory.

Given that, for James,

8. Being satisfactory is maximizing desire–satisfaction.

it follows again that

5. A proposition is true when believing it maximizes desire–satisfaction.

James never explicitly asserted either the Master Syllogism or the Truth Syllogism, even though the premises of both clearly are defended in his text. One possible explanation is his abhorrence of doing philosophy in a rigorous, by-the-numbers manner. Another is that their premises are too abstract to be of any practical guidance in making concrete ethical decisions. Due to radical limitations in our predictive powers, we rarely are in a position to determine which option among those that are open to us will in fact maximize desire–satisfaction in the long run. Therefore, proposition 3, which is the application of 1 to the special case of belief options, will not give us sufficient guidance in the vast majority of cases in determining what to believe. They need further supplementation.

Bertrand Russell's objection to James's desire-maximizing account of truth and belief acceptance, that "It is far easier... to settle the question of fact: 'Have Popes been always infallible?' than to settle the question whether the effects of thinking them infallible are on the whole good," is based on just this limitation in our predictive powers. Because 3 cannot give sufficient guidance in making concrete belief choices, many people will believe whatever gives them immediate comfort, thus encouraging wishful thinking and gullibility. I'm back to believing that I'm the Sultan of Wisconsin ("No one eats any cheese in this state without my permission!").

The prediction problem also plagued act utilitarians and was remedied by their arming the chooser with a number of empirically well-founded generalizations to guide her, just as the navigator goes to sea supplied with empirically well-founded navigational charts. It was seen in Chapter 1 that James followed their example by supplementing his casuistic rule with the guiding principle that we should follow the dictates of traditional morality, unless we have very good epistemic reasons for believing that violating it on some occasion, or replacing it with a new code of morality, would maximize desire–satisfaction. It was the "except" qualification that distinguished James's rule instrumentalism from rule utilitarianism, whose utilitarian-based rules permit of no exceptions, even when doing so maximizes utility on some occasion.

A similar sort of supplementation is needed for 3 so as to get around Russell's objection. James accomplishes this by the following principle.

9. We are always prima facie morally obligated to believe in a manner that is epistemically warranted, except when epistemic justification is not possible.

in which the "except" clause recognizes the legitimacy of a will-to-believe option. It was necessary to include the prima facie qualification, for otherwise there would be a logical clash between 9 and 3 consisting in 3 giving pride of place to pragmatic reasons and 9 to epistemic ones. The moral obligation in 3 is absolute, admitting of no exceptions, whereas 9's moral obligation is only prima facie, being subject to being overridden when doing so will maximize desire–satisfaction.

It is interesting to note that when James was arguing for his will-to-believe doctrine he omitted the prima facie qualification from 9, thereby giving pride of place to epistemic reasons over pragmatic ones. There is a good reason for this surface inconsistency in his philosophy: James was wisely following the principle of minimal ordinance enjoining us to use the weakest, least controversial premises that are required to establish the desired conclusion, since thereby we cut down on the risk of one of our premises being false or rejected by our opponent. James is sweating with conviction that if he only can get his audience to agree that they are morally permitted to believe certain propositions upon insufficient evidence, especially that God and free will exist, great benefits will accrue to them and their society. To win them over he does not need to use the very strong, controversial premise that the only justification for a belief is pragmatic, which almost everyone would reject out of hand. All that he needed was the weaker and therefore less challengeable premise that there are both epistemic and pragmatic modes of justification of belief, with the former taking precedent over the latter, thereby allowing pragmatic reasons to be appealed to only when epistemic ones are of no avail. In order to placate those of Cliffordian leanings in his audience, James is willing *for the time being* to work with a hierarchical dualism of justifications for belief that gives a dominant position to epistemic reasons, as does an unqualified version of 9. James even argues for the weaker conclusion that we are morally *permitted* to believe upon insufficient evidence when doing so will maximize desire–satisfaction rather than the stronger one that we are morally *obligated* to do so, as is required by 3.

There is good textual evidence that James intended 9 as a guiding principle or instrumental rule that is adopted because

10. By having beliefs that are epistemically warranted, desire–satisfaction is maximized in the long run.

He claimed that "True ideas would never have been singled out as such, would never have acquired a class-name, least of all a name suggesting value, unless they had been useful from the outset," and that "Our obligation to seek truth is part of our general obligation to do what pays. The payments true ideas bring are the sole why of our duty to follow them" (*P* 98 and 110). He says further that pragmatists do not deny truth but "have only sought to trace exactly why people follow it and always ought to follow it" (*P* 38). The intellectualist critics who stress truth for truth's sake should

follow the pragmatic method and ask: "What is truth *known-as*? What does its existence stand for in the way of concrete goods?" – they would see that the name of it is the *inbegriff* of almost everything valuable in our lives. The true is the opposite of whatever is instable, of whatever is practically disappointing, of whatever is useless, of whatever is lying and unreliable, of whatever is unverifiable and unsupported, of whatever is inconsistent and contradictory, of whatever is artificial and eccentric, of whatever is unreal in the sense of being of no practical account. Here are pragmatic reasons with a vengeance why we should turn to truth. (*MT* 48)

And, for good measure, James says that he cannot conceive "that the notion [of truth] would ever have grown up, or that true ideas would ever have been sorted out from false or idle ones, save for the greater sum of satisfactions" (*MT* 89).

There is an apparent clash in these quotations between James's contrast between, on the one hand, true ideas and what it pays to believe and, on the other, his acceptance of

5. A proposition is true when believing it maximizes desire–satisfaction.

This seeming clash is easily neutralized once it is seen that James means by "true ideas" and "truth" in these quotations what people *ordinarily* take to be "true." These will be ideas that people take to be epistemically warranted relative to the best available evidence. On the other hand, when he speaks of a belief that "pays" (*PP* 98, 110), he means one that maximizes desire–satisfaction – achieves "the greater sum of satisfactions." It is such a belief that will count as true belief relative to his *revisionary* analysis of truth in terms of 5. If James were to have meant by "true ideas" and "truth" in these quotations his favored 5-based sense of "true," he would have been uttering, in essence, the uninformative proposition that we seek true ideas – ideas that are such that believing them maximizes desire–satisfaction – so as to maximize desire–satisfaction, which is a special instance of "We seek X so as to obtain X."

There are two other guiding principles in addition to 9 that James employs in his rule-instrumentalist account of belief acceptance and truth.

11. Make sure that your web of beliefs is internally consistent.
12. Whenever a contradiction breaks out in your web of belief revise the web in a way that makes the minimum changes in it.

As was the case with 9, there is good empirical evidence that following them will maximize desire–satisfaction in the long run.

13. By following the rule of consistency, 11, we maximize desire–satisfaction in the long run.
14. By following the rule of conservative belief-revision to eliminate a contradiction in our web of belief, 12, we maximize desire–satisfaction in the long run.

We know from our past experience that people who hold contradictory beliefs are less effective in bringing about what is desirable and that because of limitations in our time and energy we do better by eliminating tensions and inconsistencies in our web of belief by making the smallest changes that are necessary to reestablish consistency. Again, it must be stressed that these guiding principles impose only prima facie obligations, since they admit of exceptions when a better job of maximizing desire–satisfaction can be done by violating them.

There is an interesting internal inconsistency in the rule instrumentalism I attribute to James. The only reasons that can be given for why we are well advised to accept his three instrumental rules, namely 9, 11, and 12, are based on inductive reasoning from past experience. Thus, there are three propositions – 10, 13, and 14 – that are believed on exclusively epistemic grounds, which violates

3. We are always morally obligated to believe in a way that maximizes desire–satisfaction over the other belief options available to us.

We would be launched on a vicious infinite regress were we to say that our justification for believing 10, 13, and 14 is that we thereby maximize desire–satisfaction, for, again, the only justifications for these claims are inductive arguments based on our past experience. Maybe the best that can be done on James's behalf is to make an ad hoc restriction of 3 to first-order beliefs – beliefs that are not about other beliefs or propositions. This would permit second-order beliefs, of which 10, 13, and 14 are instances, to be acquired on exclusively epistemic grounds, such as inductive arguments from past experience. Even with the ad hoc restriction, 3 still is a very bold and exciting thesis.

Central to James's instrumental rules of consistency and conservatism is that of a web of belief. Exactly what is contained in the web? Is it comprised exclusively of propositional beliefs or does it contain conative and emotional states as well? For the most part, James treats the web as exclusively a web of opinions: "The individual has a stock of old *opinions* already, but he meets a new experience that puts them to a strain.... He saves as much of it as he can, for in this matter of *belief* we are all extreme conservatives" (*PP* 34–5; my italics). "A new *opinion* counts as 'true' just in proportion as it gratifies the individual's desire to assimilate the novel in his experience to his *beliefs* in stock" (*PP* 36; my italics). His use of "opinion" seems to be a synonym for "belief." In the following, "belief" occurs explicitly: "Experience is a process that continually gives us new material to digest. We handle this intellectually by the mass of *beliefs* of which we find ourselves already possessed, as-similating, rejecting, or rearranging in different degrees" (*MT* 42; my italics). There are other passages in which "knowledge" is used in place of "belief," but knowledge involves belief (*MT* 82–3). And, for good measure, there is, "The amount of accord which satisfies most men and women is merely the absence of violent clash between their usual thoughts and statements and the limited sphere of *sense-perceptions* in which their lives are cast," which, by the use of "sense-perceptions," seems to exclude conative and emotional states (*MT* 59; my italics).

There are, however, some passages in which James portrays his web as including, in addition to beliefs, conative and emotional states, thus making his web of belief a web of mentation or thought, which was James's generic term for any conscious state (*PP* 186). The web of mentation will include, in addition to propositional beliefs, conative states, such as desires and wants, and emotional ones consisting in feel-ings of satisfaction and the like. Here is one such passage. "Somebody contradicts them [his stock of opinions]; or in a reflective moment he discovers that they contradict each other; or he hears of facts with which they are incompatible; or *desires* arise in him which they cease to satisfy" (*PP* 34–5; my italics). Up until the final disjunct the web is of beliefs exclusively, but suddenly, in the final disjunct, he injects desires into it. Thus your desire that there not be a chair in the room (because you bet that there aren't any in the room) gets into your web, along with your perceptually based beliefs that a chair is present, and must be weighed in with the latter in determining whether you should believe that a chair is present. Therefore, conative states, along with beliefs, count as evidence for and are partially confirmatory of a belief. Needless to say this is shocking to most philosophers, coming close to mortal sin in their eyes.

That this injection of desire into the web is not due to a momen-tary careless lapse on James's part becomes clear when it is compared with what James says about the confirmation of empirical beliefs, such as that there is a house along the cow path. Initially, James seems to restrict the confirmatory experiences to sense experiences alone: "Following our mental image of a house along the cow-path, we actually come to see the house; we get the image's *full* verification" (*P* 99; my italics). But, at other places, he seems to require personal satisfaction as well as confirmatory sense experiences for full verification. "The true

thought is useful here because the house which is its object is useful"
(*P* 98). This makes it appear as if the truth of your belief depends in
part upon how pleased you are with coming upon the house, so that if it
should contain a wicked witch who eats you alive, your belief would not
be true!

This seems to be the implication of these further claims. "Truth
[is] essentially bound up with the way in which one moment in our
experience may lead us towards other moments *which it will be worth
while to have been led to* (*P* 98; my italics). "Agreement thus turns out
to be essentially an affair of leading – leading that is useful because
it is into quarters that contain objects that are *important* (*P* 103; my
italics). That the confirmatory experiences for an empirical belief are
of the mixed-bag sort seems to be the implication of James's claim
that "ideas [that are true] must point to or lead towards *that* reality
and no other, and . . . the pointings and leadings must yield satisfaction
as their result" (*P* 104). Herein, James is concerned with reference,
a topic for the next chapter, and is requiring that the referent be
one that we are pleased to come upon. No wicked witches allowed
for true beliefs. Because the satisfactions or dissatisfactions you have
upon reaching the house are confirmatory or disconfirmatory of your
belief, they will become part of your future web and thereby will play a
role in determining which candidates for admission to the web will be
accepted.

One problem with allowing the personal satisfactions that one experiences upon arriving at the house to count as confirmatory is that
it renders confirmation, and thereby truth, subjective because of the
variability among persons in regard to what satisfies them. One person
abhors the idea of getting eaten alive by the wicked witch in the house
at the end of the cow path but another, of a Jamesian hipster mentality who is willing to try anything once, finds the idea attractive. The
person who bet against there being any chair in the room is dissatisfied upon perceiving, and thereby verifying, at least for most people,
that a chair is there, but the person she bet is quite pleased with this
perceptual outcome. It would be implausible in the extreme for James
to try to escape this Protagorean relativistic nightmare by appeal to
a general agreement among people as to what gives satisfaction, due
to their sharing a common human nature. This fails to square not
only with patent facts about the widespread diversity among people in

regard to what outcomes give them satisfaction, but also with James's "sentiment of rationality" doctrine, according to which people differ with respect to which philosophy they find attractive because of their psychological differences. Furthermore, allowing personal satisfaction to be confirmatory is inconsistent with James's rule-instrumental theory of belief-acceptance and truth based on the guiding principle

9. We are always prima facie morally obligated to believe in a manner that is epistemically warranted, except when epistemic reasons are not available.

Another problem concerns the incommensurability between conative and emotional states, on the one hand, and perceptual ones, on the other, in respect to their confirmatory or evidential force. How are we to weigh the evidential value of your desire that there be no chair in the room in relation to your seeming to perceive one there? Whereas we have rough and ready procedures for hefting one piece of sensory evidence against another, we have no idea of how to factor in conative and emotional states. When this deleterious consequence of allowing the latter to be confirmatory is conjoined with the subjectivistic consequences of doing so, it renders our notion of truth totally inoperative, which is a most unfortunate outcome for a pragmatist. Given all of these problems, I think James's rule-instrumentalist theory of belief acceptance and truth would do well to work with a web of belief rather than one of mentation.

But even when so interpreted, his theory faces many objections. One is that James's account of truth fails to accord with common sense or ordinary language. The leading proponents of this objection were G. E. Moore and Bertrand Russell. Both failed to detect James's rule instrumentalism. This is evident in Russell's objection that it is easier in most cases to find out whether a proposition is true than whether believing it maximizes desire–satisfaction, an objection that is easily deflected by James's rule instrumentalism, as has been shown. I will recast their objections so that they take into account James's rule instrumentalism.

James's "definition" of truth based on 3 was

5. A proposition is true when believing it maximizes desire–satisfaction.

Moore, in his typical arrogantly humble fashion, goes to excruciating lengths to show that this definition fails to square with ordinary usage. He does this by showing that there are true sentences in which "is true" is used (not mentioned within quotation marks) that become false when James's alleged synonym, "is such that believing it maximizes desire-satisfaction," is substituted for "is true." It certainly is true that it is possible that believing proposition p maximizes desire–satisfaction, even though it is not the case that p is true; but, when the substitution is made, this true proposition turns into the necessarily false one that it is possible that believing proposition p maximizes desire–satisfaction, even though it is not the case that believing p maximizes desire–satisfaction. Descartes' evil genius, for example, could rig things so that our beliefs that maximize desire–satisfaction, as well as propositions that are epistemically warranted, are out of correspondence with reality.

Moore's objection runs through open doors. James not only grants that his analysis departs from ordinary usage, he boasts that it does, for he charges the ordinary sense of truth and reference, based as it is "on a static relation of 'correspondence'," with being an "an absolutely empty notion" (P 39). "Common-sense theories [of truth] left the gap untouched, declaring our mind able to clear it by a self-transcending leap" (MT 61). The postulation of some absolute reality with which our true ideas must correspond is totally vacuous, for how can "the partisan of absolute reality know what this orders him to think?" (MT 47). In response to another one of his ordinary language critics, J. B. Pratt, James counters that Pratt's unanalyzable notion of correspondence "ought to consist in something assignable and describable, and not remain a pure mystery" (MT 93). The same tactic is employed in an exchange of letters in the *Journal of Philosophy, Psychology and Scientific Methods* for 1907 against another of his realist critics, John E. Russell, who also takes the truth or reference relation to be unmediated and transcendent. James charges that this permits an idea to be true of some reality although it is in principle unverifiable that it is. "There might be no empirical mediation between it [the idea] and its object, no leading either to the object, or towards it, or into its associates, and yet it might still be true as 'agreeing' with the object" (*ERE* 152).

At the basis of James's objection to the common-sense notion of an unmediated, transcendent correspondence relation is his lifelong commitment to empiricism. This notion is empirically vacuous and thus empty, mysterious, and unintelligible. "The popular and traditional position" of a true idea corresponding with "a standard beyond itself," an absolute reality, is based on the fallacious inference from the fact that "finite experiences must draw support from one another [to] the notion that experience *uberhaupt* must need an absolute support" (*MT* 55). He calls this transcendence relation "saltatory," because it involves an idea mysteriously jumping out of its own skin and hitting some distant target. In contrast, his eliminative analysis of the truth or reference relation is based on "ambulatory relations," in which an idea leads us to a direct perception of its referent, or one of its associates if it be an unobservable scientific entity or another person's conscious state, through a series of intermediate experiences that are constitutive of the idea's meaning (*MT* 245). This will be the topic of the next chapter.

In general, James had no compunction about giving revisionary analyses of common-sense concepts when they did not measure up to his empirical standards. Common-sense concepts are not hardwired into our brains, as are our necessary beliefs about logical and mathematical concepts, but are the result of ancient inventions by past geniuses that caught on and stood the test of time. But they are challengeable and have been challenged with some success by science and critical philosophy, and therefore James tells us that "We have seen reason to suspect it [common sense]" (*P* 94). One of the reasons that James felt common sense to be fair game for philosophical criticism, and ultimately for revision, is that he saw it as incorporating a "popular philosophy" that really was a repository for past metaphysical theories, as is seen in his comment that "noumenal substances as matter, nature, power, are admitted alike by metaphysics and by popular philosophy *or* common sense" (*ECR* 323; my italics). He once quipped that "Every philosopher pretends that all the others are metaphysicians against whom he is simply defending the rights of common sense" (*LWJ* 2, 232–3).

James himself challenges our common-sense concepts of the soul, material substances, the mental-physical dualism, and essences as lacking proper empirical credentials. "Scholastic psychology and common-sense have always believed in a simple immaterial soul substance (*PP* 181; see also 15, 314). In basic accord with Locke, James claims that "the substantial Soul explains nothing and guarantees nothing [and has] only proved its superfluity for scientific purposes" (*PP* 331–2). It will be seen in Chapter 8 how James replaced common sense's soul substance with a psychologically connected succession of states of consciousness in the manner of the bundle theory of traditional British empiricism. "Scholasticism has taken the notion of [material] substance from common sense and made it very technical and articulate," and it "has tried to eternalize the common-sense categories by treating them very technically and articulately" (*P* 46, 90). But "vainly did scholasticism, common-sense's college-trained younger sister, seek to stereotype the forms of the human family had always talked with, to make them definite and fix them for eternity" (*P* 92). Berkeley succeeded in showing on pragmatic grounds the meaninglessness of "the scholastic notion of a material substance unapproachable by us, behind the external world, deeper and more real than it, and needed to support it" (*P* 47; see also 111). James follows the phenomenalistic strain in Berkeley's philosophy by attempting to reduce a material object to a set of actual and possible percepts.

"Common sense and popular philosophy," James tells us, "are as dualistic as it is possible to be" (*ERE* 69). But James, as will be seen when his doctrine of pure experience is expounded, goes on to challenge this dualism on phenomenological grounds, for he is unable when he introspects his own mind to separate off a mental component of a percept from its physical one. Our common-sense concepts of the nature or essences of things are "prejudices, so petrified intellectually, that to our vulgarest names, with their suggestions, we ascribe an eternal and exclusive worth" (*PP* 961). There could be good empirical reasons, such as science supplies, to reconstruct our classificatory systems of concepts.

But to show that the common-sense notion of truth as a saltatory correspondence relation is empirically vacuous is not alone sufficient to justify James's revisionary analysis of truth in terms of maximizing desire–satisfaction for believers. After all, there are many other ways to reconstruct the concept of truth, such as a warranted assertibility theory of truth. Some positive justification is needed, and for James it seems to be the moral one that by getting us to think about truth, the most honorific of honorific terms, in his new way we shall be better motivated to believe in a way that will maximize desire–satisfaction, his summum bonum. The things that counted as true under the old definition will no longer be esteemed as highly, this being reserved for the denotata of James's persuasive definition of "true" in terms of maximizing desire–satisfaction for the believers. By getting us to speak in his new way about truth, James gives us an incentive to follow the path of his promethean pragmatism so as to promote maximal human flourishing.

An obvious, but unfounded, objection is that there are possible worlds in which Descartes' evil genius brings it about that the beliefs that maximize desire–satisfaction are out of whack with what is true in the ordinary sense, or at least with what is warranted by the best evidence that it is possible for us to acquire under those circumstances. As indicated in Chapter 1, James's analyses are not meant to hold for every conceivable world but only for the actual world. Not only is there no reason to think that the actual world is an evil genius world or one in which we are brains in vats and the like, but the very intelligibility of such worlds is suspect for James's empiricistic philosophy, since they are empirically indiscernible from worlds devoid of the evil genius or the horrible Doctor Input. This is James's reason for refusing to take scepticism-in-general seriously. Against those who think that the actual world holds counter-examples to James's revisionary analysis, he is ready to reply that a "true" belief "is what works best in the way of leading us, what fits *every* part of life best and combines with the *collectivity* of experience's demands, *nothing being omitted*" (*P* 44; my italics). "The true is what works well, even though the qualification 'on the whole' may always have to be added" (*VRE* 361). These quotations are typical of James's repeated insistence on taking the broadest view possible of the effects of a belief. Beliefs that are, *in the actual world*, epistemically *un*warranted, not just *non*warranted, are notoriously unsatisfactory, all things considered, in the long run.

I wish that my interpretation of James as a revisionary, rule-instrumental theorist about truth and belief acceptance were the whole story, because I think that this view not only is consistent but also bold and original, well deserving of respect and serious consideration, if not acceptance. Unfortunately, James went on and made concessions to the realists with the hope of placating them. They believe that reality goes on its own merry way quite independently of its relation to us as knowers or language users. They capture this deep intuition by the law of bivalence, which holds that every proposition is either true or false. James cannot accept this *categorical* version of bivalence for two reasons. First, it involves the reviled nonempirical saltatory truth relation. Second, this relation is between an abstract proposition, which James was seen to reject in Chapter 1, and the worldly event it reports. Following Berkeley's strategy of speaking with the vulgar but thinking with the learned, James grants them their law of bivalence, provided he can give his learned reformulation of it. What he proposes is a conditionalized version of bivalence, coupled with the view of absolute truth as an ideal limit of inquiry. You can almost hear him saying to his realist critics in his attempt to win them over, "Ich bin ein 'Realist'." Unfortunately, each of these attempts to placate the common-sense realist winds up in total disaster, the former accepting the realist's categorical version of bivalence and the latter violating his own empiricistic and humanistic commitments.

James's conditionalizing of bivalence denies that there are *actual* truths about unthought-of events, since, for James's nominalism, the bearer of truth is a thought or idea in someone's mind. There are, however, *virtual* or *possible* truths about them. The truth about any such unthought-of event, however, "is thus already generically predetermined by the event's nature; and one may accordingly say with a perfectly good conscience that it virtually pre-exists. Common sense is thus right in its instinctive contention" (*MT* 155). This does not mean just that if there were to exist someone who formed the appropriate belief in her mind about this event, her belief would actually be true. James requires more for there to be actual truth, namely a successful act of verification consisting in a sequence of empirically vouchsafed steps that terminates in a direct perception of the event or one that goes proxy for it, as in the case of subatomic events or events in other minds. Only upon its successful completion does the virtual or possible truth become actual. "Truth *happens* to an idea. It *becomes* true, is *made* true by events. Its verity *is* in fact an event, a process: the process namely of its verifying itself, its veri*fication*" (*P* 97). The requirement that a true idea be actually verified amounts to equating truth with knowledge. "Truth and knowledge are terms correlative and interdependent" (*MT* 158). Wherever there is the one there is the other. A lot more will be said about this in the next chapter.

This sense of "virtual truth" in terms of being inductively supported stands in sharp contrast with his possibility-of-verification sense based on what would be discovered if an idea were properly tested. Such a possible truth is not verifiable in the sense that it admits of the mere possibility of being tested or verified but in the stronger sense that if it were properly tested it would be verified in the sense of being discovered to be true.

> The truth of an event, past, present, or future, is for me only another name for the fact that *if* the event ever *does* get known, the nature of the knowledge is already to some degree predetermined. The truth which precedes actual knowledge of a fact means only what any possible knower of the fact will eventually find himself necessitated to believe about it. (*MT* 157)

Before some human witness actually counted the number of stars in the Big Dipper constellation, "they were only implicitly or virtually" seven in number (*MT* 56). This definition of "virtually (possibly) true" implicitly appeals to the notion of an ideal limit toward which *properly* conducted inquiries converge, which is to be the next issue to be considered. This is why there is "the possibility of only one answer" and why the possible knower "will eventually find himself necessitated to believe" the proposition in question. Thus, James's conditionalizing of bivalence requires his ideal limit account of absolute truth.

James employs this strong sense of being virtually or possibly verifiable or knowable to give a subjunctive conditional version of the realist's categorical law of bivalence. Instead of saying that every proposition is actually true or its contradictory is, he conditionalizes bivalence by holding that every proposition is possibly true or its contradictory is, meaning that if there were to be a thinker who properly tested this proposition, either it would be discovered that it is true or it would be discovered that its contradictory is.

James's attempt to finesse common-sense realism is an exercise in futility, since his conditionalized version of bivalence entails the categorical version. This becomes obvious once it is realized that the proposition that if *p* were to be properly tested, *p* would be discovered to be true logically entails that *p* is true; for a proposition cannot be verified or discovered to be true unless it is true.

Not only does James's conditionalized version of bivalence yield the categorical version, it also commits him to countenancing the realist's abstract propositions, or at least something just as queer from a nominalistic point of view. He responds to the realist that "when you try to impale me on your second horn [in which James departs from common sense by rejecting bivalence], I think of the truth in question as a mere *abstract possibility*, so I say it does exist, and side with common sense" (*MT* 159; my italics). The abstract possibility consists in the possibility of there existing a knower who performs a proper verification. The realist's abstract truth is "only another name for a *potential* as distinguished from an actual knowledge of the reality.... It is knowledge anticipated, knowledge in the form of *possibility* merely.... truth *possible* or *virtual* exist, for a knower might *possibly* be brought to birth" (*MT* 157–8; my italics). Unfortunately for James, the *abstract possibility* that there should exist a knower is ontologically on all fours with the realist's abstract proposition. Like the latter, it is not locatable in space or time and is devoid of any sensible properties. From a nominalistic point of view, replacing abstract propositions with these abstract possibilities is like jumping from the frying pan into the fire.

James's attempt to capture the realist's intuition that there is a reality that is independent of the knower defines the absolutely true as an ideal limit of *properly* conducted inquiry, for a proposition that is virtually true is one that would be verified if the appropriate tests or inquiries were properly conducted. "The 'absolutely' true, meaning what no farther experience will ever alter, is that ideal vanishing-point towards which we imagine that all our temporary truth will some day converge" (*P* 106–7). There is a convergence toward a limit with respect to both agreement and the content of our scientific theories. This is clearly brought out by his claims that there is "an ideal opinion in which all men might agree, and which no man should ever wish to change" and that "Truth absolute ... means an ideal set of formulations towards which all opinions may in the long run of experience be expected to converge" (*MT* 142, 143).That there is an ultimately true solution to the casuistic rule also makes use of the ideal limit doctrine: "Actualized in God's thought already must be that ethical philosophy which we seek as the solution.

There is no problem with the empirical credentials of the convergence to agreement, since it could be empirically determined that there was such convergence over time, but there is a problem with empirically determining when we are at last in possession of the absolutely true theory or that the succession of theories is converging toward some specific theory as a limit. Certainly, there is no way in principle of determining that we have arrived at the scientific millennium. In fact, James's commitment to fallibilism – that we can never be certain that our theories will not be replaced by some better theory in the future – precludes the possibility of empirically determining this.

Maybe it is possible to determine empirically that there is a contentful convergence to a limit by the theories which are successively accepted by the scientific community. Not only does James deny that there is, as a matter of contingent fact, such convergence, his account of scientific theories precludes the very possibility of it. Any given phenomenon will be equally well explainable by more than one scientific theory. In the first place, every scientific theory will contain factors that appeal to aesthetic predilections, but, notoriously, they vary among persons. "The superiority of one our formulas to another may not consist so much in its literal 'objectivity,' as in subjective qualities like its usefulness, its 'elegance' or its congruity with our residual beliefs' (*MT* 41). Even more important is that the very idea of a scientific theory being a literal copy of reality as it is in itself has lost scientific creditability in modern science. According to Mach, Ostwald, and Duhem "no hypothesis is truer than any other in the sense of being a more literal copy of reality. They are all but ways of talking on our part, to be compared solely from the point of view of their *use* (*P* 93). All of our theories "are instrumental, are mental modes of *adaptation* to reality, rather than revelations or Gnostic answers to some divinely instituted world-enigma" (*P* 94).

Up to about 1850 almost everyone believed that sciences expressed truths that were exact copies of a definite code of non-human realities. But the enormously rapid multiplication of theories in these latter days has well-nigh upset the notion of any one of them being a more literally objective kind of thing than another. There are so many geometries, so many logics, so many physical and chemical hypotheses, so many classifications, each one of them good for so much and yet not good for everything, that the notion that even the truest formula may be a human device and not a literal transcript has dawned upon us. (*MT* 40)

Science, thus, is an all too human creation, an instrument that we forged to do certain jobs. This humanistic view of science seems to preclude the possibility of there being a contentful limit to which successive scientific theories converge.

Because James's empiricism and humanistic views of scientific theories preclude the very possibility of empirically determining either that some theory is absolutely true or that there is a contentful convergence to a limit among successive theories, it must be concluded that James's ideal limit doctrine of absolute truth must go; for the former doctrines are much more deeply entrenched in his promethean pragmatism than is the ideal limit theory of truth.

6

The Semantics of "Truth"

James was interpreted in the previous chapter as giving a morally based revisionary analysis of belief acceptance and truth that held us to be morally obligated to believe in a way that maximizes desire–satisfaction, with the result that a proposition counts as true when believing it maximizes desire–satisfaction. He supplemented this account with guiding principles enjoining us to have beliefs that are both consistent and epistemically warranted, and to follow a conservative strategy when it becomes necessary to revise our web of belief, which really was a web of mentation since it included conative states and emotions along with beliefs. It was suggested that things would go best if James went with a web comprised exclusively of beliefs. Because the rationale for accepting these guiding principles is to help us maximize desire–satisfaction in the long run, they admit of exceptions when doing so on some occasion can achieve this. Thus, they are merely instrumental rules.

James motivated his revisionary analysis by both therapeutic and moral considerations. By accepting his moralizing of epistemology we avoid commitment to the empirically vacuous truth or correspondence relation of common sense, with all of the mental cramps and perplexities that this occasions, which, in turn, aids our promethean endeavor to achieve our summum bonum, that being the full self-realization for each of our many selves.

A conceptual system is a *system* in that its concepts are logically interconnected. Thus, a revisionary analysis of some concept requires, for the sake of consistency, that systematic revisions be made in surrounding concepts in the system. The concept of truth is logically intertwined with that of meaning, since the meaning of a sentence is supposed to supply truth conditions for the proposition it expresses, with a proposition being true when these truth conditions are fulfilled. Think in this connection of Tarski's convention T that holds a sentence "s" to be true if and only if s. The topic of this chapter is James's theory of meaning and its connection with his theory of truth. First, his theory of meaning will be presented and then it will be shown why the theory of truth that falls out of it cannot be taken to be a theory of truth but only of the conditions under which a proposition is epistemically warranted, which is why "truth" is placed within scare quotes in the title of this chapter.

The one constant in James's philosophy, from the first to the last words he wrote, was his passionate commitment to empiricism. It was, however, a most liberal form of empiricism that countenanced not only the sensible qualities of the external senses and the sensations of inner sense but also relations, which were excluded from Hume's empiricism, as well as the contents of religious and mystical experiences, in which the subject has an apparent direct nonsensory perception of some purely spiritual, supernatural being. Although James's empiricism is a constant, the particular form or species it took varied. We shall see him making unannounced shifts between two different species of empiricism: One is the exclusively future-oriented operationalistic or pragmatic empiricism that he officially endorses as his pragmatic theory of meaning according to which the whole meaning of an idea is a set of conditionalized predictions stating what experiences would be had in the future upon performing certain actions, and the other is that of classical British empiricism that finds the meaning of an idea in terms of the sensory or experiential contents that its analysis comprises, regardless of whether they are future or not. The latter species of empiricism will be called "content empiricism" and the former "operationalist or pragmatic empiricism."

A good example of his failure to distinguish between these two different species of empirical meaning is the subtitle of his book *Pragmatism: A New Name for Some Old Ways of Thinking.* The "*Old Ways of Thinking*" refers to the empiricistic reductions given by Locke,

Berkeley, and Hume, whom James claims to be the forerunners of pragmatism (*P* 30). These reductions were based upon content empiricism, the meaning of an idea of *X* consisting in the experiences that would be had upon experiencing *X*. But the operationalistic form of empiricism that James espouses in *Pragmatism* and officially dubs "pragmatism" is quite a different species of empiricism from that of these classical British empiricists, since it is exclusively future oriented and concerns the actions required by the subject as well as the experiences attendant upon these actions.

Certain claims that James made about the relation between his pragmatism and radical empiricism make sense only if he countenances a distinction between the operationalist and content species of empiricism, assuming that meaning gives truth conditions. Pragmatism is a theory of both meaning and truth. An idea's meaning is a set of conditionalized predictions, with its truth consisting in the actual fulfillment or verification of these predictions, as is required by this assumption. Pragmatism, therefore, is a conjunction of an operationalist empiricism (*O* for short) with a theory of truth (*T* for short) based on it, on the assumption that meaning gives truth conditions.

Radical empiricism, on the other hand,

consists first of a postulate, next of a statement of fact, and finally of a generalized conclusion.

The postulate is that the only things that shall be debatable among philosophers shall be things definable in terms drawn from experience. . . .

The statement of fact is that the relations between things, conjunctive as well as disjunctive, are just as much matters of direct particular experience, neither more so nor less so, than the things themselves.

The generalized conclusion is that therefore the parts of experience hold together from next to next by relations that are themselves parts of experience. The directly apprehended universe needs, in short, no extraneous transempirical connective support, but possesses in its own right concatenated or continuous structure. (*MT* 6–7; my italics)

James was none too clear about the relation between radical empiricism and his pragmatism – the conjunction of *O* and *T*. At first he says "that there is no logical connexion between pragmatism, as I understand it, and a doctrine which I have recently set forth as 'radical empiricism'" (*P* 6). But later he says that the establishment of the pragmatic theory of truth "is a step of first-rate importance in making radical empiricism prevail" (*MT* 6). Both remarks are correct but they need further explanation.

Some commentators have mistakenly thought that radical empiricism entails pragmatism but not vice versa. The reason for this is that they thought that radical empiricism's postulate of empiricism *is identical with* the O conjunct of pragmatism, its operationalist theory of meaning; and, since O entails T and radical empiricism entails O, radical empiricism entails the conjunction of O and T (pragmatism). Pragmatism, thus, is a logically necessary condition for radical empiricism, since one of the conjuncts in radical empiricism, its postulate of empiricism, entails pragmatism. What these commentators failed to realize is that pragmatism's operationalist theory of meaning, O, is only one species of empiricism; and, since the empirical postulate refers to a generic empiricism, of which content empiricism, along with O, are different species, this postulate does not entail O. For, whereas a species entails the genus, the converse does not hold: That something is a tiger entails that it is an animal but not vice versa.

The reason why the establishment of the pragmatic theory of truth "is a step of first-rate importance in making radical empiricism prevail" is that it eliminates certain prominent counter-examples to the empirical postulate of the latter, consisting in the truth, correspondence, and reference relations. The pragmatic theory of meaning shows how these relations can be empirically analyzed in terms of a succession of experiences that terminates in a percept of the correspondent or referent in the truth or reference relation. Thus, pragmatism, although it does not entail radical empiricism, helps it to prevail by protecting its flank against some seemingly powerful counter-examples.

Whereas Peirce's version of pragmatism is derived largely from the operationalistic habits of laboratory scientists, especially their preoccupation with finding ways to measure physical properties, and was confined to general concepts that admitted of precise operationalistic analyses, James's version applies to *all* concepts and derives from Darwinian biology's depiction of man as an organism who must use his intelligence as a practical instrument to aid him in his endeavor to survive, and survive well, in a hostile environment. It is the coming to fruition of his labors in chemistry, anatomy, and physiology during the 1860's and 1870's. The Darwinian view of man, which James recasts as the promethean view of man, informs all of James's writings. Basically,

James wants a theory of meaning that will connect a belief's meaning with the role that it plays in guiding the believer in his effort to cope successfully with his environment. It is for this reason that he makes an idea's meaning completely prospective, a matter that will concern us later.

The basis of James's pragmatic theory of meaning is the view of a belief as "that upon which a man is prepared to act." Peirce's claim that "our beliefs are really rules for action," which is endorsed by James, gives a variant on this claim (*P* 29, *VRE* 351). It is, however, a potentially misleading ellipsis, for neither the psychological belief state, the believing, nor the what-is-believed, the content of the belief, can be identified with a rule without absurdity. Whereas the believing is temporally locatable, a rule is not itself so locatable, although its being followed or enforced is. Furthermore, what is believed when one believes that snow is white is not a rule, such as the rule to assert "snow is white" when asked what is the color of snow; for one could believe that there is such a rule but have no disposition to follow it. What Peirce and James meant, no doubt, is that to believe that snow is white is to have the disposition to follow this rule, as well as other rules that specify how one ought to act toward snow, such as to infer that one will have white visual images when confronted with snow under standard conditions. A belief, therefore, is a habit of acting, "the establishment in our nature of a rule of action," as Peirce said.

James unwittingly gives both a normative and a nonnormative account of this disposition. The former makes room for evaluating the believer's behavior, whether intentional or nonintentional, as being correct or incorrect in respect to the way in which it is connected with the original belief or thought but the latter does not, it being confined to a mere causal account of the relation between the belief and the subsequent behavior.

James's initial definitions of pragmatism give the normative account when they speak of "conduct to be *recommended*" in the Baldwin's *Dictionary* and of "what conduct it is *fitted* to produce" in *Pragmatism* (my italics. See also *VRE* 351). There are other normative sounding expressions that James uses to characterize the behavioral disposition of the believer. He speaks of the conduct that a belief "dictates" or "calls for" (*EP* 124). He also speaks of the "conduct that *should* be followed" by the believer or that is "*required*" by the belief (*EP* 335,

WB 3; my italics). When contrasting the meanings of pluralism and absolutism, he says that whereas a belief in either "permits" our leading the morally strenuous life, only the belief in pluralism "demands" it (*MT* 123). A conception of God is meaningful only if it "*implies* certain definite things that we can feel and do at particular moments of our lives, things which we could not feel and *should* not do were no God present" (*EP* 127; my italics). "Should" seems to be a synonym for "ought" or "require" here. What a believer ought or is demanded to do is different from what she will be caused to do by her having the belief in question. The use of "recommended," "fitted," "calls for," "should," "required," "demanded," "implies," and "deduced from" makes it look as if the believer's behavioral disposition is normatively based. Before investigating the source of this normativity, it will be shown that James inconsistently gave a purely causal, nonnormative account of these dispositions, often in the very same paragraph in which he gave the normative account, thereby precluding any attempt to dispel the apparent inconsistency diachronically in terms of a development in James's views of the dispositional relationship.

Usually James characterizes the behavioral disposition in purely causal terms, devoid of any type of oughtness or shouldness. He says that a belief "inspires" (*ER* 124, *WB* 32) and "instigates" (*P* 97) certain behavior. "We know an object by means of an idea, whenever we ambulate towards the object under the *impulse* which the idea communicates" (*MT* 80; my italics). The idea of the Absolute, for example, is meaningful if it "can be shown to have *any consequences* whatever for our life" (*P* 1; my italics). "Consequences," "impulses," "inspires," and "instigates" appear to be purely causal, nonnormative terms. Sometimes James describes the relation between a belief and the attendant behavior in purely temporal terms, as when he speaks of the "conduct consequent upon" or that "follows on" a belief (*ER* 125, *MT* 34). There is not even a hint of anything normative in these temporal and causal characterizations.

The problems with James's causal theory of meaning were adumbrated in Chapter 4. They resulted from the fact that the behavior that is *caused* or *followed* by a given belief or thought is determined by features of the believer's psychological make-up, but they are notoriously variable among persons. This results in a subjectivistic Protagorean nightmare in which meanings become so person-relative that communication becomes practically although not theoretically impossible, since in principle enough could be known about a person's external behavior so that his behavior upon hearing certain words could be predicted. This is nicely illustrated in the "Niagara Falls" comedy routine in which every time Lou Costello would innocently mention "Niagara Falls" it would cause Bud Abbott to go berserk and start pounding on him. There also was the odd chap who would be disposed to act so as to make

> *R.* Good will win out over evil in the long run.

become true by the performance of good-making actions only if he first believed the irrelevant proposition that Verdi wrote *Ernani.* These examples, of course, are exaggerated, but they serve to remind us of how variable the connection between belief and action is among persons.

It was necessary in Chapter 4 to protect James's doctrine of the will to believe against counter-examples based on such variability between belief and action by stipulating that 9. *A*'s belief that *p* is a rational reason for him to act so as to help make *q* become true.

Fortunately, James's nonnormative causal theory of meaning is not his final word. For the most part, James gives this theory only when engaged in his perverse nutshelling activity of giving one- or two-sentence accounts of his theory of meaning, but when he is actually working out the details of this theory, with regard to both general and singular terms, he goes with the normative account. Unlike Peirce, who found the source of the normative in the way in which the community of scientists agreed upon the use of general terms, James eschews any appeal to normatively rule-governed human practices to explain the normative. It will be seen that his account of the normative basis for the proper use of both general and singular terms is in terms of an intention to follow a "private rule," and thus he is still left with the problems of relativism and subjectivism. An account first will be given of his account of general concepts, then singular ones.

General Concepts. James's account of general concepts waffles between content empiricism and operationalism. According to his operationalistic or pragmatic theory of meaning, the meaning of your idea is determined by what "difference . . . its being true will make in some possible person's history, and we shall know, not only just what you are really claiming, but also how important an issue it is, and how to go to work to verify the claim" (*SPP* 38). But he then immediately countenances content empiricism as bringing out part of the meaning of a concept when he says that in obeying this pragmatic rule for determining meaning "we neglect the substantive content of the concept, and follow its function only." The *function* of a concept or idea – what it portends for future experience and conduct – is only a part of its meaning; it has in addition a *substantive content.* This content will be, for James, an experiential one, as is required by content empiricism.

To understand a concept you must know what it *means.* It means always some *this,* or some abstract portion of a *this,* with which we first made acquaintance in the perceptual world, or else some grouping of such abstract portions. All conceptual content is borrowed: to know what the concept 'colour' means you must have *seen* red, or blue, or green. (*SPP* 46)

In this passage James espouses Hume's concept empiricism, which requires that all concepts are derived by a process of abstraction from sense experience. These sense experiences constitute the "substantive content" of a concept's meaning. They need not be future experiences that are attendant upon the performance of certain operations.

A similar distinction between function and content underlies James's remark that "The meaning of a concept may always be found, *if not in some sensible particular which it directly designates,* then in some particular difference in the course of human experience which its being true will make" (*SPP* 37; my italics). The sensible particular that is directly designated supposedly constitutes its substantive content. The distinction between a concept's pragmatic function and its substantive empirical content also is found in his account of the three forms that a concept can take. "The concept of 'man,' to take an example, is three things: 1. the word itself; 2. a vague picture of the human form which has its own value in the way of beauty or not; and 3. an instrument for symbolizing certain objects from which we may expect human treatment when occasion arrives" (*SPP* 36). Condition 3 concerns the function or pragmatic meaning of the concept, which in the case of abstract contents is the only form that the concept takes. 2, on the other hand, is the substantive content since it involves the "vague picture" or the image part of the concept. James goes on to add that "however beautiful or otherwise worthy of stationary contemplation the substantive part of a concept may be, the more important part of its significance may naturally be held to be the consequences to which it leads" (*SPP* 37). But this countenances the substantive content as part of the meaning of certain concepts. This distinction between the substance and function of a concept gives reason to think that James had a theory of pragmatic meaning rather than a pragmatic theory of meaning, given that he recognized a nonpragmatic cognitive or substantive meaning in addition to a pragmatic one.

Since a singular or individual concept can also be carried by a word or image, what is it that makes a word or image general, applicable to more than one individual? James's answer is that it is not any intrinsic feature of the word or image but the intention of the subject to apply it generally that makes for the difference. Whether we mean a given word or image to function as a singular or general concept "*is an entirely peculiar element of the thought*" that accompanies it (*PP* 446). "This added consciousness is an absolutely positive sort of feeling, transforming what would otherwise be mere noise or vision into something *understood*; and determining the sequel of my thinking, the later words and images, in a perfectly definite way" (*PP* 446). It is a "vague consciousness," a fringe or halo that "surrounds the image" and "constitutes an intention that the name or mental pictures employed should mean all the possible individuals of the class" (*PP* 451). Via this intention "we always do know which of all possible subjects we have in mind" (*PP* 454).

But exactly how does the subject's intention succeed in collecting together an extension of individuals that satisfy or are instances of his general concept? What makes it correct for him to apply it to all of them? James's answer is based on

a fundamental psychical peculiarity which may be entitled "*the principle of constancy in the mind's meanings*," and which may be thus expressed: "*The same matters can be thought of in successive portions of the mental stream, and some of these portions can know that they mean the same matters which the other portions meant.*" One might put it otherwise by saying that "the mind can always intend, and know when it intends, to think of the Same." (*PP* 434)

This principle rests on a fundamental law of psychology: "That we can at any moment think of the same thing which at any former moment we thought of is the ultimate law of our intellectual constitution" (*PP* 920).

This principle or law is of a subjective character, since it is the subject's "intention . . . to think of the same," about which he cannot be mistaken, that determines the extension of his general concept over time (*PP* 435). "Each thought decides, by its own authority," whether its present content is an instance of what it formerly intended to count as an instance of some concept. In other words, each subject follows an in-principle private rule in determining which individuals count as instances of a given general concept. He and he alone knows whether he is correctly following his intention to call these experiences instances of this concept.

This commitment to an in-principle private language in *The Principles of Psychology* becomes fully explicit in his last publication, *Some Problems of Philosophy*. A general word for a sensible quality, say for white, can collect together into its extension instances of white that differ in their color-qualities, provided "we mean that our word *shall* inalterably signify" a color common to them. "The impossibility of isolating and fixing this quality physically is irrelevant, so long as we can isolate and fix it mentally, and decide that whenever we say 'white,' that identical quality, whether applied rightly or wrongly, is what we shall be held to *mean*. Our meanings can be the same as often as we intend to have them so" (*SPP* 57). James uses "we" in this passage in the distributive sense, since each one of us must adhere to his own private intention always to call things "white" that have the same color as the specimen he has mentally isolated and officially dubbed as the standard of whiteness. James does allow for the possibility of the speaker "rightly or wrongly" applying "white," but only the speaker is able to determine whether he is correctly adhering to his own private rule. The reason is that his paradigm of whiteness, which is a mental image private to himself, is not in principle accessible to anyone else. It is Wittgenstein's beetle in the matchbox that is observable only by the matchbox's owner. Therefore no one else can check up on the speaker to determine whether he is consistently adhering to his rule always to call things "white" that have the same color as his mental paradigm of whiteness. It was this commitment to an in-principle private language that made James the major whipping boy of the later Wittgenstein.

Singular Concepts. Singular concepts or ideas have a special philosophical importance, since it is through them that our thought and language gets hooked onto reality. In order for us to say something true or false about the world we must ultimately employ some singular concept that refers to a real-life individual, even if it be just a place or time. It was for this reason, no doubt, that James implicitly reduced questions about truth to ones about knowledge, and the latter, in turn, to questions about singular reference. (See, for example, *ERE* 28, 31–3, 152, and *MT* 128–30.) James begins by asking a question about the conditions under which a belief is true but immediately replaces it by a question about how the belief can be known, which he then replaces by the question about how we can refer to or be acquainted with the real-life individual(s) that the belief is about.

James presents his account of singular reference as a way of escaping from Royce's ingenious reference-based argument, in his 1885 *The Religious Aspect of Philosophy*, for the thesis that everything is a part of a single Absolute Mind. The argument proceeds by rejecting the representative realist or, in James's terminology, intellectualist, view of reference that has a mental image mysteriously jump out of its own skin and hit some transcendent target. A person's image of the Empire State Building or its name in some unexplained way manages to reach out and grab hold of the Empire State Building itself. Royce finds this account unacceptable because the reference relation is a non-mediated, primitive relation that is empirically vacuous, being an instance of James's reviled nonempirical saltatory relation. It is incapable of explaining how the finite mind is able to aim at and hit its Empire State Building target. As James put it in his exposition of Royce, "If thought be one thing and reality another, by what pincers, from out of all the realities, does the thought pick out the special one it intends to know?" (*ECR* 386). So far James is in complete agreement with Royce.

Having disposed of the representative realist or intellectualist account of reference, Royce goes on to contend that the only possible way in which reference could succeed is if the referring idea in the finite mind, along with its real-life referent, are parts of a single mind, the Absolute, that brings it about via its intention that the former refers to the latter. This results in an idealism in which everything, along with our finite minds and their contents, is an idea in the Absolute Mind.

James, of course, rejects Royce's argument that reference can be secured only in this way. But at exactly what station does James get off the Royce Express? He agrees with Royce that there is nothing problematic about how a mind is acquainted with or refers to one of its own ideas. Following Grote, he dubs it "knowledge as acquaintance" (*MT* 18–19). To be conscious of a content or a "that" ipso facto is to know or refer to it. It was seen in James's account of general concepts that there is nothing problematic about a mind's identifying and reidentifying one of its ideas, this serving as the basis for his in-principle private language. James further agrees with Royce that there is nothing problematic about how a mind uses one of its ideas to refer to another of its ideas. For here the referent aimed at is an empirical content of the mind of the referer, unlike representative realism in which it is transcendent. In response to James's challenge to explain how it is possible for the representative realist to know what is the target of his purported reference, John Russell responded, "When I think, I know what I am thinking about, just as I know what mark I am aiming at when I am engaged in target-shooting" (*ERE* 152–3). But this analogy misfires since, for the representative realist, the referential target is a transcendent one and thereby cannot be aimed at. If the target were itself a content of the mind of the referer there would be no such problem, for it would know what target is aimed at by its referential thought. And, moreover, it can bring it about via its own intending that this thought refers to this target.

James agrees with all this, so how does he escape from Royce's argument? In his summary of Royce's argument, James writes that it assumes "that we *could* make anything in our own mind refer to anything else *there*, – provided, of course, the two things were objects of a single act of thought" (*ECR* 386). While James agrees that the mind has this power to intend that one of its ideas refers to another one of its ideas, he rejects the requirement that the relata in this referential relation be co-present in "a single act of thought." An earlier idea can refer to a later idea in the same mind via an ambulatory relation that *guides* or *leads* the thinker through a connecting sequence of intermediary experiences. For example, a person located at 37th Street and 5th Avenue at time t_1 entertains an image of the Empire State Building or its name that guides or leads him, quite literally, through a sequence of intervening steps to 34th Street and 5th Avenue at the later time t_4, at which time he has a vivid percept of the building. If the initiating idea at t_1 involved the use of the name "Empire State Building," it would not resemble the terminating percept. When the 1884 essay

"The Function of Cognition" was reprinted in *The Meaning of Truth* in 1909, James added a note saying that it gave "undue prominence . . . to resembling, which altho a fundamental function in knowing truly, is so often dispensed with" (*MT* 32).

James's alternative analysis of reference, at least on its face, seems to be as idealistic as Royce's, for the referential relation is between *ideas in a single mind*, albeit successive rather than simultaneous ones. James claims that "Experiences are all" (*ECR* 552) and that "experience and reality come to the same thing" (*MT* 64). He boasts that his pragmatism converts the "empty notion of a static relation of 'correspondence' [reference] . . . between our minds and reality, into that of a rich and active commerce . . . between particular thoughts of ours, *and the great universe of other experiences in which they play their parts and have their uses*" (*P* 39; my italics). "The only function that one experience can perform is to lead into another experience; and the only fulfillment we can speak of is the reaching of a certain experienced end" (*P* 65). It will be seen in Chapter 7 that James attempted to show that experience is neither intrinsically mental nor intrinsically physical but instead some kind of neutral stuff.

James's account of how the earlier thought *leads* or *guides* the thinker to the later one through a sequence of connected experiences contains the same clash between the normative and nonnormative causal accounts as was found to infect his account of the connection between a general idea and its associated behavioral disposition. (See *MT* 29, 34, 64, 80, 96, and *P* 97–9 for the nonnormative causal account and *ERE* 23, 25, 29, 31, 43, and *MT* 63, 129 for the normative account.) The normative account, which he gives for the most part, makes a crucial use of the conscious intent of the initial idea in which the subsequent steps are anticipated. This idea is surrounded by a "penumbra," "halo," or "fringe" consisting in vague feelings of anticipation of the kinaesthetic sensations and visual sensations that the referer will experience as he goes through the successive steps that are required. As he progresses this halo will change.

Differently located people will have different causal recipes for guiding them to a common referent, but this does not preclude their coming upon one and the same referent at the termination of their respective sequence of steps. James has an account for their terminating percepts being of one and the same object based on a coincidence between their indexical references, a touching of their index fingers as they point to the building.

It is via overt acts of ostension that they ultimately are able to hook their referring terms onto the world and, moreover, know that they are coreferers. In his Syllabus of Philosophy 3 for 1902–3 James wrote, "'Two can't have the same object, because each has its object inside of itself.' Pragmatic answer: How can I tell *where* your object is except by your acts? To show where, you point to *my* object with your hand which I see" (*ML* 269). When the index fingers of two referers actually touch each other it establishes that their respective referents are spatially coincident and thus one and the same. James speaks of "that spot wherein our hands meet, and where each of us begins to work if he wishes to make the hall [our common referent] change before the other's eye" (*ERE* 41). It is not just the spatial coincidence of different acts of ostension that establishes coreference but also the coordinated manner in which the coreferers act upon their common referent. "Your hand lays hold of one end of a rope and my hand lays hold of the other end. We pull against each other. Can our two hands be mutual objects in their experience, and the rope not be mutual also? What is true of the rope is true of any other percept" (*ERE* 38). Although persons who indexically corefer to the Empire State Building at a given time cannot together lift or push the building, they can jointly act on it in various ways; imagine that they are realizing the pipe dream of every tin man and are jointly aluminum siding the building. It is through such shared activity that Berkeley's "congeries of solipsisms" is escaped (*ERE* 38–9). This emphasis on the need for shared activity for two people to be coreferers is in the spirit of the Mead–Dewey requirement that there be a social community of people engaged in cooperative pursuits for there to be linguistic communication. James would have to apply the same communitarian requirements to general concepts if he is to escape the radical subjectivism of his in-principle private language account of them; however, it would be beyond the scope of this book to attempt this on his behalf.

Even if James's theory of singular reference can avoid the problem of subjectivism, it still faces what Lovejoy aptly called "the paradox of the alleged futurity of yesterday." The paradox arises from James's theory of meaning, along with those of Peirce and Dewey, being completely future oriented. Recall that James, following Peirce, said that "to develop a thought's meaning we need only determine what conduct it is *fitted to produce*: that conduct is for us its *sole* significance" (*P* 28; my italics).

It was just seen that for James the meaning of a singular concept is a causal recipe for grabbing the referent by the lapels in the *future*. This is in accord with the underlying promethean spirit of his philosophy in which our whole way of conceiving the world is geared to furthering our quest to gain control and mastery over objects so that we can use them to maximize desire–satisfaction. Toward this end we must be able to concoct recipes that will lead us to these objects so that we can effectively use them. This exclusively future-oriented causal theory of reference stands in stark contrast with the past-oriented causal or historical theories of singular reference championed in recent times by Kripke, Donnellan, Putnam, and Burge in which the causal chain begins in the past with a baptismal-type bestowal of a proper name that then gets continuously passed on from one referer to a subsequent one in an ongoing linguistic community that terminates in a present use of the name. Whereas this theory of reference fails to do justice to the pragmatic aspect of reference, James's theory seems to make it impossible to refer to a past object.

When confronted with this paradox James responded by appeal to the way in which we ordinary indirectly verify statements about the past. In regard to the problem of referring to the past person Julius Caesar, James wrote that "Caesar had, and my statement has, effects; and if these effects in any way run together, a concrete medium and bottom is provided for the determinate, cognitive relation, which, as a pure *actio in distans*, seemed to float too vaguely and unintelligibly" (*MT* 121). He also said that "All human thinking gets discursified; we exchange ideas; we lend and borrow verifications, get them from one another by means of social intercourse," which seems to bring in the ongoing linguistic community of the historical theory of reference of Kripke et al. (*P* 102). But James failed to realize that, according to his exclusively future-oriented pragmatic or operationalist theory of meaning, his claims that "Caesar *had* effects" or that "we lend and borrow verifications" have as their *whole* meaning a set of conditionalized predictions that report what experiences we will have in the future if we perform certain operations. The apparently retrospective meanings get converted into exclusively future-directed ones.

That it is impossible to refer to a past individual creates the following problem for reference to individuals in the future, which I owe to Henry Jackman. Imagine that I have a cap that I have continuously owned since I purchased it seven years ago. I left it on a table in the next room and now entertain a thought of it. According to James the meaning of this thought for me is a recipe that will guide me step by experiential step from where I now am to the cap on the table in the next room so that I can grab it by the "lapels." I follow this recipe and reach a cap that exactly resembles my initiating thought of it, even down to having a dark spot on its bill where the dog had had an accident, but unbeknownst to me some practical joker, out to give a counter-example to James, had replaced it with an exact duplicate. I take the cap to be the referent of my initiating thought because it not only resembles my original cap but also satisfies all of the pragmatic functions of the original cap, such as discouraging panhandlers from approaching me for money. But it isn't my cap, and there seemingly is no way to explain why it is not without tracing the past history of this cap against that of my original cap in order to show that it is not spatio-temporally continuous with the original cap. Thus, unless it is possible to refer to a past object *qua* past object, it is not possible to determine that a present object is the referent of a past act of reference.

James has available to him the resources to escape from the problem of how reference can be made to an individual, as well as the more general paradox of the alleged futurity of yesterday. It was shown that he sloshed back and forth between an operationalist and content version of empiricism. What he needs to do is explicitly to recognize content empiricism as an additional species of empirical meaning in addition to that of operationalism. Thus the meaning of my thought that Caesar crossed the Rubicon need not be exhausted by statements predicting what experiences I will have if I read certain books and the like but also involves a subjunctive conditional statement describing what experiences someone *would* have had if he *were* to have directly observed the crossing. The latter, of course, can be contrary to fact. In the case of my cap that is now in the next room, my causal recipe for getting my hands on it must be supplemented by a description of the cap's past history, its continuous history since I purchased it seven years ago, that is, a description of the experiences that would have been had were an observer to have continuously observed it over this seven-year interval.

What is the textual support for this way of interpreting, or should I say reinterpreting, James? Although for the most part James identified an idea's whole meaning with its operationalist meaning, especially when he was explicitly presenting his pragmatic theory of meaning, there are several crucial passages in which he countenanced content empiricism as another species of meaning. We have already seen him make a distinction between the "function" of an idea and its "substantive content," with the latter being an idea's content empirical meaning (*SPP* 38). James introduced this distinction in a casual manner, failing to alert the reader that it undercuts his previous official commitment to a univocal operationalist theory of meaning. A similar sort of sudden and casual qualification of the latter occurs in a footnote (!) in *The Varieties of Religious Experience* in regard to the "objective truth" of religious experiences: "The word 'truth' is here taken to mean something additional to bare value for life, although the natural propensity of man is to believe that whatever has great value for life is thereby certified as true" (*VRE* 401). This crucial qualification of his former pragmatic theory of truth deserved to be put up in bright lights rather than to be buried in a footnote.

So far it has been found that, in spite of James's official endorsement of the pragmatic theory of meaning as capturing the *whole* meaning of a concept, he also recognized a content empirical sort of meaning. Thus, when all is said and done, James did not have a pragmatic theory of meaning but only a theory of pragmatic meaning. What James would fight in the last ditch for, however, is that a *necessary* condition for an idea to be meaningful is that it have a pragmatic meaning. This seems to be maintained in James's final letter to John E. Russell.

Dear Russell: We seem now to have laid bare our exact difference. According to me, 'meaning' a certain object and 'agreeing' with it are abstract notions of both of which definite concrete accounts can be given.

According to you, they shine by their own inner light and no further account can be given. They may even 'obtain' (*in cases where human verification is impossible*) and make no empirical difference to us. To me, using the pragmatic method of testing concepts, this would mean that the word truth might on certain occasions have no meaning whatever. I still must hold to its having always a meaning, and continue to contend for that meaning being unfoldable and representable in experiential terms. (*ERE* 153; my italics)

What James is saying is that without our being able in practice to verify a belief, which, it will be recalled, requires our being able to pin down the referents of its referring terms, the belief is meaningless. If we were completely causally cut off from the past Caesar, so that no future indirect verification is practically possible, the belief that Caesar crossed the Rubicon, in spite of having a content empirical meaning, would not be meaningful. James's point can be recast in terms of a distinction that was made by subsequent logical positivists. Schlick distinguished between a statement's actual and logical verification, Carnap between its practical and theoretical verifiability, and Ayer between its practical and in-principle verifiability. The latter member of each of the three distinctions corresponds to James's content empirical meaning, since it concerns what an *ideal* observer who was suitably equipped and stationed in space and time would have observed. The former concerns how it is practically possible for a present person to verify a statement, this often involving indirect verification. James does not think that the mere "logical," "theoretical," or "in principle" possibility of verification is enough for meaningfulness. There also must be the practical possibility of verification by a present person. This completes my account of James's theory of meaning, and it now can be asked what theory of truth falls out of it, *on the assumption that a theory of meaning supplies truth conditions for sentences.*

The following argument attempts to show what theory of truth is entailed by James's pragmatic theory of truth on this assumption.

The Truth-Conditions Argument

(i) A belief is true if and only if it corresponds with reality. necessary truth in virtue of the definition of "true"

(ii) A belief is true if and only if its meaning corresponds with reality. necessary truth (*P* 131)

(iii) The meaning of a belief is a set of conditionalized predictions of the form "If you do act *A*, then you will have experience *E*." pragmatic theory of meaning

(iv) Reality is the totality of experiences. premise based on *P* 39, *MT* 64–5, and *ECR* 552

(v) A belief is true if and only if the set of conditionalized predictions that constitute its meaning agrees with experience, in
that upon doing act *A* you have experience *E*, and so on for the
other conditionalized predictions in the set.   from (ii)–(iv)

James stresses over and over again that he accepts premise (i), which
is the correspondence theory of truth, provided he is free to supply
his own pragmatic account of what correspondence and reality mean,
this being another case of his speaking with the vulgar but thinking
with the learned. Conclusion (v), which is James's pragmatic theory
of truth, requires actual, as contrasted with potential, verification. It
is this requirement that underlies his claim that "Truth *happens* to an
idea. It *becomes* true, is *made* true by events" (*MT* 3). A belief acquires
the property of truth when it becomes actually verified, and this is
something that we bring about through our activities as verifiers. What
the truth-conditions argument establishes is that James's pragmatic
theory of meaning, premise (iii), logically entails his pragmatic theory of truth, conclusion (v), thereby satisfying the requirement that a
theory of truth supply truth conditions for beliefs and sentences. The
reason is that the conjunction of (iii) with the necessarily true correspondence theory of truth, (i), entails (v), his pragmatic theory of
truth. This shows that (iii) logically entails (v), it being a law of modal
logic that if (p and q) entail r and q is necessary, then p entails r.

It must be stressed again that (v) follows from (iii) only if it is assumed that a theory of meaning supplies truth conditions for a belief
or sentence, an assumption that almost every philosopher made up
until James. James cannot make it, for, if he does, a serious aporia
breaks out within his philosophy due to the fact that (v) clashes with
his morally driven revisionary account of truth

5. A proposition is true when believing it maximizes desire–
satisfaction.

The clash is due to the fact that (v) holds that truth is determined *exclusively* by epistemic considerations having to do with a set of conditionalized predictions being borne out by empirical experience, whereas
5 holds that a belief's truth is determined *exclusively* by its maximizing desire–satisfaction for those who believe it. This aporia cannot be
escaped by replacing or supplementing James's pragmatic theory of

meaning with a content empirical theory of meaning, for there still will remain the clash between an epistemically grounded theory of truth with one based on maximizing desire–satisfaction. This replacement or supplementation changes only the account that is given of the epistemic grounds of truth. Thus, if (iii) should be replaced by

(iii)′ The meaning of a belief is its substantive empirical content.

it will follow that

(v)′ A belief is true if and only if its substantive empirical content agrees with experience.

But (v)′ is just as incompatible with 5 as is (v).

It is the task of the James interpreter to try to find on his behalf some way out of this aporia, being guided by the desiderata of finding an interpretation that is textually well motivated, agrees with the underlying spirit of his philosophy, and makes for the most interesting philosophical doctrine in its own right, matters about which there can be considerable disagreement among equally competent James interpreters. It has been argued at length in previous chapters that 5's account of truth is in accord with the underlying promethean spirit of James's philosophy – his quest to have it all – and, in addition, has ample textual support, though James is not consistent on this issue. Furthermore, this account makes James's theory of truth a bold and original contribution to the history of philosophy, qualifying him for induction into the Philosophical Hall of Fame, and which deserves to be taken seriously even if not ultimately accepted. For these reasons I suggest that we interpret James as rejecting the assumption that a theory of meaning gives truth conditions for beliefs and sentences and instead take his theory of meaning as supplying only the conditions under which a belief is epistemically warranted. It is important that James have a well grounded theory of epistemic warrant, since it is necessary for him to supplement 5 with the guiding principle

9. We are always prima facie morally obligated to believe in a manner that is epistemically warranted, except when epistemic justification is not possible.

His meaning-based account of epistemic warrant explains what is meant by "epistemically warranted" and "epistemic justification" in 9.

7

Ontological Relativism

William James Meets Poo-bah

The promethean James is engaged in the grand quest to have it all, which requires having each of his many selves fully realize itself. But among James's desires is a second-order desire that all of these first-order desires be realized in a harmonious way. He wants to be able, for example, to do science, lead the morally strenuous life, and be religious with a clear metaphysical conscience because there is no inconsistency between these different ways of being in and viewing the world. But there appear to be conflicts between them, and pragmatism is recommended as a *reconciler* or *mediator*, but not synthesizer or unifier, between these different selves or perspectives. Consider our "tough- and tender-hearted" selves. The former, of whom the prime example is the absolute idealist, is "rationalistic, intellectualistic, idealistic, optimistic, religious, free-willist, monistic, and dogmatical," while the latter is of a reductive scientistic bent, being "empirical, sensationalistic, materialistic, pessimistic, irreligious, fatalistic, pluralist, and sceptical" (*P* 13). Most of us have a hankering for the good things in both the tough- and tender-minded ways of taking the world, in spite of their apparent clashes, and pragmatism is advertised as giving us a way to have both without there being any clashes between them.

I. Methodological Univocalism

The gospel preached by pragmatism is reconciliation through methodological univocalism. It shows that the tough- and tender-minded selves employ the very same method for determining meaning and truth. Because no one wants to impugn the legitimacy of doing science, if it can be shown that in our moral and religious lives we employ the very same method that science does, morality and religion will ride the coattails of science to intellectual respectability, becoming subject to all the rights and privileges thereunto appertaining. James uses Papini's simile that likens pragmatism to a hotel corridor

from which a hundred doors open into a hundred chambers. In one you may see a man on his knees praying to regain his faith; in another a desk at which sits some one eager to destroy all metaphysics; in a third a laboratory with an investigator looking for new footholds by which to advance upon the future. (*EP* 146)

This is a much higher class hotel than any I have ever been in, even though it allowed guests to use Bunsen burners and, supposedly, cook in their rooms. All the occupants, regardless of what they are up to in their different rooms, must pass through the common corridor to get to their rooms in the sense that they have to employ the same pragmatic method for determining meaning and truth in their respective activities. Through methodological univocalism we can form a live-and-let-live alliance, though not synthesis or unification, between our tough- and tender-minded selves. James recommends that we adopt his pragmatism on a "try it, you'll like it" basis. By affording us complete freedom to "come and go" between the different rooms (maybe it wasn't such a high class hotel after all), pragmatism should eventually prove itself "the most completely impressive way to the normal run of minds" (*P* 25). James is assuming that the normal run of minds shares his penchant to have it all and thus is looking for a way to reconcile the seemingly conflicting demands and claims made by their many selves.

It has been seen that James's pragmatic theory of meaning was exclusively future oriented because it had as its underlying raison d'etre to give us a way of conceiving things that will enable us to gain power over them so that we can use them as instrumental means in our quest to have it all. Thus the concept of a general object is a set of conditionalized predictions that prepares us to interact with objects of that sort in a fruitful manner, and a singular concept is an action-guiding recipe for getting hold of its referent for the purpose of using and enjoying it.

Although scientific concepts seem to be amenable, at least for the most part, to such an operationalistic analysis, it is questionable whether the sort of concepts that figure prominently in the life of the moral agent and religious person are. The challenge to James is to show that they are. Toward this end James attempted to give pragmatic or operationalistic analyses of these concepts, the most prominent of which are God, freedom, and design. According to James they "have for their *sole* meaning a better promise as to this world's outcome" (*P*6; my italics). The use of "sole" indicates that the future consequences of a belief in the realization of one of these concepts exhausts its meaning. That their meaning is exclusively pragmatic is borne out by his remark that "Taken abstractly, no one of these terms has any inner content, none of them would retain the least pragmatic value in a world whose character was obviously perfect from the start. . . . Free-will thus has no meaning unless it be a doctrine of relief. . . . Other than this practical significance, the words God, free-will, design, etc., have none" (*P*61). Because the meaning of these concepts is what they portend for the future, they would have no meaning in a futureless world (*P* 50ff.). What they portend for the future, moreover, must have consequences for what attitude and stance we should adopt toward the world.

Take for example the mystic's concept of the Absolute One or Nirvana. According to James's pragmatic rendering it "means safety from this everlasting round of adventures of which the world consists" and thus would have us adopt a passive, accepting attitude toward the world (*P* 140; see also 75). James makes it appear as if we are committed to calling a pill "God" or "Nirvana" if it should cause those who ingest it to feel blissful and safe. The "cash value" of the concept of the God of the absolutist or mystic is that it licenses us to take an occasional moral holiday, because we are assured that good will triumph no matter what we do or that evil is only an illusion and thus not in need of elimination (*P*41). The concept of determinism also requires us to take a passive or quietistic stance toward the world and the evils thereof, which served as the basis of the Dilemma of Determinism Argument that to accept determinism requires lapsing into pessimism. It was because of this undesirable consequence of a belief in determinism and the epistemic undecidability of determinism that James claimed we had a will-to-believe justification for rejecting determinism. James's analysis of God in terms of the conditionalized prediction that if we collectively exert our best moral effort, then good will win out over evil in the long run is another example of his rendering metaphysical concepts solely in terms of what they portend for the human future and thereby the stance and attitude that it is appropriate for us to adopt.

It is to James's credit that his vivid sense of reality prevented him from going all the way with these outlandishly reductive pragmatic analyses. In the last chapter it was shown how James enriched his pragmatic meaning with a type of content empiricism – the "substantive content" of the concept. He even countenanced an irreducibly theoretical meaning for metaphysical concepts such as the soul and the Absolute. What basically is missing in his pragmatic analysis of God is God himself – a being who has conscious intents and personally interacts with us. At other places he brings in this personal God when he says that God "must be conceived as the deepest power in the universe; and, second, he must be conceived under the form of a mental personality. . . . A power not ourselves, then, which not only makes for righteousness, but means it, and which recognizes us – such is the definition which I think nobody will be inclined to dispute" (*WB* 97–8). Herein James combines the personal and pragmatic features of God.

II. Ontological Relativism

Unfortunately, methodological univocalism does not go far enough in eliminating all the clashes between our many different selves. Our scientific self accepts determinism, epiphenomenalism, and the bifurcation between man and nature, but our moral agent self believes that there are undetermined acts of spiritual causation in a world that has human meaning. Furthermore, whereas both use concepts as teleological instruments for gaining power to control the world, mystics eschew concepts altogether so that they can penetrate to the inner core of a cotton-candyish reality through an act of sympathetic intuition. A true reconciliation of the quests and worldviews of these many selves needs something more than methodological univocalism.

The something more that is needed is found in Poo-bah, that delightful character in *The Mikado* who holds all the offices of state and avoids the apparent inconsistencies between the various things he says by restricting them to the perspectives or interests of different officials. William James will be seen to be a metaphysical Poo-bah. Instead of being many different officials, he has many different selves hungering for self-realization, each of whose interests are directed toward its own corresponding world. The seeming inconsistencies between the claims made by these different selves are neutralized by restricting them to a certain perspective or interest. *Qua* the tough-minded scientist, James affirms determinism and that there is no psychosis without neurosis, but *qua* the tender-minded moral agent, he rejects both and instead accepts the reality of undetermined acts of spiritual causation. *Qua* promethean man of action, he carves reality up into a plurality of discrete individuals in terms of pragmatically based classificatory systems; but, *qua* mystic, he eschews concepts altogether so as to penetrate to intuit reality as it is in itself. And so on, and so on. What is real depends upon the purposes and interests that are freely selected by a self, analogous to Poo-bah freely choosing which official's perspective to adopt.

James's democratic plurality of equally real worlds, each awaiting the Midas touch of interest to qualify it as the real world, is worked out in the chapter on "The Perception of Reality" in *The Principles of Psychology*. Herein an attempt is made to unearth what we mean by "existence" through a genetic analysis of the reasons why we call something existent. The existence of objects, when approached in this manner, is found to consist in their relation to ourselves. "Existence is thus no substantive quality when we predicate it of any object; it is a relation ultimately terminating in ourselves, and at the moment when it terminates, becoming a *practical* relation" (*PP* 919). By "practical" James means what appeals to our emotional and active life, what is of interest and importance to us. Because it is such an appeal that leads us to attribute reality to something, it follows that

reality means simply relation to our emotional and active life. This is the only sense which the word ever has in the mouths of practical men. In this sense, whatever excites and stimulates our interest is real.... *The fons et origo of all reality, whether from the absolute or the practical point of view, is ourselves.* (*PP* 924–5)

That existence or reality is relative to a person at a time is due to the fact that interests vary across persons and over time for a single person.

In spite of the fact that attributions of existence are based on an object's emotional appeal to an agent due to its interest or importance,

James holds that the agent chooses whether or not to believe in the existence of a conceived object. Immediately after saying that "in its inner nature belief, or the sense of reality, is a sort of feeling more allied to the emotions than to anything else," he adds that belief also involves an act of "consent" that "is recognized by all to be a manifestation of our active nature" (*PP* 921). The choice enters in as an *effort to attend* to some idea of which we are conscious. Thus, "Each of us literally chooses, by his ways of attending to things, what sort of a universe he shall appear to himself to inhabit" (*PP* 401).

James claims that every object thought of has some type of reality. "For, in the strict and ultimate sense of the word existence, everything which can be thought of at all exists as *some* sort of object, whether mythical object, individual thinker's object, or object in outer space and for intelligence at large" (*PP* 923). The use of the "strict and ultimate" qualification is a tip-off that a revisionary analysis is in the offing. Each sort of object is a denizen of a world of related objects. *"Every object we think of gets at last referred to one world or another.* . . . It settles into our belief as a common-sense object, a scientific object, an abstract object, a mythological object, an object of someone's mistaken conception, or a madman's object" (*PP* 922). Not only do we believe in the existence or reality of every object that we attend to in an uncontested manner, that is, that fills our conscious without a competitor, we assign that object to a world of related objects and thereby take this world also to be, not only existent, but *the* real world. "Reality, starting from our Ego, thus sheds itself from point to point – first, upon all objects which have an immediate sting of interest for our Ego in them, and next, upon the objects most continuously related with these"– their fellow world mates (*PP* 926).

James identifies "the Universe" or "the total world" with the totality of these worlds, sometimes called "sub-worlds" or "sub-universes" (*PP* 921). "The total world of which the philosophers must take account is thus composed of the realities *plus* the fancies and illusions" (*PP* 920). Again, "The reality believed by the complete philosopher" comprises every object of thought along with its world of related objects. This "complete philosopher," furthermore, "seeks to determine the relation of each sub-world to the others in the total world which *is*" (*PP* 921). James correctly points out that "the various worlds themselves . . . appear . . . to most men's minds in no very definitely conceived relation to each other" (*PP*922). This raises the question of what James took the unifying relation between worlds to be, in virtue of which they form a universe. Unfortunately, nowhere in any of his writings, either published or unpublished, does he explicitly address this issue. James was hard at work in his final years on a metaphysical magnum opus, posthumously published as *Some Problems in Philosophy*, that would "round out my system, which now is too much like an arch built on one side" (*SPP*xiii). In Chapter 11 an attempt is made to develop from James's writings various ways in which this arch might be finished so as to effect a unification of the many worlds, assuming that it was this lacuna in his philosophy that he had in mind.

The solution to the unifying relation between worlds that is implicit in *The Principles of Psychology* and, in general, in his pragmatically-based writings, is what I will call the "promethean solution." Each of the worlds is a self-contained unity, some even having their own ontology, conceptual system, presuppositions, and doxastic principles for making and justifying claims made within that world. There are no direct relations between the worlds, only the mediated one consisting in their all being possible objects of interest-based selection by a promethean subject. Thus, the many worlds enjoy only an indirect, subject-mediated unification.

The reconciliation between the different selves and their corresponding different worlds is of a first-I-am-this-sort-of-a-self-and-then-I-am-that-sort-of-self type. James makes this very point when he speaks of the philosophical layman as "living vaguely in one plausible compartment of it [his metaphysical scheme] or another to suit the temptations of *successive hours*" (*P* 14; my italics). Another example of this temporalized schizophrenia is his claim that "Of course as human beings we can be healthy minded on one day and sick souls on the next" and thereby take different worlds to be the real one on these different days (*P* 141). More of this "taking turns" strategy for avoiding conflict is seen in his claim that "The interest of theoretic rationality. . . . is but one of a thousand human purposes. When others rear their heads it must pack up its little bundle and retire till its turn recurs" (*EP* 56). While this "taking turns" strategy might work in preventing conflicts in a nursery school between children all of whom want to use the swing, it does not succeed in enabling each of us to become an integrated self.

By effecting this sharp separation between the worlds and making their very actualization consist in being accorded reality by the interests of a promethean subject, James gives carte blanche to each of his many selves to assert itself with a clear conscience, providing the proper "*qua* this world" relativization is made so as to avoid any interworld conflict. "Each of us literally chooses, by his ways of attending to things, what sort of a universe he shall appear to inhabit" (*PP* 401). This enables James to reconcile his scientific and moral agent selves. In a published letter of 1888 to the editor of the *Open Court*, James replies to Professor von Gizycki's criticisms of the Dilemma of Determinism that "We claim indeterminism, we claim that good things were *possible* where bad things now are, in the interests of moral activity, just as we claim determinism in the interests of scientific activity" (*WB* 445). This is repeated two years later in *The Principles of Psychology*. "Nor do I see why for scientific purposes one need give it [determinism] up even if indeterminate amounts of effort really do occur... Science, however, must be constantly reminded that her purposes are not the only purposes, and that the order of uniform causation which she has use for, and is therefore right in postulating, may be enveloped in a wider order, on which she has no claims at all" (*PP* 1179). He warns that "the aspiration to be 'scientific' is... an idol of the tribe to the present generation," which must be avoided by seeing it as the "one-sided subjective interest which it is" (*PP* 1236). "The popular notion that 'Science' is forced on the mind *ab extra* and that our interests have nothing to do with its construction, is utterly absurd" (*PP* 1260).

And in the same Poo-bah fashion James claims that the physiologist, *qua* practicing physiologist, is justified in refusing to admit "that there may be mental events to which no brain-events corresponds." But this same physiologist, *qua* moral agent, is permitted to believe that there are undetermined spiritual acts of causation. "The believers in mechanism do so without hesitation, and they ought not to refuse a similar privilege to the believers in a spiritual force" (*PP* 429). This spiritual force is the active inner self, and its nature changes with a shift in our perspective. *Qua* introspective psychologist attempting to ascertain "in what the feeling of this central active self consists" (*PP* 286), he holds that it is nothing but "the collection of... peculiar motions in the head or between the head and throat" (*PP* 288). But *qua* moral agent, he identifies this active self, which is "the substantive thing which we *are*," with our "sense of the amount of effort we can put forth" quite independently of past causal determinants (*PP* 1181).

Underlying James's Poo-bahism is his will-to-believe doctrine. Throughout his career James argued that our intellect cannot determine which world is the real world. For example, in regard to the common-sense, scientific, and philosophical stages of thought, James says that "It is impossible . . . to say that any stage as yet in sight is absolutely more *true* than any other" (*P* 92). Given these intellectual limitations, the will-to-believe doctrine permits us to choose which world to take as real, at least for the time being, on the basis of our interests, since this will help us to satisfy these interests, which certainly is a desirable state of affairs, at least according to James's underlying axiological intuition that the satisfaction of a desire is in itself a good thing, in fact the only thing that is good in itself (*WB* 153). Usually it is the workaday world of sensible objects that engages our interest, so much so that there is no need to preface what we say with a restrictive "*qua*"-clause, since the background context makes manifest that we are speaking from the perspective of this practical world.

While the many worlds and selves might get *reconciled* by Poo-bahism, they fail to get *unified*. As James matured as a philosopher he attempted to find ways of unifying the worlds so as get beyond this unsatisfying schizophrenic outcome. It is the task of Chapter 11 to explore in depth the various ways in which the many worlds can get unified.

III. Pure Experience

There is another way in which James attempted reconciliation between conflicting points of view, that being via his extremely bold and original doctrine of "Pure Experience," which is rightly considered to be his most significant contribution to technical philosophy. It denies that there is any irreducible ontological dualism between the mental and the physical – nothing is mental or physical *simpliciter* – and instead claims that *every* individual is composed of some sort of neutral stuff called Pure Experience and has both the potentiality to become physical and the potentiality to become mental, the former being realized when it actually enters into a lawlike sequence of events and the latter when the sequence is a rhapsody of causally unconnected events that comprise a person's mental history since later members of the sequence can remember earlier ones. It will turn out that the scope of the "every" quantifier is quite limited for James, applying only to sensible particulars within the phenomenal world. It does not apply to the denizens of abstract worlds, such as numbers and properties, since they cannot enter into any temporal sequences, given that they are nontemporal. Nor does it apply to purely spiritual individuals in supernatural worlds, since they cannot occupy space. It will be seen that James included all of these nonphenomenal entities in his ontology. Thus, the doctrine of Pure Experience does not yield interworld unification but only an intra-world unification within the world of sensible particulars.

The doctrine of Pure Experience achieves reconciliation within the sensible world by giving a therapeutic analysis that dissolves perplexing and stultifying epistemological dualisms, primarily that between the subject and object of experience. The value of pure experience, according to James, is that "You escape the noetic 'chasm,' with its discontinuity" (*ML* 319). "Throughout the history of philosophy the subject and its object have been treated as absolutely discontinuous entities; and thereupon the presence of the latter to the former, or the 'apprehension' by the former of the latter, has assumed a paradoxical character which all sorts of theories had to be invented to overcome" (*ERE* 27). For reasons that will be given in Chapter 10, the dualism between the conscious subject and the physical object renders it impossible for the subject to perceive the object or have any other sort of relation to it. But, if the subject and object are made of the same underlying ontological stuff, namely pure experience, there ceases to be an unbridgeable ontological chasm between them. In the perception of a pen, say, there is only a single individual, the pen percept, that can be placed in two sequences such that it functions physically in one and mentally in the other. James says in Poo-bah-like fashion that "The double functioning of the identical pen swings round the phrases 'in so far forth as,' or 'as,' or 'qua, or 'quantenus' or 'en tant que,' etc. In so far as it acts physically, in so far as it acts mentally, etc. the results differ" (*MEN* 98). The point of the "*qua*"-clause is to restrict the claim to a certain sequence of events in which the pen is included, it being up to the speaker which sequence it is.

The extreme rival doctrines of idealism, which makes the object part of the subject's consciousness, and materialism, which reduces consciousness to physical processes and states, are seen to be "solutions" to a bogus problem. By neutralizing the problem of how the "inner" and the "outer," the "subjective" and "objective" are connected, the clash between them is neutralized. This is reconciliation with a vengeance. The clash between the insider approach of introspection also gets reconciled with the apparently rival outsider approach of laboratory psychology. By dissolving conceptual cramps and puzzlements, James helps us to get our intellectual house in order so that we can function more effectively as promethean agents engaged in the grand quest to have it all. A fly in a bottle cannot achieve any important flylike goals.

The doctrine of Pure Experience, which was tentatively developed in a series of papers of 1904–5 (posthumously published as *Essays in Radical Empiricism*), maintains:

I. No event is mental or physical *simpliciter*, but is so only when related to earlier and later events in a certain manner;

II. All sensible events are made of the same neutral stuff – Pure Experience; and

III. For every sensible event there are *actual* sequences of events such that it qualifies as mental in some of them and as physical in others; or, more weakly

III'. For every sensible event there are *possible* sequences of events such that it qualifies as mental in some of them and as physical in others.

Before discussing each of these tenets in detail, it is important to point out two things. First, no tenet entails any other one, thus allowing us to be pick-and-choose shoppers. Tenet I, however, is the core of the doctrine and gets explained in III. Many have accepted I and some version of III but rejected II. Second, the doctrine of Pure Experience is logically independent of Radical Experience, not being entailed by nor entailing either its postulate of empiricism (that only empirically definable entities are to be discussable in philosophy), statement of fact (that relations are perceptually given), or generalized conclusion (that relations stand in no need of a transcendental source). Many commentators muddy the waters by including the doctrine of Pure Experience within Radical Empiricism, and there are passages in James that encourage them to do so. As far as I can see the only connection between the two doctrines is that, according to James, the doctrine of Pure Experience is supposed to gain partial support by following Radical Empiricism's empirical postulate. But if we are to include everything discovered by following this postulate, Radical Empiricism becomes an unhelpful compendium of all empirically ascertained truths, such as that humans require water to survive. It is important to bear in mind this terminological point, for, when I argue that James abandoned the doctrine of Pure Experience after 1905, it must not be taken to imply that he abandoned Radical Empiricism, which is something that he never did.

Tenet I. James, no doubt wanting a grabber to get the reader's attention, makes the startling assertion that "'consciousness' . . . is the name of a nonentity" (*ERE* 3). What he means is that there are no conscious or mental entities, be they substances or processes, *as understood by common sense*, according to which an individual is conscious or mental *simpliciter*, meaning that the predicate or function "__ is conscious (or mental)" is one-place or monadic. But grammatical appearances deceive, just as they were found in Section II to do for "exists" or "is actual," both of which also falsely appeared to be monadic predicates when they really are relational predicates for James that mean "World __ is of interest to person __ at time __," which makes "is actual" a triadic or three-place predicate. Similarly, James is going to argue that "is conscious" is really a relational predicate, and likewise for "is physical." By denying that "is mental" and "is physical" are monadic predicates James in effect is rejecting the Cartesian dualism between the mental and the physical, each of which is supposed to be an ultimate monadic form of stuff.

James's claim that what is experientially given is neither mental nor physical *simpliciter* can be viewed as following up the British phenomenalist tradition by adding that what it took the immediately given to be, namely a sensum or sense-datum, is in itself neither mental nor physical. Although the mental-physical dualism does not apply to a given piece of pure experience taken in isolation, it does apply to temporal sequences of events so that an individual piece of pure experience qualifies as mental or physical when it is taken as a member of a mental or physical type of sequence respectively. James leans very heavily on the analogy of a pure experience with a letter in a crossword puzzle that can be placed in either a vertical or horizontal series, thus forming a part of different words in these two ways of being taken, the "a" in "cat" and "bat" for example (*MT* 36 and *ERE* 269). Analogously, by taking a piece of pure experience in a certain way, we make it to be mental or physical. This is yet another instance of James's promethean humanism that the world is what we make it. Just as we determine by our interest-based acts of attending which world is the actual world, we determine by these acts whether a sensible particular is mental or physical.

James initially characterizes the difference between a physical and mental type of temporal sequence of events in a viciously regressive manner, because he fails to use topically-neutral words to describe the members of the sequences. He winds up saying, roughly, that an event qualifies as mental when it is placed in a succession of other mental events, and physical when placed in a succession of physical events. An experience counts as mental if it "is the last term of a train of sensations, emotions, decisions, movements, classifications, expectations, etc., ending in the present, and the first term of a series of similar 'inner' operations extending into the future" and the very same experience counts as physical if it is the "*terminus ad quem* of a lot of previous physical operations, carpentering, papering, furnishing, warming, etc" (*ERE* 8–9). James's placing of "inner" within scare quotation marks does not protect him against the charge that he is analyzing a mental sequence in terms of mentalistic concepts that themselves refer to inner episodes or states that are conscious *simpliciter*, which are the very states that he wants to eliminate through his analysis. But his more considered account is based on whether the events comprising the succession are connected in a stable, lawlike manner, which is a close cousin of Kant's Second Analogy of Experience criterion for objectivity. The percept of a pen counts as physical if "it is a stable feature, holds ink, marks paper.... So far as it is unstable, on the contrary, coming and going with the movements of my eyes, altering with what I call my fancy" it counts as mental (*ERE* 61). James seems to appeal to Kant's irreversibility of the order in which a sequence of events is experienced as a criterion for objectivity and thus for being a physical sequence: If I can reverse the order in which I sense a succession of events, as by moving my head for example, it is not an objective order. To speak more accurately, in a mental ordering it is the contents of the related experiences, what they represent, that do not stand in lawlike connections: the experiences *qua* events can stand in cause and effect relations, as happens in sequences of experiences in a dream whose contents are not nomically connected according to scientific laws but which can stand in cause and effect relations to each other in which a later dream experience is caused by an earlier one, my dream experience of fear being caused by my early seeming to see a monster in my dream. But the contents of dream experiences, what they represent, are not connectable according to scientific laws with either each other or the contents of waking experiences that precede or succeed the dream. Causal anomalies break out between these contents. I dream I am swimming in Georgian Bay and the next instant am walking in Pittsburgh.

James gives the misleading impression that every piece of pure experience belongs to either a physical or mental sequence, even to both types of sequence, but this can't be right. For there are two types of nonphysical sequences. One is a mental sequence that constitutes someone's mental history. It will be seen in the next chapter that this requires that the later members remember the earlier ones in some noncausal sense that involves the later members appropriating earlier ones because of their having a special sort of warmth and intimacy. Another is a sequence whose member experiences are not nomically connected but do not constitute a personal series, since the later members do not remember the earlier ones. Thus, the dichotomy between mental and physical sequences is not exhaustive, since there is the third possibility of a temporal sequence of pure experiences in which the members are neither nomically connected nor psychologically continuous in virtue of the later members remembering the earlier ones. This will have repercussions for tenet III.

That immediate experience is neutral in the sense of being neither intrinsically mental nor intrinsically physical is supported by appeal to both therapeutic and introspective considerations. The therapeutic advantages concerning the overcoming of mentally paralyzing dualisms between the subjective and the objective, the inner and the outer worlds, have already been indicated. In particular, James hoped to dissolve the perennial epistemological puzzle concerning the problem of other minds and how two minds could know one and the same object and thereby escape from their separate solipsistic worlds. The problem of other minds is rooted in the supposed conceptual truth that a state of consciousness cannot be common to two or more minds, with the result that the only way in which one mind can know what is going on in another is through the risky Cartesian argument from analogy in which the person makes correlations between her overt behavior and mental states and infers that other persons satisfy the same correlations, thus allowing her to infer their conscious states from their observed overt behavior. Because she is conceptually barred from ever directly verifying that these correlations in fact hold for other persons, since she can't have their mental states, the door is left wide open for scepticism.

James puts his doctrine of Pure Experience to work in undermining the alleged impossibility of a conscious or mental state being had or shared by two minds, thereby closing the conceptual gap between them that invited scepticism. Just as a point can be a common member of intersecting lines, a piece of pure experience can be common to the mental histories of two minds in virtue of later members of each historical sequence remembering this experience. A pen percept is a piece of pure experience, in itself neither mental nor physical. For it to qualify as conscious requires that it be known by being remembered by a later piece of pure experience. There is no absurdity in this pen percept being remembered by both you and me, which would involve "its being felt in two different ways at once, as yours, namely, and as mine" (*ERE* 66; see also 269).

But if it is possible for our mental histories to share a common pen percept when each of us remembers it, it must be possible for our earlier perceptions of the pen to be one and the same percept. James waffles over whether this is possible and finally comes to a negative view. Initially, James sides with a common-sense "natural realism" that holds that "Your mind and mine *may* terminate in the same percept, not merely against it, as if it were a third external thing, but by inserting themselves into it and coalescing with it" (*ERE* 40). "We believe that we all know and think about the same world, because *we believe our PERCEPTS are possessed by us in common*" (*MT* 30). Common sense believes that "my percept is held to *be* the pen for the time being – percepts and physical realities being treated by common sense as identical" (*MT* 87).

This direct realism, however, seems to be taken back when James says that "when you and I are said to know the 'same' Memorial Hall, our minds do [not] terminate at or in a numerically identical perception," the reason being that "we see the Hall in different perspectives" because of our different spatial locations (*ERE* 40). James is assuming that among the conditions for percept identity is having the same look, feel, appearance, and the like. Your percept of the Hall has a different shape than mine. Because the Hall is felt equivocally by us,

felt now as part of my mind and again at the same time *not* as part of my mind, but of yours (for my mind is *not* yours), and this would seem impossible without doubling it into two distinct things, or, in other words, without reverting to the ordinary dualistic philosophy of insulated minds each knowing its object representatively as a third thing – and that would be to give up the pure-experience scheme altogether. (*ERE* 63)

The only way in which our percepts could be one and the same is if our heads were to be spatially coincident at that time, like Siamese twins joined at the head. To assume that this is possible is to assume more than many would grant. Judging by the fact that James repeatedly gives the Cartesian argument from analogy for other minds and their contents (*ERE* 36, 38 and *MT* 24, 30), it would appear that he has failed to convince even himself that an experience can be owned by different minds. In Chapter 9 it will be seen that implicit in James's writings is a completely different solution to the problem of how we can know another mind that is based on his theory of acts of sympathetic intuition in which one person I–Thous another.

Although tenet I seems to fail in its therapeutic intention to eliminate the "noetic chasm," it still might find support from the deliverances of introspection. Furthermore, even if it were to achieve its intended therapeutic purpose, the defenders of the doctrine that experience involves an "impalpable inner flowing" that is "pure diaphaneity" would not accept it. Like G. E. Moore in his 1903 "A Refutation of Idealism," they claim that when they introspect their own mind upon experiencing a sense-datum, such as a yellow patch, they can separate off the yellow patch content from the conscious sensing that accompanies it, analogous to separating a paint into a menstruum and a pigmental mass (*ERE* 6). James challenges their introspective reports, claiming that, at least in his own case, he is not able to make any such distinction. "I am as confident as I am of anything that, in myself, the stream of thinking . . . is only a careless name for what, when scrutinized, reveals itself to consist chiefly of the stream of my breathing" (*ERE* 19; see also 268–9). This clash between rival introspectors should raise suspicions about the legitimacy of appeals to what is introspectively given.

Tenet II. This thesis, which holds "that there is only one primal stuff or material in the world, a stuff of which everything is composed," has created great consternation for interpreters, since James seems to be back with the Milesians seeking the underlying metaphysical stuff that composes all things. Many commentators cannot get themselves to believe that James was serious when he claimed that there is an underlying metaphysical stuff, since it would violate the empirical postulate of his Radical Empiricism, "that the only things that shall be debatable among philosophers shall be things definable in terms drawn from experience." But, as seen in the previous chapter, James was quite willing to countenance metaphysical entities, such as God, free will, and the soul, as well as the theoretical entities of science, that could not themselves be analyzed in terms of empirical contents, provided they played a worthwhile explanatory role. Thus, to be consistent with his actual practice as a philosopher he must amend his empirical postulate so that it holds that the only things that shall be debatable among philosophers shall be things definable in terms drawn from experience, *or that are useful in explaining empirical phenomena.*

But a mere eleven pages after he claims that pure experience is the common stuff of which everything is composed he seemingly takes it back. "Although for fluency's sake I myself spoke early in this article of a stuff of pure experience, I have now to say that there is no *general* stuff of which experience at large is made. There are as many stuffs as there are 'natures' in the things experienced" (*ERE* 14). James, however, does not stand by his retraction, for five pages later he says that "*thoughts in the concrete are made of the same stuff as things are*" (*ERE* 19). And in two subsequent articles he reiterates his Milesian metaphysical view, saying in "On the Notion of Consciousness" that "things and thought are not at all fundamentally heterogeneous; they are made of one and the stuff, which as such cannot be defined but only experienced; and which, if one wishes, one can call the stuff of experience in general" (*ERE* 271) and in "The Place of Affectional Facts in a World of Pure Experience" that "thoughts and things are absolutely homogeneous as to their material" (*ERE* 69). If we are just counting heads, it looks as if the metaphysical interpretation of pure experience wins.

How can this apparent inconsistency be dissolved? James's explanation that it was for "fluency's sake I myself spoke early in this article of a stuff of pure experience" is no help, for it is just as easy to say that there is no primal stuff of which everything is composed as it is to say that there is. The solution must reside in finding suitably different senses of "stuff" and "composed of" in the affirmation and denial. The text amply supports such a dual meaning solution. To see how it does we must look again at James's rival claims.

Thesis
There is only one primal stuff or material in the world, a stuff of which everything is composed, which is to be called "pure experience." (*ERE* 4)

Antithesis
There is no *general* stuff of which experience at large is made. There are as many stuffs as there are "natures" in the things experienced. (*ERE* 14)

The Thesis speaks of a "primal stuff" and the Antithesis of a "general stuff." There would be no contradiction if "primal stuff" means a metaphysical stuff that is wholly indeterminate because it is pure potentiality, and "general stuff" means stuff that is natured because already partially informed, in other words, some sort of empirical or scientific stuff. It is consistent to say that there is a wholly indeterminate metaphysical stuff of which everything is "composed" but no empirical stuff of which everything is "composed." There is a corresponding shift in the sense of "composed" from the Thesis, where it means "metaphysically composed" of something like prime matter, to the Antithesis, where it means "empirically composed," in the sense in which materialists believe that everything is composed of ultimate scientific particles. The Antithesis is a rejection of such a materialism. Plainly, Aristotle and James are not saying that if you physically decomposed a chair you would eventually come upon prime matter or pure experience, something which you do only when you "look" at the chair through your metaphysical "microscope," that is, when you try to answer the question of the ultimate grounds of individuation of individuals or how seemingly distinct individuals can be related to each other.

There is some textual support for this double-meaning interpretation. "There is no thought-stuff different from thing-stuff, I said; but the same identical piece of 'pure experience' (which was the name I gave to the *materia prima* of everything) can stand alternately for a 'fact of consciousness' or for a physical reality, according as it is taken in one context or in another" (*ERE* 69). James imputes to pure experience the same role as pure potentiality as Aristotle did to prime matter. "The instant field of the present is at all times what I call the 'pure' experience. It is only virtually or *potentially* either object or subject as yet. For the time being, it is plain, *unqualified* actuality or existence" (*ERE* 13; my italics). At one point James seems to identify his universal metaphysical stuff with a Platonic type receptacle of being. "Save for time and space (and, if you like, for 'being') there appears no universal element of which all things are made" (*ERE* 15). The formless space of Plato's receptacle, which should be upgraded to space-time, plays the same metaphysical role as does prime matter of offering a realm of pure potentiality that grounds the possibility of forms being instantiated and explains the ultimate ground of individuation of empirical particulars. It was seen in the previous chapter that James's account of how different perceivers can be coreferers requires that they ultimately must use spatial indexical terms such as "here" and "this place" that denote one and the same region of space as such, a region of James's "universal space."

It is not just pure experience that James holds to be potentiality but also "baby's first sensation" of the "big, blooming, buzzing confusion"; however, they are not identical for two reasons. First, pure experience, in virtue of being pure potentiality, does not instantiate any properties, except possibly for being spatio-temporal, whereas sensations, although not conceptualized by the subject, do instantiate sensible and relational properties for James. Second, sensations have the potentiality of being conceptualized by a subject and thereby becoming in James's terminology a *perception*. Therefore, the potentiality of sensations is relative to a subject who can learn to make discriminations and eventually conceptualize them, whereas the potentiality of pure experience is absolute. Sensations are to the new born babe as a block of marble is to a sculptor. In both cases there is something propertied that presents a subject with the opportunity of fashioning something meaningful out of it, a statue in one case and a cosmos in the other.

Tenet III. This tenet holds that for every sensible event there are *actual*, for the strong version, and, for the weak version, *possible* sequences of events such that it qualifies as mental in some of them and as physical in others. The strong version obviously is too strong, since there are numerous sensible experiences, such as unobserved events, for which there are no actual sequences of events in which they qualify as mental and/or physical. James was well aware of these types of counterexamples to the strong thesis. "It is possible to imagine a universe of experiences in which the only alternative between neighbors would be either physical interaction or complete inertness. In such a world the mental or the physical *status* of any piece of experience would be unequivocal" (*ERE* 71). Herein James realizes that an event could qualify only as mental or only as physical, and thus be *per accidens unambiguously mental or physical*; however, he fails to realize that an event could *per accidens* fail to qualify as either, since there could be an event that stands in no causal or memory relations to what precedes or follows it and thus fail to qualify as either physical or mental. Thus only the weak version, tenet III', is to be taken seriously.

James has three ways of protecting it against apparent recalcitrant cases – by appeal to (i) "alternate worlds," (ii) "nonenergistic properties," and (iii) "panpsychism." (i) yields a sound but unexciting version of pure experience, (ii) a false but exciting version, and (iii) an unwitting abandonment of the central idea of the doctrine of Pure Experience.

(i) *Alternate Worlds.* This attempted solution is found in a passage that James quotes from Hugo Munsterberg with full approval: "The objects of dreamers and hallucinated persons are wholly without general validity. But even were they centaurs and golden mountains, they still would be 'off there,' in fairy land, and not inside of ourselves" (*ERE* 11). This gets developed by James in terms of his many worlds, engaged in a competition with each other to capture the subject's passing interest so as to qualify for the time being as the "actual world." Were there no perceptual world that primarily engaged our interest and precluded one of these imaginary, merely thought-of worlds, "our world of thought would be the only world, and would enjoy complete reality in our belief. This actually happens in our dreams, and in our day-dreams so long as percepts do not interrupt them" (*ERE* 12).

All of the recalcitrant cases of a piece of unaccommodated pure experience can be handled by including them in an alternative world to the sensible one, such as was discussed in Section II on ontological relativism. In regard to the unobserved falling of the tree in the forest, James can avail himself of the sort of counterfactual analysis that is supplied by phenomenalism: If there were to have been an observer present in the forest (though there wasn't) who took the requisite steps, she would have been visually appeared to in a tree-falling-like manner. This counterfactual proposition describes some alternative world to the one that we now take to be actual on the basis of our present sensible interests. We can create a counterfactual world for any recalcitrant piece of pure experience you please. A free-floating bit of conscious experience is such that there is a counterfactual sequence of events in which it is remembered by later members and thus qualifies as mental. In other words, if the multiple personality subject of the original experience were to have had, though she didn't, subsequent experiences that remembered this experience, it would have qualified as mental. If the totality of history were to consist in a single event, a brief loud noise, it would satisfy tenet III', because if there were to exist the right sort of successions of events, ones in which it is remembered and others to whose members it is nomically connected, it would qualify respectively as both mental and physical in James's relational sense.

The worry is that this version is too weak, because the counterfactual alternative possible worlds it must invoke are not possible enough. On the basis of James's own analysis of possibility, he would be among those most dissatisfied. In league with Aristotle, as he is on all matters concerning possibility, James claims that a possibility must be grounded in actuality. For something to be possible in the weakest sense, a "bare" possibility, it is required that

there is nothing extant capable of preventing the possible thing. The absence of real grounds of interference may thus be said to make things *not impossible*, possible therefore in the *bare* or *abstract* sense. But most possibles are not bare, they are concretely grounded, or well-grounded, as we say. What does this mean pragmatically? It means not only that there are no preventive conditions present, but that some of the conditions of production of the possible things actually are here. (*P* 136)

A campfire burning unattended in a strong wind in a dry forest is a possible forest fire in James's "concretely grounded" sense, since nothing is afoot that will prevent its developing into a forest fire and moreover there are actual forces favoring its so developing.

The sort of counterfactual possibilities that must be employed to save tenet III' fail to qualify as either bare or concretely grounded possibilities. The unobserved falling of the tree might occur in a world devoid of all observers, and thus there would be nothing in actuality that concretely grounds the possibility of there being someone who observes this event. What is more, this possibility is not even a bare possibility, since its realization is prevented by what exists in this observerless world, namely that every individual that exists in this world has some property that is incompatible with being an observer. Imagine that its sole members are the tree, a clump of soil, and a rock. Being a tree logically precludes being an observer, and so on for the sortal properties possessed by the other members of this world.

(ii) *Nonenergistic Properties.* Although James did not explicitly deploy his analysis of possibility against the "alternative world" version, it is clear that he felt a need to find another version that would not invoke its ungrounded possibilities. He played around with a second way of dealing with recalcitrant cases that made use of a distinction between two ways in which an object can possess a causal power or disposition – "energetically" and "nonenergetically." A delusory or purely imaginary object need not be placed in some counterfactual physical sequence in order to have physical properties, such as the causal powers that are possessed by the kind of object it is, and thereby qualify as physical. Rather, it can possess them in the actual world and thus qualify as physical relative to the actual world alone but have them in a funny sort of "nonenergetic" manner.

We find that there are some fires that will always burn sticks and always warm our bodies, and that there are some waters that will always put out fires; while there are other fires and waters that will not act at all. The general group of experiences that *act*, that do not only possess their natures intrinsically, but wear them adjectively and energetically, turning them against one another, comes inevitably to be contrasted with the group whose members, having identically the same natures, fail to manifest them in the 'energetic' way. (*ERE* 17; see also 70)

It should be obvious to the reader that something has gone radically wrong. Imagine that you have ordered a set of ginzu knives for $19.95 from the Williams Sonoma James Company that you saw advertised on television as having exceptional sharpness, capable of cutting through even a two-by-four. You get the knives and to your dismay find that they quite literally can't even cut the mustard, no less a two-by-four. You write a letter of complaint to the company demanding a refund because the knives do not have the advertised property of sharpness. You would not be satisfied if the company were to respond that the knives sold to you are sharp, as advertised, only they are not sharp "energetically," meaning that they do have the causal power to cut but only in respect to imaginary objects. "Mental knives may be sharp, but they won't cut real wood" (*ERE* 17). Enjoy your ginzu knives, you are told, but remember to cut only imaginary objects with them.

What has gone wrong here? James fails to realize that "nonenergetically" is a reality-canceling modifier in the way that "toy" and "decoy" are, a toy or decoy duck not being a duck. Similarly, to have a causal power or disposition nonenergetically is not to have it. As a result, James's claim that some fires have the causal power to warm and some water has the causal power to put out fires but only nonenergetically commits him to there being fire and water that are devoid of their relevant causal powers. But this is conceptually impossible, since their causal powers are essential to them. If something cannot quench thirst or put out fires and the like, it isn't water, only "fool's water." Your $19.95 ginzu knives are only "fool's ginzu knives."

(iii) *Panpsychism.* Obviously, James was not fully satisfied with the ways (i) and (ii) handle recalcitrant cases, especially ones involving unobserved events. This third solution applies only to these types of recalcitrant cases. It contends that "unobserved events" really aren't unobserved, since they are at least present for themselves. Of such an event James says, "If not a future experience of our own or a present one of our neighbor, it must be . . . an experience for itself whose relation to other things we translate into the action of molecules, etherwaves, or whatever else the physical symbols may be. This opens the chapter of the relations of . . . [pure experience] to panpsychism, into which I cannot enter now" (*ERE* 43). Ten years earlier, in *The Varieties of Religious Experience*, James embraces this panpsychism. "The only meaning we can attach to the notion of a thing as it is 'in itself' is by conceiving it as it is *for* itself; i.e., as a piece of full experience with a private sense of 'pinch' or inner activity of some sort going with it" (*VRE* 394). This means that when a rock falls off a ledge without any observers being around its fall is at least present "for itself," which, I assume, means that it is conscious of its own falling, and, if it could talk, might say, "I have fallen down and I can't get up." This is panpsychism, because it imputes an inner consciousness to every sensible particular, even apparently insentient ones like rocks.

It is not an accident that James did not develop his panpsychic suggestion for dealing with unobserved events in his articles of 1904–5, for it amounts to a complete abandonment of the central idea of Pure Experience – that nothing is mental or conscious *simpliciter* but only in relation to other bits of pure experience. The rock's inner consciousness of its own fall does not seem to depend on its being related to any earlier or later world mates. James's suggestion of panpsychism is more than just a suggestion, since he commits himself to panpsychism in his writings both prior and subsequent to the 1904–5 articles. This will be a major topic in Part II, to which we now turn.

PART II

THE PASSIVE MYSTIC

8

The Self

James's promethean pragmatic self, being a restless, indefatigable desire–satisfaction maximizer, was seen in Part I to be always on the make in his quest to have it all. Toward this end he had to adopt an externalized stance toward worldly objects, since his concern was with successfully manipulating them for his own purposes. His pragmatic theory of meaning and truth supplied him with recipes for successfully riding herd on them. In addition they served as a univocal methodological reconciler or mediator between the projects and interests of his many different selves, but only a partial reconciler since conflicts still remained between the perspectives of these selves, especially those of the moral agent and scientist with regard to the issue of determinism, free will, and bifurcationism. The stronger medicine of a Poobahistic ontological relativism was needed, requiring him never to go anywhere or do anything without being armed with a "*qua*"-clause. Even the doctrine of Pure Experience, which turned out to be a failed though noble experiment, had a reconciling intent within the world of sensible objects. The will-to-believe doctrine served his promethean self by permitting him to believe in epistemically undecidable matters, such as that God and free will exist, in a manner that would enable him to be an active agent in bringing about the flourishing of his many selves. It doesn't get any more promethean than this.

All references in this chapter are to *The Principles of Psychology*, unless otherwise noted.

But the stance of the externalized promethean pragmatist toward worldly objects, including other persons, did not satisfy James's deep mystical longings for a more intimate personal relation to them, a relation so intimate that it would ultimately involve a union with them, but one that stopped short of the numerical identity of monistic mysticism. To experience such union it was necessary to overcome his active promethean self and learn to become passive so that he could penetrate to their inner consciousness through acts of conceptless sympathetic intuition. The promethean quest to have it all has given way to the mystical quest to spiritually penetrate all.

If there were to have been "Personals" in the newspapers in his time, James's would have read: "Harvard Professor, equally at home in a Norfolk Jacket or a backwoodsman's outfit, doing science or leading the morally strenuous life. Desperately seeking to penetrate to the inner conscious life of others. Animals and fishes okay. No kooks please."

This mystical quest for intimacy and union was both deeply rooted in William James, the man, and endemic to his era, which felt threatened by the seemingly meaningless, impersonal world that had become the professed official view of science since the rise of the "new physics" in the seventeenth century. (Everyone in Cambridge and half of Boston would have responded to his ad!) It seems as if everyone in New England in the second half of the nineteenth century had been inoculated by the Concord bacilli of mystical transcendentalism as an immunization against this threat. Along with Peirce and Dewey, James made the overcoming of this pernicious bifurcation between man and nature the chief goal of his philosophies.

James asserted, over and over again, that science supported the bifurcation between man and the world. "The essence of things for science is not to be what they seem, but to be atoms and molecules moving to and from each other according to strange laws" (1230). What James means by this cryptic remark is that "Sensible phenomena are pure delusions for the mechanical philosophy" based on modern science (1258). "Even today, secondary qualities themselves – heat, sound, light – have but a vague place in the scheme of understanding. In the common-sense meaning and for practical purposes, they are absolutely objective, absolutely physical. For the physicist, they are subjective. For him, only form, mass, and movement have an outer reality" (*ERE* 266).

This scientific image of the world challenges our deepest humanistic longings and aspirations. Some of the most eloquent and poignant passages in James attest to the sense of alienation and forlornness wrought by this bifurcation. Science holds that "all the things and qualities men love, *dulcissima mundi nomina*, are but illusions of our fancy attached to accidental clouds of dust which will be dissipated by the eternal cosmic weather as carelessly as they were formed" (1260). "The romantic spontaneity and courage are gone, the vision is materialistic and depressing. Ideals appear as inert by-products of physiology; what is higher is explained by what is lower and treated forever as a case of 'nothing but' – nothing but something else of a quite inferior sort" (*P* 15). Our "personal" and "romantic" view of life is incompatible with the mechanistic and materialistic worldview of science.

Not only does the mechanistic and materialistic worldview of science undermine our personal and romantic ways of thinking, it renders the world an unfit habit for a moral agent, since it gives him no reason for wanting to take life seriously, and this is the worst defect in a philosophy since it does not give our active propensities any

object whatever to press against. A philosophy whose principle is so incommensurate with our most intimate powers as to deny them all relevancy in universal affairs, as to annihilate their motives at one blow, will be even more unpopular than pessimism. . . . This is why materialism will always fail of universal adoption . . . For materialism denies reality to the objects of almost all the impulses which we most cherish. . . . We demand in it [the universe] a *character* for which our emotions and active propensities shall be a match. (940–1)

Any philosophy that presents a view of the world that is devoid of human significance is unacceptable. "Nothing could be more absurd than to hope for the definitive triumph of any philosophy which should refuse to legitimate and to legitimate in an emphatic manner, the more powerful of our emotional and practical tendencies" (943). "It surely is a merit in a philosophy to make the very life we lead seem real and earnest" (*PU* 28). Herein James is speaking both as a man and as a sociologist of philosophy.

James's panacea for the evils of scientifically based bifurcationism is to follow the way of inwardness, something that was to be later advocated by the existentialists and contemporary continental philosophers.

> The only form of thing that we directly encounter . . . is our own personal life. The only complete category of our thinking . . . is the category of personality, every other category being one of the abstract elements of that. And this systematic denial on Science's part of personality as a condition of events, this rigorous belief that in its own essential and innermost nature our world is a strictly impersonal world, may . . . be the very defect that our descendants will be most surprised at in our own boasted Science. (*EPR* 136–6)

This passage reveals the most fundamental assumption of James's philosophy – that the true nature of reality is to be ascertained not through the employment of symbols or concepts but rather through personal experience. "So long as we deal with the cosmic and the general [as does Science], we deal only with the symbols of reality, but *as soon as we deal with private and personal phenomena as such, we deal with realities in the completest sense of the term*" (*VRE* 393). "Individuality is founded in feeling; and the recesses of feeling, the darker, blinder strata of character, are the only places in the world in which we catch real fact in the making, and directly perceive how events happen, and how work is actually done" (*VRE* 395).

James's advocation of the inner approach to understanding reality develops an important theme in Emerson, who wrote in his *Diary* for 1833, "There is a correspondence between the human soul and everything that exists in the world; more properly, everything that is known to man. Instead of studying things without, the principles of them all may be penetrated into within him. . . . The purpose of life seems to be to acquaint man with himself. . . . The highest revelation is that God is in every man." Through looking into our own souls, that is, introspecting our own minds, we discover the way things really are, and, not surprisingly, they will turn out to be of a like kind to ourselves. Thus, by giving pride of place to introspection, James assures that our view of the universe will be a personal, romantic one. As will be seen in the next chapter, it will enable each of us to address our universe as a "Thou."

In recommending that we follow the way of inwardness or subjectivism, James, in effect, is giving pride of place to introspection over the way of objective analysis in terms of cause and effect. In *The Principles of Psychology* James held these approaches in a precarious dynamic equilibrium, ultimately siding with the introspective approach. Not only did he say that "Introspective Observation is what we have to rely on first and foremost and always," but let it have the final say when he dealt with humanistically valuable concepts, such as the self and its free will. The story to be told in Part II of this book is how James ultimately relied on the inner approach of introspection to ascertain the nature of reality, projecting onto reality at large what he discovered from introspecting his own consciousness, and, not surprisingly, wound up espousing consciousness to be the stuff of everything, with the subject of experience partially merging with what he experiences in the way in which different phases of a conscious process melt into eacʰ other. The story will begin in this chapter with an account of James'ᵣ theory of the self and how he relied solely on the revelations of introspection to reveal its nature.

Of the many different selves that James recognizes only the "spiritual self" – the flow of one's consciousness – is made use of in his account of personal identity over time. This is significant, since the nature of a given type of enduring individual is determined by its criteria of identity over time; for whatever it is that makes for its enduring as numerically one and the same individual constitutes what that type of individual is. These criteria for personal identity over time can be of either a "first-person" or "third-person" sort. The former is based on what is available to the subject through introspection and the latter on what is publicly observable. First, an exposition will be given of James's phenomenological analysis in terms of first-person criteria and then it will be asked what role, if any, he assigns to third-person criteria.

James holds the spiritual self to be a bundle of successive stages of consciousness. The members of the bundle are "Thoughts," a Thought for James being the total way in which a person is conscious at a time. All of the psychological states, processes, and dispositions that were formerly predicable of the person or Self now are to be predicated of a momentary Thought. By anchoring everything to the present Thought James hoped to escape any need to bring in an enduring Cartesian soul substance. The bundling relation is based on the feeling of warmth and intimacy that the present Thought has for an earlier one (314, 316). A past Thought is self-ascribed by a present one – taken to be co-personal with it – when it is recaptured in memory with the same warmth and intimacy it had when present, thereby agreeing with Locke that the grounds for self-ascribing a past Thought are the same as those for self-ascribing a present one.

There are several ways in which James describes this recapturing of the original warmth and intimacy of a past Thought by a present one. Most often, it is said that the latter "appropriates" or "adopts" the former. The present Thought is said also to "own" the past one. Each Thought, other than the first or last in a personal history, is "born an owner, and dies owned, transmitting whatever it realized as its Self to its own later proprietor" (322). At another place he uses the simile of the passing on of "the 'title' of a collective self" from one Thought to another (322). You might say that every Thought goes from Champ to Chump in a brief moment, rather than in the fifteen minutes envisioned by Andy Warhol. This comparison with the successive holders of a title misfires, since they are not co-personal whereas the successive appropriators are.

Plainly, James thinks of the appropriation or ownership relation as transitive. "Who owns the last self owns the self before the last, for what possesses the possessor possesses the possessed" (322). It might be true that *propositional-memory*, in which it is a proposition that is remembered, is transitive (if I remember that I remembered that I went to the circus, then I remember that I went to the circus); however, *image-memory*, in which there is a representation of a former experience of one's own through an affective or phenomenal reenactment of it, does not seem to be transitive. And it is clear that he is concerned exclusively with image-memory. James uses a diagram to illustrate the manner in which a Thought appropriates every thought appropriated by any Thought it appropriates (324). It consists in a series of Chinese boxes with their bottom halves cut away. Each box represents a single Thought, with its phenomenal content included within the box. The initial (present) Thought-box in the series includes within itself its phenomenal content and the phenomenal content included within each Thought-box included within it. As a consequence, the visual image content of a Thought contains the visual image content of any Thought it appropriates, just as a painting of a scene including a painting contains the represented painting in miniature.

The worry is that there is a finite bound to the number of possible successive appropriators and thus a rupture in transitivity, due to a limiting threshold on the smallness of the images we can be conscious of, just as there is a limiting threshold on how many contained paintings there can be in a painting that contains a miniature version of itself, in this case due to limitations imposed by materials and skills, as well as on our power of making visual discriminations. Furthermore, usually when I affectively recapture a past Thought through image-memory I do not have an image of every one of its phenomenal contents. I affectively recall my agonizing over this chapter yesterday evening, but I do not have a phenomenal awareness of every content of my total state of consciousness at that time, such as my itching from a mosquito bite.

Given the function that James assigns to his bundling relation, there is no need for him to fight in the last ditch for its having an image-memory based transitivity. This function is to secure sufficient qualitative similarity between successive phases of the stream of thought so that they can qualify as co-personal. His image-memory is only a device, as it was for Hume, for securing the kind of qualitative continuity that is necessary for the identity over time of any enduring individual or continuant.

The sense of our own personal identity, then, is exactly like any one of our other perceptions of sameness among phenomena. It is a conclusion grounded either on the resemblance in a fundamental respect, or on the continuity before the mind, of the phenomena compared. (318)

James follows Locke in holding that the temporal phases of a continuing individual can vary qualitatively, provided that they do so in a gradual and continuous manner.

If James grants, as he should, that image-memory, for the reasons just given, is not transitive, he will have to complicate his account so as to handle cases in which transitivity fails to hold. He could avail himself of the grandfather relation to image-memory and say that successive Thoughts are co-personal just in case either one of them has an image-memory of the other or they are connected by an unbroken succession of image-memories. This, of course, will not meet the problem posed by the logical possibility of the same Thought being image-remembered by different simultaneous Thoughts. James would not worry about such mere *logical* possibilities, since his analysis had the modest aim of describing how things *actually* are. In general, as has been pointed out in the discussion of truth in Chapter 5, James never claimed that his analyses or accounts gave logically or conceptually sufficient and necessary conditions.

Another aspect of the appropriation relation requiring further consideration is the role played by the qualities of warmth and intimacy upon which it is based. The charming example by which James attempts to illustrate this is fraught with difficulties: "Peter, awakening in the same bed with Paul, and recalling what both had in mind before they went to sleep, reidentifies and appropriates the 'warm' ideas as his, and is never tempted to confuse them with those cold and pale-appearing ones which he ascribes to Paul" (317). This fails as a phenomenological analysis of the grounds on which a person self-ascribes an idea. Imagine that Peter's own ideas prior to falling asleep were quite "cold and pale-appearing" compared with the ideas of Paul that were then related to him. Peter was thinking about a boring departmental meeting he had just attended in which five hours were given over to discussing whether a graduate student representative should be allowed to vote on junior faculty appointments at the very time Paul was relating to him the exciting details of his evening with some lady. Peter is not under any temptation, either at that time or when he reconsiders these ideas upon waking, to take Paul's ideas as his own, in spite of their greater warmth and interest.

A similar objection applies to James's phenomenological account of how we identify our own body. Our bodies "too are percepts in our objective field – they are simply the most interesting percepts there" (304). The Hunchback of Notre Dame, no doubt, finds the body of his beloved far more interesting than his own without thereby taking it to be his. James also errs in making "liveliness, or sensible pungency" (928) one of the important phenomenological characteristics on the basis of which we take a sensation's object to be real. "Whilst absorbed in the novel, we turn our backs on all other worlds, and, for the time, the Ivanhoe-world remains our absolute reality" (922). Again, this is belied by the phenomenological facts, for, not only are our dreams usually more lively and vivid than our run-of-the-mill waking sense experiences without thereby being taken to be of a reality that supplants or stands alongside of the ordinary sensible world, one fails to read a novel as a novel if the actions it depicts are taken to be real-life.

What is incredible about the Peter–Paul example is that James has each of them have access to both his own and the other person's mental states in just the way that they have access to all the garments that they left in a pile on the floor before retiring. (These aren't my briefs since I wear jockey shorts.) This completes our overview of James's phenomenological analysis of the identity of the Self over time, and a more in-depth probe is now required if we are to resolve its *making versus discovering* and *first- versus third-person criteria* aporias.

A good way to broach this aporia is through the herd simile. James initially says that "There is found a *self* brand, just as there is found a herd brand," which, by its use of "found," plainly supports the discovering thesis. If the making theorist should object that the herdsman had to initially brand loose, unowned cattle, James's imagines the response that "They are not his because they are branded; they are branded because they are his" (320). (The respondent must have never heard of cattle thieves, or even settlers.) He mounts an objection to his dispensing with an enduring soul based on the analogous fact that the Thought does not capture or appropriate its own Thoughts, "but as soon as it comes into existence it finds them already its own," to which his response again is the anti-Cartesian one that the present Thought can perform all the functions that a soul substance does (321). What he fails to realize is that this fact counts against his claim that the present Thought makes the unity by its appropriative act. It renders this act otiose by requiring it to unify that which already is unified, thereby resulting in the contradiction that the unity of the Self over time is both made and discovered.

It was pointed out in Chapter 7 that the same aporia infects James's account of existence or reality. According to his phenomenological analysis, we take as real "*whatever things we select and emphasize and turn to* WITH A WILL. . . . The world of living realities as contrasted with unrealities is thus anchored in the Ego, considered as an active and emotional term" (926). But these claims in favor of the making thesis of reality were seen to clash with his claims that we take a sensation's object to be real primarily when it has "Coerciveness over attention, or the power to possess consciousness," and, secondly, on the basis of "Liveliness, or sensible pungency, especially in the way of exciting pleasure or pain" (928). These two sets of claims clash, because we do not make something lively or interesting, no less coercive, by an act of will.

The order of explanation goes from something's being interesting to its being attended to rather than vice versa. A similar aporia also runs throughout his general account of belief. On the one hand, his sentiment of rationality doctrine stresses that our beliefs are determined by our emotions and passions, which renders them nonintentional. On the other hand, his promethean will-to-believe doctrine requires that we be able to choose our beliefs at will, something which we accomplish by making the intentional effort to concentrate our attention in a certain way, as was shown in Chapter 2. James would like to believe that each of us is a *causa sui*, totally responsible for everything we are and do, but he is too good a psychologist to go down the line with this promethean doctrine, with the result that an aporia appears.

But the herd simile can also be put to use in service of the making thesis. James now imagines that "wild cattle were lassoed by a newly created settler and then owned for the first time" (321). We can further imagine that upon lassoing them, the herder imprints his unique self brand on them, thereby making them his, this being analogous to the present Thought appropriating a Thought, be it present or past, as its own. The herd simile, since it permits both the discovering and making interpretation, limps on all four hoofs and should be permanently retired to Gabby Hayes's Wild West Museum in Canton, Ohio. A new start is needed.

James's account of the self-ascription of a Thought, be it present or past, begins with the phenomenal fact that some Thought is given to a present Thought with the qualities of warmth and intimacy of a special sort. "Our own past states of mind...appear to us endowed with a sort of warmth and intimacy that makes the perception of them seem more like a process of sensation than like a thought" (218). So far there is no intentional act, only passiveness, since one cannot choose to make something warm or interesting. The Thought simply discovers via passive sensation its co-personality with other Thoughts, which fits squarely with his passionate insistence that "The knowledge the present feeling has of the past ones is a real tie between them" (340). The relation of co-personality, like all relations, *pace* Hume and Mill, are experientially given and inhere in the real world.

James's problem is this. What work is left over for the intentional act of appropriation or adoption to do after a past Thought appears warm and intimate to a present Thought, since this supposedly makes them co-personal? It was this problem, no doubt, that led James to remark that "the only point that is obscure is the *act of appropriation* itself" (323). James finds two different jobs for the appropriative act to do.

First, an appropriative act is one of self-ascription that involves selective emphasis. Such a self-ascription, necessarily, requires that the present Thought refer to itself by the use of a first-person indexical expression, such as "I" or "me." But they, along with every other indexical expression, according to James, "are at bottom only names of *emphasis*" (324). Herein we find the sought for intentional act of selective attention, because "the distinction between *I* and *you*, like that between *this* and *that, here* and *there, now* and *then* . . . is the result of our laying the same selective emphasis on parts of place and time" (273). Furthermore, we can think of the appropriative act as influenced, but not determined, by what appears warm and intimate, thereby finding some role for these feelings to do in the account of co-personality.

Unfortunately, this way of finding something for the appropriative act to do in determining co-personality between Thoughts rests on a radically mistaken view of how first-person indexical words work, wrongly assimilating them to selective indexical terms such as "this." A use of "this" is indeed selective among objects, because if the user had chosen on that very occasion of use to point in a different direction than he had in fact pointed, he would have pointed to a different object than he in fact did. Because a use of "I" cannot refer to anyone other than the user, it is not selective in this counterfactual manner. Similarly, a use of "now" does not select or choose some time from out of a group of other times that could have been denoted instead *on that very occasion.*

A second job for the appropriative act is to make actual what was only possible through an intentional judgment of co-personality. When a past Thought appears warm and intimate to a present Thought, they are only potentially co-personal and become so in actuality only when the present Thought judges them to be on the basis of the warmth and intimacy relation between them (321; see also *MT* 56). This seems to get things backward, since what makes the judgment true is that the Thoughts are co-personal rather than the other way around.

I believe that some useful work can be found for the appropriative act on the basis of some remarks that James makes in passing about the

forensic aspect of self-identity over time, an aspect which James for the
most part rightfully neglects, given that his analysis is a phenomenological one. He endorses what he takes to be the dictates of the law
and "common sense" that a man should not be punished for what he
no longer remembers, because "he is not the same person forensically
now which he was then" (352). When a present Thought appropriates
a past Thought or deed, it assumes moral responsibility for it, making
itself a fit subject of praise or blame. Appropriative acts of judgments
of co-personality, in general, convert a *bare* personal numerical identity
over time into a significant identity. Without a conscious judgment of
appropriation of a past Thought, the present Thought cannot make
a meaningful use of this thought in taking stock of itself guiding its
future conduct. The appropriative act gives pragmatic significance to
a person's past. Maybe this is what James was after or should have been
after.

This completes the exposition of James's phenomenological analysis of personal identity over time in terms of first-person criteria. Is this
the whole story about our identity over time or is there a need to invoke third-person criteria? James occasionally flirts with third-person
criteria as defeaters or overriders for judgments of personal identity
based on first-person criteria, as in the following quotations.

The psychologist, looking on and playing the critic, might prove the thought
[of self identity] wrong, and show there was no real identity, there might have
been no yesterday, or, at any rate, no self of yesterday; or, if there were, the
sameness predicated might not obtain, or might be predicated on insufficient
grounds. In either case, the personal identity would not exist as a *fact*; but
it would exist as a *feeling* all the same; the consciousness of it by the thought
would be there, and the psychologist would still have to analyze that, and show
where its illusoriness lay. (315–16)

"The way in which the present Thought [one's momentary total state
of consciousness] appropriates the past is a real way, so long as no
other owner appropriates it in a more real way, and so long as the
Thought has no grounds for repudiating it stronger than those which
lead to its appropriation" (341). James seems to anticipate the contemporary "best (or only) candidate" requirement for self-identity over
time. James gives an early indication of what these objective defeaters
or overriders could be when he says that "The experiences of the body

are thus one of the conditions of the faculty of memory being what it is" (17). This seems to imply that neurophysiological facts about brain processes and states could defeat a personal identity claim based on apparent memory by showing that the right sort of causal process was not in operation within the body. The later chapter on "Memory" in *The Principles of Psychology* will be seen to give some support to this interpretation.

James's phenomenological analysis takes an "inner" approach to understanding the nature of persons. It stands in stark contrast with the "outer" or objective approach that treats persons as what I will call, in a somewhat extended sense of the term, a "natural kind," meaning a type of object whose nature is to be determined through natural science. These contrasting approaches are at the foundation of the split in twentieth century philosophy between so-called Continental and analytical approaches. They also form the real basis of James's contrast between the tough- and tender-minded given in *Pragmatism*, in spite of their not appearing explicitly in his account. The traits listed under "The Tender-Minded," for the most part, are those that assure an unbifurcated world and are vouchsafed through the inner approach, as contrasted with those listed under "The Tough-Minded," which represent the natural scientist's temper of mind, with its natural kinds approach to understanding persons and their world.

I think that, in general, James takes the inner, introspective approach to understanding reality. His method of analysis is to infer both what we mean by "*X*" and what *X* really is from an introspective analysis of what we experience *X* to be – the experiential reasons for calling something "*X*." Five prominent examples of this derivation of semantic and metaphysical conclusions from an introspective analysis are his analyses of good, truth, matter, negation, and reality. In Chapter 1 James's attempt to define *good* in terms of the experiential conditions under which we take something to be good, namely when it satisfies a desire or demand, was expounded. James's claims in *Pragmatism* that "The reasons why we call things true is the reason why they *are* true" (37) and in *The Meaning of Truth* that truth is "what truth [is] *known-as*" (48) give further evidence of his proclivity to determine the nature of something on the basis of how we experience it, as does his oft-repeated endorsement of Berkeley's reductive analysis of material objects in terms of our experiential grounds for believing that they exist.

These four cases, however, are not sufficiently probative in showing that James thought self-identity over time could be analyzed in terms of first-person criteria alone, since third-person criteria, having to do with things like the endurance of a body, also are experientially accessible, though not in as direct and immediate a way as are our own conscious states. Even so, these experiences of bodies would not be the whole nor even a significant part of what we experience our own personal identity as and thereby our reasons for taking ourselves to endure over time.

Of more moment are his analyses of negation and reality. From the analysis of the psychological grounds for a negative belief – "we never disbelieve something except for the reason that we believe something else which contradicts the first thing" – he draws a conclusion concerning the nature of the logical concept of negation – "Compare this [just mentioned] psychological fact with the corresponding logical truth that all negation rests on covert assertion of something else than the thing denied" (914). The most telling example is that of reality. He begins with the psychological question, "*Under what circumstances do we think things real?*" (917), to which his answer is that we do so when they "appear both *interesting* and *important*" (924). But from this psychological analysis he draws the semantic conclusion that "*reality means simply relation to our emotional and active life*" and that "this is the only sense which the word ever has in the mouths of practical men" (924).

James's account of self-identity over time shows a similar inference of semantic and metaphysical conclusions from a psychological or introspective analysis. To start with, he asks "what the consciousness may mean when it calls the present self the *same* with one of the past selves which it has in mind" (316). He boasts that the introspective analyses given by himself and his Associationist predecessors "have taken so much of the *meaning* of personal identity out of the clouds and made of the Self an empirical and verifiable thing" (319; my italics). And a few pages later he makes the strong statement that "It is impossible to discover any *verifiable* features in personal identity which this sketch does not contain," which seems to render third-person criteria otiose, given that his "sketch" is exclusively in terms of first-person criteria (322). These quotations still are not decisive, since it could be argued that his use of "mean" is short for "psychologically means," since it occurs within the scope of the section entitled "The Sense of Personal Identity."

What really nails down my case are the unrestricted endorsements of an exclusively introspective analysis given in publications subsequent to *The Principles of Psychology*, thereby escaping this scope problem. In the 1902 *The Varieties of Religious Experience* James praises Locke for analyzing "personal identity" in terms of "its cash-value," meaning what it is "*known as*" (*VRE* 350). In his series of articles on Pure Experience published during 1904–5 he argued that no experiential datum is conscious or physical *simpliciter* but only in a relational manner. Placed in one kind of network of relationships to other experiential data it qualifies as physical but in a different kind of network as conscious. The latter kind of network is said to be that of the history of a single Self over time, which he explained as follows:

In the chapter on 'The Self,' in my *Principles of Psychology*, I explained the continuous identity of each personal consciousness as a name for the practical fact that new experiences come which look back on the old ones, find them 'warm,' and greet and appropriate them as 'mine'. (*ERE* 64; see also 39 and 270)

Herein he is asserting without qualification or restriction what constitutes the identity of the self over time.

I take it that some good reasons have just been advanced for taking James's analyses based exclusively on first-person criteria as an analysis of self-identity over time as such. But, it will be objected, this cannot be the whole story. To be sure, James's introspective approach to understanding self-identity supports his antibifurcationism, since it gives an account of the Self in terms of what has importance for our emotions and active propensities, which, it will be recalled, formed the underlying leitmotiv of his analysis. The dramatic portrayal of personal endurance that it gives secures a central place for our values and aspirations, thus helping to prevent our world from becoming a bifurcated one devoid of human meaning. James, however, is not exclusively an "inside man," for he wrote *The Principles of Psychology* primarily for the purpose of establishing psychology as a *natural* science, and, toward that end, gave prominence to the "outside"-based work (actually it was done indoors in a laboratory) of his German friends and colleagues, about whose exact scientific method he said that "it could hardly have arisen in a country whose natives could be *bored*" (192). There is a tension that runs throughout the book between the outer and inner methodological approaches, or between his functional psychology and phenomenological psychology. But, as has been already shown, there unquestionably are places in *The Principles of Psychology* where one of the approaches becomes dominant and is appealed to as being revelatory of the true nature of the phenomenon under investigation, and some good reasons have been advanced to show that he gave priority to the inner approach for revealing the true nature of personal identity.

A more serious objection is that there are strong materialistic undercurrents in *The Principles of Psychology*, in particular his reductive phenomenological analysis of our prized active inner Self, that Self of all the other Selves, which is the source of will and effort, to a collection of bodily sensations, primarily movements in the head (287–8). Herein James seems to come close to Dewey's natural kinds view of a person, which speaks against his having exclusively first-person criteria for self-identity over time. But surface appearances deceive here. First, James's reductive analysis is explicitly restricted Poo-bah style to phenomenal appearances, and, when he waxes metaphysical and moral in the chapters "Attention" and "Will," this active Self turns into something nonmaterial that defies description and explanation by natural science, as was shown in Chapter 3 (424, 1179–82). It must be remembered that James is an arch relativist who always speaks *qua* some human perspective or interest. The apparent contradiction between his claim in *The Principles of Psychology* that "there is no neurosis without psychosis" (133; see also 18) and his account of the independence of consciousness from matter (his filtration theory of the brain) in his later writings, especially the lecture on "Human Immortality: Two Supposed Objections," *The Varieties of Religious Experience*, and *A Pluralistic Universe*, vanishes once it is realized that the former claim is restricted to our perspective as natural scientists. Similar considerations hold for his comments about determinism. *Qua* scientists, we assume determinism, but, *qua* moral beings, we must reject it. This is in accord with his Poo-bahism, as seen in the previous chapter.

What has been primarily overlooked by those, like Dewey, who have attributed a naturalistic or materialistic view of persons to James on the basis of his phenomenological reduction of the inner Self to a collection of bodily movements is that James nowhere bases self-identity over time on that of the body or even some core part thereof, such as the brain, that is causally responsible according to science for what is most important and distinctive about persons. He does not hold it to be even a necessary condition for such identity, as is attested to by his claim that "The same brain may subserve many conscious selves, either alternate or coexisting" (379). If a person were identical with a living human body or brain, then they should have the same criteria of identity, but plainly they do not for James, otherwise he would have said so somewhere.

But, it could still be objected, we must take the quotations given earlier in which James alluded to the possibility of defeating an introspectively based claim of self-identity over time by appeal to third-person criteria. He does not explicitly tell us what they are, but if we dig deeply enough we might find them, and they might very well involve a requirement of some sort of spatio-temporal continuity of a body, thereby showing that his phenomenological analysis is not the whole story about personal identity over time.

The most likely place to look for these defeaters is in James's "Memory" chapter, the reason being that his introspective analysis based on the state of *seeming* to remember inevitably leads to the question of when such an apparent memory is veridical, and thus the apparent identity a real one. The hope is that we shall find in this chapter some causal requirement for an apparent memory to be veridical that could serve as the sought for third-person criteria by which a claim of personal endurance based on apparent memory could be challenged or defeated. That this chapter is placed six chapters after the chapter "The Consciousness of Self" does not preclude it containing these defeaters, since James had some reason for placing it where he did in *The Principles of Psychology*, namely, that he might have wanted to contrast the account of immediate memory given in the chapter that immediately precedes it on "The Perception of Time" with its account of secondary memory of what has lapsed from consciousness. Nevertheless, that there is such a wide separation between the chapters should give us some pause.

The plot of the "Memory" chapter is the familiar one in which an introspective analysis is given initially and then followed by an historical or causal one. The phenomenological analysis merely repeats the one given in the "The Consciousness of Self." For me to remember a past event I must have "directly experienced its occurrence. It must have that 'warmth and intimacy' which were so often spoken of in the chapter on the Self, as characterizing all experiences 'appropriated' by the thinker as his own" (612). The historical analysis of the causes of memory, in contrast, is a straightforward neurophysiological one.

Whatever accidental cue may turn this tendency [to recall] into an actuality, the permanent *ground* of the tendency itself lies in the organized neural paths by which the cue calls up the experience . . . the condition which makes it possible at all . . . is . . . the brain-paths which *associate* the experience with the occasion and cue of recall. (616)

Retention "is no mysterious storing up of an 'idea' in an unconscious state." It is "a morphological feature, the presence of these 'paths' . . . in the finest recesses of the brain's tissue" (617).

The big question, which James makes no attempt to answer, is how the phenomenological and causal accounts of memory are connected, this being just a special instance of his general failure to connect together the "inner" and "outer" approaches of *The Principles of Psychology*, which is one of the big unresolved aporias in his philosophy. James now has before him everything that is needed for placing a causal requirement on memory. BUT HE DOESN'T. Were he to opt for making the neurophysiological causes of memory necessary for memory, his memory theory of personal endurance would in effect be treating persons as natural kinds in the manner of contemporary memory theorists, such as Shoemaker and Perry, the reason being that he would be giving natural science the prerogative of determining the identity conditions and thereby the nature of persons. BUT HE DOESN'T!

Based on what James both says and fails to say when the opportunity presents itself, his criteria for memory are, as they are for Locke and Quinton, of a coherentist sort, subject to the only these two defeaters: someone experienced the event in question; and there is no other equally good or better claimant under these coherentist criteria, which is my construal of his remark that the present Thought veridically appropriates a past one "so long as no other owner appropriates it in a more real way" (341). The role of this defeater is to save the transitivity of identity in the case in which coexistent persons are equally good claimants under these criteria for having memories of the same past Thought. The Mayor of Queensbury's apparent memories of the

Thoughts of Socrates are veridical, and thereby he is identical with Socrates, just in case his apparent memory corresponds with the past and properly coheres with a sufficiently rich set of other historically accurate apparent memories he has of Socrates' past, and there does not exist at that time anyone who qualifies at least as well under this memory-coherence account to have memories of Socrates. James, with his life-long passion to investigate paranormal phenomena, is the last person to balk at the possibility of such a case of reincarnation.

My coherentist version of James's analysis allows apparent memories alone to be sufficient for personal identity over time. It does, however, recognize two defeaters based on third-person criteria – that the apparent memories match the past of some real-life person and that there is no equally good or better claimant under the apparent memory-coherence criterion, both of which are determined by public observation. But that the coherence criterion is alone sufficient shows that James does not treat the self as a natural kind, for there is no caused-in-the-right-way requirement that is left for science to determine.

9

The I–Thou Quest for Intimacy
and Religious Mysticism

The preceding chapter presented the first lap of William James's quest for intimacy, in which he adopted the insider's approach to understanding the nature of his own self through an introspective analysis of its conditions of identity over time. The next lap in his journey is his attempt to achieve a deep intimacy, ultimately a union, with the inner life of other persons, both natural and supernatural, even with the world at large, including the animals and fishes that were mentioned in his ad in the Personals.

I. The I–Thou Experience

James begins with a special inward manner in which one person experiences another as a "Thou" rather than an "It," and then extends this to the experience of the world at large, resulting in panpsychism. His analysis of the I–Thou experience bears a striking resemblance to that offered by Martin Buber some thirty years later. In his book *I and Thou*, Buber distinguishes between the I–It and the I–Thou modes of experience. The former is James's pragmatic mode of experiencing worldly individuals in terms of how we can ride herd on them and use them for the achievement of our goals. Toward this end we conceptualize them in a way that enables us effectively to use them. But in an I–Thou experience the relata enter into each other. Through a fusing of their originally separate consciousnesses they enter into what

Buber terms "relational processes and states," in which they partially fuse or mush together.

The best place to begin the exposition of James's version of the I–Thou experience is with his great account of the lovers Jack and Jill. To a disinterested, objective observer they might look completely uninteresting, just another ordinary guy and gal. Each of them, however, because they have a deep empathetic awareness of the other's inner consciousness, experiences the other as something wondrously unique. Through this reciprocal merging of psyches each expands their own consciousness and gains a deeper knowledge of the other than could be gotten from an objective, scientific account. James's description of their reciprocal I–Thou-ing of each other, though he doesn't yet use this language, reserving it for the religious person's experience of nature at large, warrants full quotation.

Every Jack sees in his own particular Jill charms and perfections to the enchantment of which we stolid onlookers are stone-cold. And which has the superior view of the absolute truth, he or we? Which has the more vital insight into the nature of Jill's existence, as a fact? Is he in excess, being in this matter a maniac? or are we in defect, being victims of a pathological anaesthesia as regards Jill's magical importance? Surely the latter; surely to Jack are the profounder truths revealed; surely poor Jill's palpitating little life-throbs *are* among the wonders of creation, *are* worthy of this sympathetic interest; and it is to our shame that the rest of us cannot feel like Jack. For Jack realizes Jill concretely, and we do not. He struggles towards a union with her inner life, divining her feelings, anticipating her desires, understanding her limits as manfully as he can, and yet inadequately, too; for he also is afflicted with some blindness, even here. Whilst we, dead clods that we are, do not even seek after these things, but are contented that that portion of eternal fact named Jill should be for us as if it were not. Jill, who knows her inner life, knows that Jack's way of taking it – so importantly – is the true and serious way; and she responds to the truth in him by taking him truly and seriously, too. May the ancient blindness never wrap its clouds about either of them again! Where would any of *us* be, were there no one willing to know as we really are or ready to repay us for *our* insight by making recognizant return? We ought, all of us, to realize each other in this intense, pathetic, and important way. (*TT* 150–1)

This might be the most profound passage in James, hardly, as James feared, "the mere piece of sentimentalism which it may seem to some readers" (*TT*4). There are features of another person's consciousness that can be known in the full-blooded existential sense only through an act of sympathetic intuition. To know what-it-is-like-to-be-Jill, which is the really important fact about Jill for James, one must enter into her inner life and experience the world the way she does. This is what is meant by James's claim that "Jack realizes Jill concretely." Because he does, he has a "truer" grasp of Jill than does the detached observer: "The truer side is the side that feels the more and not the side that feels the less" (*TT* 133). This has the consequence that you can *really* know someone only if you love them.

James's romanticism comes to the fore in his ecstatic descriptions of the marvelous ponderousness of the inner life that one grasps through the I–Thou experience. He speaks of its "vital secrets," "zest," "tingle," "excitement," "mysterious inwards," and "mysterious sensorial life" (*TT*132, 135, 137, 149), along with its "acutest internality" and "violent thrills of life" (*ERM* 99). To miss the joy of this inner consciousness in another person is to miss all, for it is this that makes her life significant, provided it is coupled with the requisite strength of character to see to it that it gets properly expressed in her overt behavior. James prizes this inner life so highly that he holds that "In every being that is real there is something external to, and sacred from, the grasp of every other" (*WB* 111).

James deduces different normative conclusions from this "sacredness" of an individual's inner life, some benevolent and others less so. Among the benevolent consequences is his principle of democracy requiring us to respect other persons, even nations, and adopt a live-and-let-live hands-off policy. He calls this "respect for the sacredness of individuality...the outward tolerance of whatever is not itself intolerant." It served as the basis of his opposition to what he saw as American imperialism in the Philippines (*TT*4). He even goes so far as to deploy this democratic principle to oppose the "Aristocratic" or snob objection to immortality, namely, that if there were immortality, heaven would become too crowded with a bunch of undesirable riff-raff. He charges this objection with displaying a blindness to other creatures due to a failure to properly I–Thou them.

You take these swarms of alien kinsmen as they are for you: an external picture painted on your retina, representing a crowd oppressive by its vastness and confusion...But all the while, beyond this externality which is your way of realizing them, they realize themselves with the acutest internality, with the most violent thrills of life. 'Tis you who are dead, stone-dead and blind and senseless, in your way of looking on. You open your eyes upon a scene of which you miss the whole significance. Each of these grotesque or even repulsive aliens is animated by an inner joy of living as hot or hotter than that which you feel beating in your private breast. (*ERM* 99)

There were, however, less benevolent uses that James made of the sacredness of the inner life. At times it led him to indulge in overly romantic sentimental glorification of the inner life to the exclusion of the social and economic conditions that are necessary for such inner flourishing. James was blind to the role that the economic conditions under which men live and work play in molding their character. James, like Emerson, glorified the ideal of an absolutely unentangled and unfettered individuality. For James, in sharp distinction from Dewey, man is *in*, but not *of*, the environment. James's socialism was one of the spirit that was divorced from economic realities. His glorification of the stoic person who manages to cultivate and keep alive a rich inner life regardless of how unfortunate her external circumstances is its result. James admitted that "society has...got to pass towards some newer and better equilibrium, and the distribution of wealth has doubtless slowly got to change," but immediately adds that such changes will not make "any genuine vital difference...to the lives of our descendants....The solid meaning of life is always the same eternal thing – the marriage...of some unhabitual ideal, however special, with some fidelity, courage, and endurance; with some man's or woman's pains. – And whatever or wherever life may be, there will always be the chance for that marriage to take place" (*TT* 166). And "no outward changes of condition in life can keep the nightingale of its eternal meaning from singing in all sorts of different men's hearts" (*TT* 167). He naively thinks that the conflicts between rich and poor, workers and owners, result largely from the fact that "each...ignores the fact that happiness and unhappiness and significance are a vital mystery; each pins them absolutely on some ridiculous feature of the external situation; and everybody remains outside of everybody else's sight" (*TT* 166). Romantic sentimentalism does have its price.

James's reactionary use of his romanticism about the inner life also underlies his account of habit.

Habit is thus the enormous fly-wheel of society, its most precious conservative agent. It alone is what keeps us all within bounds of ordinance, and saves the children of fortune from the envious uprisings of the poor. It alone prevents the hardest and most repulsive walks of life from being deserted by those brought up to treat therein . . . It is well for the world that in most of us, by the age of thirty, the character has set like plaster, and will never soften again. (*PP* 125–6)

In a letter to sister Alice in 1865 from the Amazon he expresses the same conservative sentiment. "The boy has acted so far as cabin boy. His blue black hair falls over his eye brows, but he is a real willing young savage & we hope, by keeping him low & weak to make an excellent servant of him for all the time we are on the Amazons" (*CWJ* 4, 114).

The same reactionary spirit runs throughout his *Talks to Teachers on Psychology*. Instead of making his pragmatism the basis of his theory of education, as Dewey did, he leans heavily on associationist psychology and its rote methods of training, because the purpose of education is to inculcate in students the right set of habits so that they will fit into a preexistent society. Education "consists in the organizing of resources in the human being which shall fit him to his social and physical world" (*TT* 27). This conservative emphasis is especially prominent in the "Will" chapter of the book, in which it is said: "Thus are your pupils to be saved: first, by the stock of ideas with which you furnish them; second, by the amount of voluntary attention that they can exert in holding to the right ones, however unpalatable; and third, by the several habits of acting definitely on these latter to which they have been successfully trained" (*TT* 110). Whereas Dewey wanted to use the educational system to radically reconstruct society, his only difference from Plato being that Plato cultivated Dionysius of Syracuse and Dewey the teacher's union, James wanted to use the educational system to propagate a society with which he basically was quite content.

To return to the I–Thou experience, what requires further elucidation is James's all too brief description of how Jack "struggles toward a union with [Jill's] inner life." He is supposed to achieve this through an act of sympathetic or empathetic intuition, but just what is that? James, of course, cannot give a straightforward literal answer. Since the inner life that is the object of this intuition is said to be mysterious and ineffable, so is the act that intuits it. Indirect communication, of the sort practiced by mystics, is needed. Buber followed this path in his account of the I–Thou experience in the preceding quotations, which is why many readers, no doubt, were mystified. Maybe the best that can be done is to write a novel or play or, better yet, a typical Tin Pan Alley song. Jack takes one look at Jill and "Whamo! Zing Went the Strings of His Heart." As he peers deeply into her eyes he feels he has known her all his life. His focus of orientation has radically altered so that now he perceives the whole world through her. He locks in on her inner joy and tingles, which is what bestows meaning and value on her life. Jack's I–Thou-ing of Jill is reciprocated by Jill, thus bringing about a mutual partial merger of their consciousnesses.

James did not stop with I–Thou-ing his fellow humans. He even wanted to I–Thou the beasts and fishes, as well as nature. He writes in a letter of 1873: "Sight of elephants and tigers at Barnum's menagerie whose existence, so individual and peculiar, yet stands there, so intensely and vividly real, as much as one's own, so that one feels again poignantly the unfathomableness of ontology, supposing ontology to be at all" (*LWJ*, 1:224). Not to slight the fishes, in a letter of 1899 to his wife, he says: "four cuttle-fish in the Aquarium. I wish we had one of them for a child – such flexible intensity of life in a form so inaccessible to our sympathy." Maybe James would have had more luck I–Thou-ing a cat, as did Buber.

James wanted to go all the way and I–Thou the entire universe, as nature mystics have traditionally done. Clearly, James is personalizing the universe when he writes, "The Universe is no longer a mere *It* to us, but a *Thou*, if we are religious; and any relation that may be possible from person to person might be possible here" (*WB* 31). Taking a religious stance to the world "changes the dead blank *it* of the world into a living *thou*, with whom the whole man may have dealings" (*WB* 101). "Infra-theistic ways of looking on the world leave it in the third person, a mere *it*... [but] theism turns the *it* into a *thou*" (*WB* 106).

James's I–Thou-ing of nature is within the tradition of cosmic consciousness or nature mysticism. He endorses the following lines in Wordsworth's poem *The Prelude*:

> To every natural form, rock, fruit or flower,
> Even the loose stones that cover the high-way,
> I gave a moral life: I saw them feel,
> Or linked them to some feeling: the great mass
> Lay bedded in a quickening soul, and all
> That I beheld respired with inward meaning. (quoted in *TT* 139)

Wordsworth's "strange inner joy" resulted from his responsiveness "to the secret life of Nature roundabout him" (*TT* 140). It is clear that James accepts the panpsychic upshot of this sort of nature mysticism experience. Herein panpsychism enters in, not as it did in the last chapter as an intellectual device for saving the doctrine of Pure Experience against the challenge posed by unperceived events, but as something experientially vouchsafed by I–Thou experiences of nature.

Another part of James's account of the I–Thou relation that needs further elaboration is just how unified a person becomes with its Thou, be it another person or nature. There are monistic mystics who take the unification to be one of complete numerical identity, but, James, being squarely ensconced within the Western theistic mystical tradition, takes it to be something less than that, a case of what he liked to call, using Blood's marvelous phrase, "ever not quite" (*EP* 189). Throughout his career he was a self-proclaimed "pluralistic mystic." Buber was not as unequivocally committed as was James to a dualistic interpretation of the I–Thou experience, for he reports in *Between Man and Man* that he once had a mystical experience in which it appeared as if he became one and the same as God, but upon subsequent reflection (i.e. he remembered that he is Jewish) came to realize that it stopped short of strict numerical identity, which is reminiscent of Meister Eckhardt's "little point" that God gives men so that they can rotate about it and find their way back to their creaturehood and thereby realize that they are distinct from God, the Creator.

II. Religious Mystical Experiences

It is in *The Varieties of Religious Experience* that James gives his most developed account of mystical experiences. The major thesis of this book, and one which I think is successfully maintained to James's everlasting credit, is that the basis of religion, including its institutional structure, theology, and personal religious feelings and beliefs, is rooted in religious experiences of a mystical sort in which the individual has an apparent direct, nonsensory perception of a "More," an "Unseen" supernatural or purely spiritual reality into which she is to some extent absorbed and from which spiritual energy flows into her. These "perceptions" of the "More" can be viewed as a very heightened and intense form of the I–Thou experience. Through these I–Thou experiences of the More the subject gets "an assurance of safety and a temper of peace, and, in relations to others, a preponderance of loving affection" (*VRE* 383). In the introduction it was shown that this is this sort of assurance that James's "sick" or "morbid" self needed in order to face the evils of the world, especially the sort that occasioned an experience of existential angst. James's mystical self is the other side of the coin of his healthy-minded promethean self, the one that is itching to engage in a Texas death match with evil without any assurance of who will emerge victorious.

Surprisingly, James claims not to have had any mystical experiences himself – "my own constitution shuts me out from their enjoyment almost entirely, and I can speak of them only at second hand" (*VRE* 301). If this is so, is not the underlying thesis of this book, that James had a mystical self who clashed with his promethean pragmatic self, especially in regard to the challenge posed by evil, wrong? How can one be a mystic, or even be so sympathetically inclined to mystical experiences as to accept their cognitivity, as James will be seen to have done, without having mystical experiences? I have two replies.

My first response is that even if it were true that James did not have any mystical experiences, at least of the more developed type, it could be the case that he had a deep sensitivity to and appreciation of them and what they seemingly reveal, just as someone who lacks the musical genius to compose an *Eroica* symphony can aesthetically resonate to it, which seems to be the point of James's claim that "we all have at least the germ of mysticism is us" (*P* 76).

Second, James is not leveling with his audience, no doubt because he didn't want to appear as some kind of a bleeding heart mystic engaged in special pleading. Mystical experiences for him cover a broad spectrum of cases, going from the relatively undeveloped experiences of a heightened sense of reality, an intensification of feeling and insight, such as occurs under the influence of alcohol, drugs, nitrous oxide, art, and even the raptures of nature, to the fully developed monistic experience of an undifferentiated unity in which all distinctions are obliterated. James never had an experience of the latter kind, but he did have more than his share of the less developed ones, given his penchant to experiment on himself with nitrous oxide and mescal. He was no stranger to alcohol either and gives glowing descriptions of its effects, along with impassioned sermons on its evils (*VRE* 307). He

even had a fairly well developed nature mysticism experience in the
Adirondacks in 1898 shortly before he caused irreparable damage to
his heart, from which he eventually died, by overtaxing himself on a
trek. James reports in the 1910 "A Suggestion about Mysticism" four
mystical experiences he had in 1906 in which he apparently became
aware of experiences not his own.

Granted that James had every right to be a sympathetic expositor
and defender of mysticism, we can now consider the specifics of his
account. The first question concerns whether our apprehension of
the supersensible reality is conceptual or via some direct presentation.
Throughout *The Varieties of Religious Experience* James works with a perceptual model of mystical experiences, likening them to ordinary sense
perceptions in that both involve a direct acquaintance with an object,
although only the latter has a sensory content. "Mystical experiences
are . . . direct perceptions . . . absolutely sensational . . . face to face presentation of what seems to exist" (*VRE* 336). A perception is "direct," I
assume, if the existential claims made by the subject on the basis of her
experience are noninferential. Another important and highly controversial assumption James makes in his likening mystical experiences
to sense perceptions is that mystical experiences, like sensory ones,
are intentional in the sense that they have an apparent accusative that
exists independently of the subject when the experience is veridical.
In this respect, they are unlike a feeling of pain, which takes only a cog-
nate or internal accusative, since feeling a pain is nothing but paining
or feeling painfully.

James tries to take a neutral stance on whether mystical experiences support a monistic or pluralistic view of the More or unseen
reality, in spite of his own strong emotional commitment to the pluralistic version. At one place he seems to come down on the side of
the modern-day mystical ecumenicalists, Suzuki, Stace, and Merton,
who contend that there is a common phenomenological *monistic* core
to all unitive mystical experiences that then gets interpreted by the
mystic so as to accord with the underlying culture of her society, as
for example Buber's imposition of a dualistic interpretation on his
apparently monistic mystical experience. "In mystic states we both
become one with the Absolute and we become aware of our oneness.
*This is the everlasting and triumphant mystical tradition, hardly altered by
differences of clime or creed*" (*VRE* 332; my italics). Some of James's major

contentions in *The Varieties of Religious Experience*, however, require a dualistic experience of the sort called "theistic" by R. C. Zaehner in his *Concordant Discord*. For example, James says that prayer is "the very soul and essence of religion," and then describes prayer as involving two-way interaction between two subjects. James's strong Protestant leanings cause him, for the most part, to give a dualistic interpretation of mystical experiences.

One of the features of mystical experiences, as well as conversion experiences in general, that James stresses, so much so that it is used as one of the four defining conditions of a mystical experience, is that the subject is passive in respect to them. While persons can take steps, such as following the mystical way, to help induce the experience, its coming is viewed by religious mystics as the free bestowal of a gift upon them by the grace of God. Through the experience the subject feels that her conscious will is held in abeyance as she finds absorption in a higher unity. "The mystic feels as if his own will were grasped and held by a superior power" (*VRE* 303). In both cases there must be a canceling out of the finite so as to open ourselves to the infinite.

James, no doubt with his sick soul's experiences of existential angst in mind, stresses how such mystically-based resignation cannot "fail to steady the nerves, to cool the fever, and appease the fret, if one be conscious that, no matter what one's difficulties for the moment may appear to be, one's life as a whole is in the keeping of a power whom one can absolutely trust" (*VRE* 230). The mystical experiences that such submission of the conscious will helps to foster are "reconciling and unifying states" that "tell of the supremacy of the ideal, of vastness, of union, of safety, and of rest" (*VRE* 330, 339). In such mystical union there is a "life not correlated with death, a health not liable to illness, a kind of good that will not perish, a good in fact that flies beyond the Goods of nature" (*VRE* 119). This is just what the promethean self's beloved religion of meliorism cannot deliver; it cannot help him make it through the dark nights of his soul, nor face the hideous catatonic epileptic youth described in the *Introduction*. A theme that runs throughout *The Varieties of Religious Experience* is the insufficiency of meliorism, condemned as being "the very consecration of forget-fulness and superficiality" (*VRE* 118–19).

Herein we see the first of several dramatic clashes between James's promethean and mystical selves. First there is the clash between the active self of the promethean moral agent and the passive self of the mystic. The promethean self *is* the active will, which, James says, is "the substantive thing which we *are*" (*PP* 1181). But for the mystic the true self, that "self of all the other selves," no longer is identified with the active aspect of a person, their free conscious will. Quite the contrary, it is that very self, along with its promethean will to believe and the meliorism it favors, that must be surrendered. The true or higher self is that aspect of us, identified by James with the subconscious or transmarginal self, that is able to enter into a complete or partial union with a supersensible reality, which is a "More" of the same kind as it.

The mystical self displaces the active will by "a willingness to close our mouths and be as nothing in the floods and waterspouts of God" (*VRE* 46). By meeting despair with religious resignation, we uncover "resources in us that naturalism, with its literal virtue, never recks of, possibilities that take our breath away, and show a world wider than either physics or Philistine ethics can imagine. Here is a world in which all is well, *in spite* of certain forms of death, indeed *because* of certain forms of death, death of hope, death of strength, death of responsibility, of fear and worry" (*ERM* 128). The death of strength and responsibility is the death of the promethean moral agent, along with its melioristic religion. The overcoming of our active self does not assure that we will achieve some kind of experiential union with God, but it is a necessary first-step along the way to such mystical illumination.

The clashes between James's promethean and mystical selves cannot be explained away as a diachronic one, since he was a highly divided self throughout his life. The clashes, rather, are synchronic. At every moment in his career he was of several minds about everything, and that is why his philosophical writings are like a philosophical wheel of fortune. Whatever doctrine it stopped on and temporarily illuminated reaped a rich payoff, since every one of his many philosophies was espoused with incredible brilliance and passion. Whether James would defend pragmatism or mysticism on any given day depended on his mood, whether he was in a healthy- or sick-minded one.

James can neutralize the clash between his morally strenuous promethean self and the passivity and quietism of his mystical self by playing Poo-bah and suitably "*qua*"-clausing the claims made by these selves, thereby allowing them to take turns in being his dominant interest; for example, he could be a promethean moral agent on the weekdays and a mystic on the weekends. This is the promethean solution, but it has the apparently unattractive upshot of making him into a temporalized schizophrenic.

Another significant clash between James's pragmatic and mystical selves is between their respective reality claims. In the first place, there is an apparent clash in the content of these claims, the promethean pragmatist asserting the existence of a multiplicity of distinct objects changing in space and time and the acosmic mystic denying the reality of this multiplicity. This contentful clash can be neutralized by Poo-bah-izing the respective reality claims – *qua* mystic I say this but *qua* moral agent I say that. A far more serious clash concerns *how* the respective reality claims are made rather than *what* they claim. In the first place, mystical claims, unlike those made by the promethean pragmatist, are not advanced in the spirit of fallibilism, as hypotheses to be tested by future experiences and thus subject to revision or withdrawal. They are, instead, claims to absolute certainty, without which there would not accrue the feeling of peace and safety so needed by James's morbid self. Secondly, and most importantly, they are advanced as noetic claims that are revelatory of an ultimate or absolute reality – the really real in comparison with which everything is a mere illusion or emanation of some sort. They are nonrelativized reality claims and therefore are incompatible with prometheanism's doctrine of ontological relativism, which played such a key role in enabling us to have it all by requiring that all reality claims be relativized to the interests of a person at a time. The mystic definitely is not saying that, *qua* the mystical point of view, reality is some kind of a unity or oneness, but rather that it is so *simpliciter*. To restrict mystical reality-claims to the mystical perspective would, in effect, be awarding an ontological status to the mystic's reality that is on all fours with Ivanhoe and Pegasus, certainly a booby prize.

Mysticism also challenges James's pragmatic theory of meaning and truth. The pragmatic theory of meaning, as contrasted with the theory of pragmatic meaning, has the meaning of "*X*" consist in a set of conditionalized predictions of what experiences we shall have upon performing certain operations, with a belief in the reality of *X* becoming warrantedly assertible when these predictions are verified. But the mystic's conception of the Absolute, the undifferentiated unity, the eternal one, or God is not based on how we can ride herd on it, for there is nothing that we do to or with this mystical reality, or ways in which it is expected to behave if we perform certain operations. It doesn't dissolve in aqua regia. It simply *is*, and is just what it *appears* to be in the immediate experience of the mystic. Herein the content of the proposition that this reality exists is not reducible to any set of pragmatic conditionalized predictions. The star performer finally gets into the act, unlike the case of the pragmatically favored melioristic religion, which reduced "God exists" to the conditionalized prediction that good will win out over evil in the long run, if we collectively exert our best moral effort. The reason James chose meliorism as his example of a religion in the final lecture of *Pragmatism* is that it can be shown to employ the same pragmatic theory of meaning and truth as does science, which fits his program of reconciliation through methodological univocalism.

In order to account for the meaning of mystical reality claims James will have to resort to content empiricism, which was found in Chapter 6 to be his other species of empiricism to that of pragmatism. Since the meaningful content of the mystic's reality claim is based on the manner in which she is phenomenologically appeared to in an of-God type experience, the truth of the claim will depend on whether her experience is objective or cognitive. The spiritual and moral benefits that the experience occasions, as will be seen, become relevant, but only as a means of indirect verification, there now being, as there wasn't for meliorism, a distinction between direct and indirect verification, with an assertion's meaning being identified primarily with the former, that being the apparent object, the intentional accusative, of the mystical experience. James seems to recognize this when he says that "the word 'truth' is here taken to mean something additional to bare value for life" (*VRE* 401). Accordingly, James makes the issue of the cognitivity or objectivity of mystical experience a central issue in *The Varieties of Religious Experience*. Concerning them, he asks about their "metaphysical significance" (308), "cognitivity" (324), "authoritativeness" (335), "objective truth" (304), "value for knowledge" (327), and "truth" (329), and whether they "furnish any *warrant for the truth* of the... supernaturality and pantheism which they favor" (335) or are "to be taken as *evidence*... for the actual existence of a higher world with which our world is in relation" (384). James is quite explicit that the answer to the "objectivity" question is independent of the biological and psychological benefits that accrue from mystical experiences.

James concludes that there is a generic content of the many different type of mystical experiences that "is literally and objectively true" (*VRE* 405). He gives two arguments to support this conclusion – one based on an analogy with sense experience and the other on an inference to the best explanation. The former is the more important one and will be considered first.

This analogical argument, which enjoys widespread popularity today, appears only in germ in the text. Its first premise claims that mystical and sense experiences are analogous in cognitively relevant respects. The second premise holds that sense experiences are cognitive, from which it is inferred by the rules of analogical reasoning that mystical experiences also are cognitive. A type of experience, E, counts as cognitive if the occurrence of an E-type experience counts as evidence for the existence of its apparent accusative in virtue of some a priori presumptive inference rule. For sense experience the rule is that if it perceptually appears to be the case that X exists, then probably it is the case that X exists, unless there are defeating conditions. These defeating conditions consist in tests and checks for the veridicality of the experience that get flunked on this occasion. Prominent among these tests are agreement among relevant observers, lawlike coherence between the experience's content and the content of earlier and later experiences, and being caused in the right way. The presumptive inference rule is said to be a priori, because it cannot be justified by appeal to sense experience without vicious circularity.

If mystical experiences are to be subject to an analogous a priori presumptive inference rule, they must be analogous to sense experiences in having defeating conditions – checks and tests that can get flunked. Mystical traditions within the great religions employ a fairly elaborate network of tests for veridicality of mystical experiences, usually including that the subject, as well as her community, display favorable moral and/or spiritual development as a result of the experience, that what her experience reveals accords with her religion's holy scriptures and the mystical experiences of past saints and notables, to name some of the more important tests of most of the great religious mystical traditions.

With a little imagination we can find most, but not all, of the elements of this analogical argument in *The Varieties of Religious Experience*. In the first place, James makes a prominent use of a perceptual model of mystical experience, which is the analogical premise of the contemporary argument for cognitivity. He comes right out and says:

> Our own more 'rational' beliefs are based on evidence exactly similar in nature to that which mystics quote for theirs. Our senses, namely, have assured us of certain states of fact; but mystical experiences are as direct perceptions of fact for those who have them as any sensations ever were for us. The records show that even though the five senses be in abeyance in them, they are absolutely sensational in their epistemological quality. (*VRE* 336)

James goes on to fill out the analogy by showing that there are mystical analogues for some of the tests for the veridicality of sense experience. What is apparently revealed by mystical experiences "must be sifted and tested, and run the gauntlet of confrontation with the total context of experience just like what comes from the outer world of sense" (*VRE* 338). Mystical experiences are also likened to "windows through which the mind looks out upon a more extensive and inclusive world" than is revealed by our senses, and just as we have checks and tests for mediating between rival sensory-based claims there are analogous ones for mediating between rival mystically based claims. Because of these background defeating conditions, it will be possible for mysticism to have "its valid experiences and its counterfeit ones, just as our world has them ... We should have to use its experiences by selecting and subordinating and substituting just as is our custom in this ordinary naturalistic world; we should be liable to error just as we are now" (*VRE* 339). Mystical experiences "establish a presumption" in favor of the thing being as it appears to be in them (*VRE* 336), which sounds very much like the presumptive inference rule.

There is one very important respect in which James differs from contemporary analogical arguers that renders his argument less attractive than theirs, namely he completely eschews any attempt to place the relevant background tests, which are the overriders or defeaters, within the shared practices of on-going religious community. In general, James's failure to see the importance of religious institutions, with their shared beliefs and communal practices, is a significant limitation in the account that is given of religious experience in *The Varieties of*

Religious Experience. This is yet another example of James's overglorifi-
cation of the isolated individual. His mystic is a lone gun mystic, cut off
from any doxastic practice of an ongoing religious community. Where
his mystic gets her tests from and how they are enforced remains a
mystery. Just as James was found in Chapter 6 to be committed to a
private language in which the speaker follows rules that only she can
determine are being followed correctly, James's mystic, in virtue of being isolated from a community of fellow believers and practitioners,
must follow her own private tests.

Contemporary analogical arguers are intent on justifying the various ongoing mystical doxastic practices as being reliable for the most
part. James, on the other hand, works only on the *retail* level, his concern being exclusively with the justification for an individual mystic
taking one of her experiences to be veridical. He fails to see that this
justification cannot be cut off from the *wholesale* justification of the
shared social practice of basing objective existential claims on mystical experiences. James fails to realize that by eschewing the wholesale
level, he significantly weakens the effectiveness of his will-to-believe
justification for the lone mystic believing that one of her experiences
is veridical. This is a very important application of the will to believe,
because what she believes in this matter could have the most important consequences for her future moral and spiritual development,
that is, for her quest for sanctification. Certainly, she will be aided
in her attempt to get herself to believe on will-to-believe grounds
that her mystical experience is veridical if she first believes that the
general doxastic practice of basing existential claims on mystical experiences is a reliable one that yields true existential beliefs for the
most part. This belief also must be based on will-to-believe grounds,
since the mystical doxastic practice, like the sensory one, does not
admit of any noncircular external justification. James's analogical argument, along with his will-to-believe justification for believing in the
veridicality of an individual mystical experience, should welcome supplementation by bringing in the doxastic practice in which his tests are
embedded.

With this in mind, a survey can now be made of the different tests
he recognized as relevant to determining the veridicality of a mystical
experience. Like the contemporary analogical arguers, James recognizes a mystical analogue to the sensory agreement and prediction

tests, though he adds a third one – the immediate luminosity test. Here, in brief, is how they work.

James makes a very broad application of the agreement test so that it concerns not only whether there is agreement among the mystics themselves but whether their reports agree with ordinary sensory-based ones. In regard to the former, he first says that there is a consensus among mystics and that "it would be odd . . . if such a unanimous type of experience should prove to be altogether wrong" (*VRE* 336). However, he immediately counters that "the appeal to numbers has no logical force" and that there is considerable disagreement among the monistic and pluralistic mystics, not to mention their collective disagreement with demoniacal mysticism. Not only doesn't the agreement test support the objectivity of mystical experience when only mystical experiences are considered, it counts against this when the sensory-based experiences are brought in. Mystical experiences "do not come to everyone; and the rest of life makes either no connexion with them, or tends to contradict them more than it confirms them" (*VRE* 22). And, against the claims of monistic mystics, James says that the "eaches" of the pluralists "are at any rate real enough to have made themselves at least appear to everyone, whereas the absolute has as yet appeared immediately to only a few mystics, and indeed to them very ambiguously" (*PU* 62).

James, I believe, tries to soften this clash between mysticism and sense experience by giving a very understated conclusion concerning what mystical experiences ultimately proclaim.

As a rule, mystical states merely add a supersensuous meaning to the ordinary outward data of consciousness. They are excitements like the emotions of love or ambition, flights to our spirit by means of which facts already objectively before us fall into a new life. They do not contradict these facts as such, or deny anything that our senses have immediately seized. (*VRE* 338)

The same protective strategy seems operative in James's bizarre initial set of four defining characteristics of a mystical experience – being ineffable, noetic, transitory, and passive (*VRE* 302–3) – in which he fails to include being a unitive experience, which is the most important and distinctive feature, but one that seems to clash with the deliverances of ordinary sense experience, which presents us with a multiplicity of distinct objects in space and time. This aptly could be called the "comic book" theory of mystical experiences, since they are supposed to function as do the field of force lines that comic books place around an object that is perceived or thought in a specifically intense manner. This, at best, fits the experiences at the undeveloped end of the mystical spectrum, such as drunkenness, but not those unitive experiences at the developed end, which not only report new facts, James's higher dimensions of reality, but also sometimes seem to contradict our sensory-based beliefs concerning the reality of space, time, and multiplicity. James does not want us to have to serve on a jury and decide whether to believe the testimony of the mystics or that of the vast majority of mankind, but he does not map out any effective strategy for preventing the matter from going to trial. He wants to find some common denominator of all mystical experiences that is sufficiently watered down so as not to conflict with the deliverances of sense experience, but this fails to address the issue of whether the more developed mystical experiences are veridical.

Whereas the agreement test did not offer any support to the objectivity claim of mystics, quite to the contrary according to James, the prediction test does. Because of the passive and transitory nature of mystical experiences, we are not able to predict their occurrence, and, to this extent, the prediction test counts against their objectivity. But this is more than offset by the fact that so many mystics grow morally and/or spiritually as a result of their experience. In attacking reductivistic causal explanations of mystical experiences he says that we must "inquire into their fruits for life," rather than their causes (*VRE* 327). This is an on-going theme in *The Varieties of Religious Experience*, especially in Lectures I, XIV, and XV.

Unfortunately, James does not clearly distinguish between these good consequences being epistemologically confirmatory of the *proposition* believed and their pragmatically justifying in the will-to-believe manner our *believing* it. The following is a typical example of this unclarity. "Believing that a higher power will take care of us in certain ways better than we can take care of ourselves, if we only genuinely throw ourselves upon it and consent to use it, it finds the belief, not only not impugned, but corroborated by its observation [of good consequences]" (*VRE* 103). Belief is being used here in a way that is ambiguous between the psychological state or act of believing and the what-is-believed, the proposition. This opens James to the standard

objection that he ran together the psychological benefits of believing
a proposition with the confirmation of the proposition believed. It
is here that James is far outstripped by his contemporary analogical
arguers, such as Alston, who make clear in his use of the prediction
test that the good consequence for the mystic and her community
are confirmatory of the objectivity of the mystical experience in virtue
of a conceptual or categoreal link between these consequences and
the nature of the apparent object of the experience. Because God is
essentially good, it is probable that those who have had an objective
experience of him will benefit morally and spiritually. By the same reasoning, one should count the deleterious consequence of a mystical
experience as evidence for it having been a veridical perception of a
malevolent being like the devil.

Immediate luminosity, the subject's intense feeling of delight and
reality, figures prominently in James's network of confirmatory tests,
sometimes being accorded pride of place over good consequences
(*VRE* 23) and at others taking second place to them (*VRE* 21–2). An
interesting question is why James, unlike his contemporary analogical arguers, used this test. The answer might be that *The Principles of
Psychology*'s interest-relative account of existence, although not explicitly endorsed in *The Varieties of Religious Experience*, still weighs heavily
in James's thinking. This might account for James's seeming relativization of *being evidence for* to persons in his first two conclusions regarding
what mystical experiences establish.

(1) Mystical states, when well developed, usually are, and have
    the right to be, absolutely authoritative over the individuals to
    whom they come.

(2) No authority emanates from them which should make it a duty
    for those who stand outside of them to accept their revelations
    uncritically. (*VRE* 335)

James's second argument for the cognitivity of mystical experience,
based on an inference to the best explanation, is only hinted at in *The
Varieties of Religious Experience* on pages 303, 304, and 381, being more
fully developed in other works. Mystical states, like many other psychic
or paranormal phenomena, among which James recognized telepathy
and alternative or secondary personality, such as prophetic speech,
automatic writing, and hypnotic and mediumistic trances, all admit

of explanation if we follow Frederic Myers and Fechner and posit "a continuum of cosmic consciousness, against which individuality builds accidental fences, and into which our several minds plunge as into a mother-sea or reservoir.... Not only psychic research, but metaphysical philosophy and speculative biology are led in their own ways to look with favor on some such 'panpsychic' view of the universe as this" (*EPR* 374). In certain exceptional states the ordinary threshold of consciousness is lowered so that we become aware of what is going on in this surrounding mother-sea-of-consciousness, the super mind or minds, since there might be more than one mother-sea. He employed this mother-sea hypothesis to explain his 1906 mystical experience in which he seemingly became aware of mental states not his own – free-floating states within this surrounding consciousness. He distinguished his experiences from the full-blown mystical states he featured in *The Varieties of Religious Experience* by pointing out that "in my case certain special directions only, in the field of reality, seemed to get suddenly uncovered, whereas in classical mystical experiences it appears rather as if the whole of reality were uncovered at once" (*EP* 160).

There are some outstanding difficulties with this inference to the best explanation for the objectivity of mystical experiences. The subconscious is far too motley a crew of oddball states and actions to warrant an inference to the objectivity of any given subconscious state or experience. Some of them are plainly noncognitive, such as hysteria, which James also assigned to the subconscious, while others, such as hypnotism and a secondary self's perceptions, are explicable in terms of ordinary sensory ways of gaining, though not processing, information, there being no need to postulate a surrounding mother-sea-of-consciousness containing free-floating bits of consciousness.

James favors the pluralistic interpretation of the mother-sea-of-consciousness hypothesis, so that there is not a single all-encompassing surrounding sea of consciousness but more than one, with God merely being the most outstanding of them in terms of power, knowledge, and goodness, but still only finite. In a mystical experience, according to the surrounding mother-seas hypothesis, the subject becomes unified with one of these super consciousnesses in a way that falls short of becoming literally numerically one and the same with it but rather in the weaker sense of becoming cognizant that it is a *part* of this enveloping consciousness. This inclusion of one consciousness's self within another raises several problems.

To begin with, the idea of an individual being a proper part of another individual of the same kind is troublesome. Aristotle argued, successfully in my opinion, that no *substance*, in his special sense, could be a proper part of another substance of the same *natural kind*: A human organism, for example, cannot be a proper part of another human organism. Aristotle would not have felt challenged by a doggy door, which is a proper part of another functioning door, because a door is an *artifact* and therefore not a *substance* in his sense.

But what about a self or mind? Is it a substance and thereby subject to Aristotle's stricture? In the last chapter, James was expounded as holding that the self is not a natural kind, because he did not leave it up to science to determine its identity conditions and therefore its nature. Maybe it is possible, after all, for a Jamesian self, understood as a succession of mental states in which the later members remember the earlier ones, to be a proper part of another self. James's rhetorical question, "Why can't I have another being own and use me, just as I am, for its purposes without knowing any of these purposes myself," seems to favor an affirmative answer (*MEN* 129). This goes along with his remark that "If we assume a wider thinker, it is evident that his purposes envelop mine. I am really lecturing *for* him" (*ERE* 89).

I believe that this inclusion doctrine is conceptually absurd for the following reason. A self, in virtue of being morally responsible for certain of her actions, must be an autonomous unit, it being the whole person, and only that person, that is held responsible for them. The reason for the "only that person" is that, according to James's libertarianism, a morally responsible action is done freely, and it is done freely only if the agent is the sole cause of it, which rules out there being another person who is responsible for the action. But if one person were a proper part of another person, both persons would be morally responsible for an intentional action performed by the former one, which is absurd.

Before concluding this chapter on James's religious mysticism, it should be pointed out that the surrounding mother-sea-of-consciousness, be it a single sea or a plurality of seas, as the monistic and pluralistic mystic respectively would have it, with which the mystic becomes wholly or partially absorbed is a supernatural entity through and through, as James repeatedly says. It is an unseen order said to be "behind the veil" (*ERM* 76, 86, 87) to those of us "here below" (*ERM* 82, 87). It is a "transcendental world" (*ERM* 93, 96) that makes "influx" into a person's ordinary consciousness when the dam or threshold of receptivity is lowered (*ERM* 93). Because the surrounding mothersea(s)-of-consciousness is said to be "supernatural," the doctrine of Pure Experience cannot be applied to it. The reason is that a physical sequence of events is a lawlike one, but a supernatural being does not behave in a lawlike manner, this being the reason for it not being amenable to scientific explanation. Thus, there is no possible sequence of events in which it would count as physical. In anticipation of this counter-example to Pure Experience, I restricted the doctrine at the very beginning to sensible individuals, thus ruling out the invisible individuals behind the veil.

The clash between James' active promethean self and his passive mystical self, along with the clash between the ontological relativism favored by his promethean self and the nonrelativized reality claims made by his mystical self, are the two deepest aporias that arise from James's quest to have it all. Readers will have to wait until Chapter 11 for an attempt to resolve these aporias.

10

The Humpty Dumpty Intuition and Backyard Mysticism

The previous two chapters have presented the first two legs of James's journey to find a cozy personal world with which he could establish an intimate communion because it would answer back to his deepest inner feelings and emotions. It began with his attempt to be intimate with himself through an introspective analysis of what made him one and the same self from one time to another. Next, he attempted to be intimate with others, be it man, beast, nature, or God, through a special type of I–Thou experience that partially unified him with their inner conscious life. To achieve this sort of mystical intimacy James found it necessary to conquer his promethean self.

This chapter will explore the third and final leg in his journey in which he cultivates a backyard mysticism based on conceptless intuition of the temporal flux. Whereas his religious mysticism was based on an effort to I–Thou other selves, most importantly supernatural ones, backyard mysticism is directed at the most mundane sort of individuals – the contents of our ordinary sense experience of the temporal flux – but it sees them in a new, mystical manner as mushing together in just the way that successive conscious states of a person do, which served as the basis for self-identity over time. Thus, what we find upon introspecting our own consciousness is the way that things, in general, are in the world. This results not just in panpsychism but spiritualism. These backyard individuals that are enmeshed in the perceptual flux

All references in this chapter are to *The Principles of Psychology*, unless otherwise noted.

are not merely imbued with but turn out to be nothing but conscious-ness, which results in about as cozy a world as one could wish for. Like the bluebird of happiness, mystical reality has been in our own backyard all along, but we have been blinded to it by our inveterate pragmatic bent of thought. As was the case with religious mysticism, we are required to overcome our active promethean self and learn to experience passively without employing concepts. James's message is that salvation can be found even in our own backyard.

James arrived at this backyard mysticism through his accounts of our perception of time. There is, to put it euphemistically, a "tension" between James's accounts of our perception of time in the chapters "The Perception of Time" and "The Stream of Thought" in his 1890 *The Principles of Psychology*. The former presents the *specious present* ac-count – that each pulse of perceptual experience has a content that comprises a succession of discrete events. The latter, on the other hand, liquefies, cotton-candifies these successive events so that they melt and fuse together, thereby denying their discreteness. It should raise one's suspicions that each of these accounts is supported by appeal to what is introspectively or phenomenologically vouchsafed. In each case the phenomenology is faked and gives a blatantly distorted account of our way of experiencing time. James, like so many phenomenologists, is a Jack Horner who is able to pull out of his phenomenological pie whatever is philosophically required.

The reason why these conflicting accounts pull out different philo-sophical plums is that they address a different datum whose presumed existence must be shown to be possible. The specious present account is an attempt to answer the *psychological* question of how it is possible for us to have, as we certainly seem to, the conceptions of temporal prece-dence and the past, the answer being that temporally successive *discrete* events are the content of a single act of perception, thereby satisfying the concept empiricist's demand to give a concept's experiential birth certificate. The stream-of-thought account, on the other hand, begins with the undoubted reality of change and addresses the *metaphysical* question of how change is possible, the answer being that change must be a processual kind of cotton-candyish glop in which temporal neigh-bors do not possess a distinct identity but instead fuse and melt to-gether. By faking their phenomenological credentials, both analyses cover over the fact that they really are transcendental deductions of the either-this-or-nothing variety. Since the specious present doctrine is the one that eventually gets spurned, we will begin with it and then go on to consider why it had to be rejected on the basis of the fundamental philosophical intuitions that motivate the stream-of-thought account.

I. The Specious Present

The motivation behind this account is to supply the required experiential credentials for our concepts of temporal succession and the past. James is a concept empiricist because he holds that "every one of our conceptions is of something which our attention originally tore out of the continuum of felt experience, and provisionally isolated so as to make of it an individual topic of discourse" (439). When James asks, "What is the original of our experience of pastness, from whence we get the meaning of the term?" he is making a specific application of this generalization (570).

To have a relational concept it is required that the relata "be known in a single pulse of consciousness for which they form one complex 'object' . . . so that properly speaking there is before the mind at no time a plurality of *ideas*, properly so called" (383). Therefore, "if we do not feel both past and present in one field of feeling, we feel them not at all" (128). As applied to the case of the relation of temporal succession, this has the consequence that "A succession of feelings, in and of itself, is not a feeling of succession" (591). This parallels a similar claim about our apprehension of spatial relations: "*If a number of sensible extents are to be perceived alongside of each other and in definite order they must appear as parts in a vaster sensible extent which can enter the mind simply and all at once*" (788).

The upshot of this is that to have the concept of temporal succession it is necessary that the conceiver have had a perception of a succession in which both the relata were presented together and moreover as successive. Fortunately, every perception represents such a complex of successive objects.

Part of the complexity is the echo of the objects just past, and, in a less degree, perhaps, the foretaste of those just to arrive. Objects fade out of consciousness slowly. If the present thought is of A B C D E F G, the next one will be of B C D E F G H, and the one after that of C D E F G H I – the lingerings of the past dropping successively away, and the incomings of the future making up the loss. These lingerings of old objects, these incomings of new, are the germs of memory and expectation, the retrospective and the prospective sense of time. (571)

He calls the temporal duration presented in each pulse of perceptual experience "the specious present," and contrasts it with the "strict present," which is the mathematically punctal one of the physicists (573). He even adds, inconsistently as we shall see, that "Reflection leads us to the conclusion that it [the strict present] *must* exist."

It would appear that the successive objects *A B C*. . . within a single specious present are discrete in the sense of being distinct from each other. Not only does this seem to be supported by his distinguishing between the successive objects *A B C*. . . and tracking them across successive specious presents, it plainly is maintained by authors whom James quotes with approval, such as Wundt, who claims that when similar pendulum strokes follow each other at regular intervals in a consciousness otherwise void, "When the first one is over, an image of it remains in the fancy until the second succeeds" (573). Furthermore, James's concept empiricism seems to require that the successive objects be discrete, for if they were not, we could not derive our idea of temporal succession from an experience of them, for, in general, we can perceive a relational complex as a relational complex only if we perceive the relata in it as distinct from each other.

James supports his doctrine of the specious present by a triumvirate of (i) introspection, (ii) neurophysiology, and (iii) experimental data. Each will be explored and found to be misinvoked.

(i) Exactly what is supposed to be revealed by an introspective analysis of a perception of a specious present? Are the successive *A B C* objects of a sensory nature – colors, sounds, and the like? And what about the relation of succession between them, is it sensory or not? The second, but not the first, question receives a clear answer. James is quite explicit that in general we do not have a sensory image or idea of any relation. So far he agrees with Hume but goes on to contend, in opposition to Hume's restriction of possible objects of introspection to sensory ideas, that we nevertheless are conscious of them (239ff.). We are said to have a "feeling" or "thought" of them, which are James's most generic terms for consciousness, of which the being aware of a sensory image is only one species (186). These feelings of relation are said to be a fringe, halo, wraith, or overtone that attaches to the relata in a relation (260).

The first question concerns whether the *A B C* relata in a relation of succession within a specious present are sensorial images. A straightforward reading of the text supports an affirmative answer and thus a sensory model of the specious present. The major support for the sensory model interpretation comes from the actual language James uses to describe our perception of a specious present. The title of the section in which he presents the doctrine of the specious present is "The Sensible Present Has Duration" (573). The claim that "*the original paragon and prototype of all conceived times is the specious present, the short duration of which we are immediately and incessantly sensible*" continues this use of sensory terms (594). Further support is found in his description of strictly past and future objects within the specious present as respectively an "echo" and a "foretaste," since echoes and tastes are sensory (571).

The sensory model is based on Jack Horner fake phenomenology. James's claim that "All the notes of a bar of a song seem to the listener to be contained in the present" is the description of someone who hears a chord, the notes of which vary in loudness according to most sensory models of the specious present, since earlier phases within a single specious present are supposed to have less vivacity or liveliness than later ones. Mozart is quoted in behalf of our perceptual present being able to encompass a succession of elements of quite some span. In regard to a symphony he composed, he wrote that he "can see the whole of it at a single glance in my mind, as if it were a beautiful painting or a handsome human being; which way I do not hear it in my imagination at all as a succession – the way it must come later – but all at once, as it were" (247). (Notice the "as it were" qualification.) If Mozart had a thirty-minute *auditory* specious present that contained the succession of sounds within an entire symphony, he must have had some terrible headaches. Furthermore, when I see your arm rise I am seeing all of the earlier positions of it when I see it at its topmost position and thereby see you as a Hindu god!

(ii) James adopts the working hypothesis of physiological psychology that there is "No psychosis without neurosis" in *The Principles of Psychology* (133). It is assumed that our sensations are caused by these neuroses. Because "The phenomena of 'summation of stimuli' in the nervous system prove that each stimulus leaves some latent activity behind it which only gradually passes away" it follows that "*there is at every moment a cumulation of brain-processes overlapping each other, of which the fainter ones are dying phases of processes which but shortly previous were active in maximal degree*" (597–8). Because these overlapping brain-processes causally condition sensations, it follows that since "the changes of neurosis are never absolutely discontinuous, so must the successive psychoses shade gradually into each other" (236). "If recently the brain tract *a* was vividly excited, and then *b*, and now vividly *c*, the total present consciousness is not produced simply by *c*'s excitement, but also by the dying vibrations of *a* and *b* as well" (235). These considerations have the consequence that a sensation has a specious present content: "All stimuli whose first nerve-vibrations have not yet ceased seem to be conditions of our getting this feeling of the specious present" (609).

Because we know that our sensations, for the most part, do not have a sensory specious present, either James's neurophysiological claims are contrary to fact or his assumption that there is a correlation between the waning and waxing of neural processes and sensory states of consciousness is unwarranted, being an instance of his own "psychologist fallacy," in which the psychologist confuses "*his own standpoint with that of the mental fact* about which he is making his report" (195). Herein it takes the form of an unwarranted assumption that the features of the publicly observable cause of a conscious state must be something of which the conscious state is aware or which has a correlate in its content.

(iii) The experimental data that James appeals to in support of his sensory model of the specious present are of no more avail than were his appeals to introspection and neurophysiology. Wundt and his student Dietze attempted "to determine experimentally the *maximal extent of our immediate distinct consciousness for successive impressions*" (577). Toward this end, they would play for a subject a sequence of rhythmically arranged sounds to determine how much of it could "be remembered as a whole, and identified without error when repeated." They found that "the *maximum filled duration* of which we can be both distinctly and immediately aware" is about twelve seconds (577).

James immediately goes on to claim that "These figures may be roughly taken to stand for the most important part of what, with Mr. Clay, we called, a few pages back, the specious present" (578). It should be obvious to the reader that the experimental data radically underdetermine the theoretical construal James places on them. All the data show is the maximum duration of strokes that, as James himself says, can "be remembered as a whole, and identified without error when repeated." This in no way establishes that when the subject is hearing the final stroke of this duration, the earlier strokes that he is immediately conscious of also are *auditorily* apprehended. A skilled drummer, like Max Roach, very likely could identify or play back without error a very intricate rhythmic pattern lasting many minutes, while the layman might be good for only several seconds worth. But this hardly shows that Max is having a Mozartian type headache when he hears the final sound in virtue of his literally hearing at that time all of the earlier sounds.

Fortunately, James abandoned the doctrine of the specious present after 1892. That he never subsequently invoked the doctrine in any of his published writings gives some but hardly conclusive evidence for this. The strongest evidence is based on the fact that his thinking became dominated by the opposing stream-of-thought view of time as a nondiscrete, promiscuous succession in which the relata get into each other because they merge, fuse, or melt together. And you can't have a discrete promiscuous affair.

II. The Stream of Thought

Consciousness is metaphorically likened to a flowing river, because neither contains distinct, isolatable parts. The specious present's discrete successive events have now become a flowing sludge. When we successively hear the words of a sentence, "They melt into each other like dissolving views," thereby showing that in the thought no "parts can be found corresponding to the object's parts. Time-parts are not such parts" (269). Herein James is making a contrast between the discrete successiveness of the objects perceived and the nondiscrete mushing together within the content of the perceptual experience.

The things are discrete and discontinuous; they do pass before us in a train or chain, making often explosive appearance and rending each other in twain.

But their comings and goings and contrasts no more break the flow of the thought that thinks them than they break the time and the space in which they lie. (233)

This stream-of-thought account is extensively elaborated on in his final two books, but with one important difference: a priori arguments are presented for the impossibility of a discrete succession, in fact for the impossibility of a discrete immediate relation of any kind. In arguing for this he winds up with an ineffable spiritualism. Let us carefully dog his steps along the way to this startling conclusion.

According to the later account, what our conceptualizing intellect falsely cuts asunder into discretely successive events really "compenetrate" and "telescope" through a sort of "endosmosis" or "conflux" (*PU* 114). "In the real concrete sensible flux of life experiences compenetrate each other so that it is not easy to know just what is excluded and what not" (113). "Boundaries are things that intervene; but nothing intervenes save parts of the perceptual flux itself, and these are overflowed by what they separate, so that whatever we distinguish and isolate conceptually is found perceptually to telescope and compenetrate and diffuse into its neighbors" (*SPP* 32). The word he uses to characterize the manner in which things within the temporal flux get inside each other, "durcheinander," has sexual connotations in German.

It is further claimed that in the mushing relation each relatum become its own other in Hegel's sense.

> every individual morsel of the sensational stream takes up the adjacent morsels by coalescing with them. . . . that no part absolutely excludes another, but that they compenetrate and are cohesive; that if you tear out one, its roots bring out more with them; that whatever is real is telescoped and diffused into other reals; that, in short, every minutest thing is already its hegelian 'own other,' in the fullest sense of the term. (*PU* 121; see also 127)

James realizes that his mushing-together relation defies the ordinary logic of identity, since it gives us an identity that is not really an identity because it is nontransitive. "For conceptual logic, the same is nothing but the same, and all sames with a third thing are the same with each other. Not so in concrete experience" (*PU* 114–15). James rightfully says that his counterlogical descriptions of our experience of change "will sound queer and dark" (*PU* 97). But an "empirical look into the

constitution of [reality shows] . . . that some of them are their own others, and indeed are so in the self-same sense in which the absolute
is maintained to be so by Hegel." Spatial neighbors also behave like
Play-Doh. "What is true here of successive states must also be true of
simultaneous characters. They also overlap each other with their being" (*PU* 130; see also *MEN* 123). James seems to be saying, if I may
paraphrase the punch line to the old shaggy dog joke, that these immediate neighbors are identical but not that identical. This is another
form taken by James's pluralistic mysticism.

James should not be interpreted as claiming that we *ordinarily* experience change in the mushing-together manner, for I no more see the
immediately adjoined temporal phases of a moving arm's trajectory as
mushing together than I see it in the Hindu godlike manner. And I do
not see spatial neighbors engaging in "endosmosis" except in the rare
cases in which they actually do engage in endosmosis or are abutting
ice cream cones in a hot sun. Thus when James claims that we see them
as having "a sort of later suffusion from one thing into another, like
a gas, or warmth, or light... [and that] what fills one place radiates
and suffuses into the other by lateral movement, 'endosmosis,'" he is
not giving a phenomenological description of our *ordinary* perceptual
experiences but of the experiences we would have if we learned how
to perceive without making use of concepts (*MEN* 91–2).

James is armed with a priori arguments to show that it is impossible that reality is the way in which we *ordinarily* perceive it to be.
And since promiscuous relations are the only alternative that we can
conceive of to discrete relations, his argument in effect is a transcendental deduction of this-way-or-no-way variety. But before we consider
these arguments, such as those based on the various paradoxes of
Zeno and Bradley, the underlying assumption that drives these arguments for James must be brought to light. William James, along
with his fellow pragmatists and their absolute idealist opponents,
was overly impressed by the fate of poor Humpty Dumpty: Once he
fell off the wall and disintegrated into separate pieces all the king's
horses and all the king's men couldn't put him back together again.
They had "Humpty Dumpty Intuition," for they believed that if we
ever allow reality to fall apart into numerically distinct substances
there is no way that all the king's philosophers can put them back

together again into relational complexes. There are stronger and weaker versions of this intuition. James had a weak version of it, since he believed that a relation could obtain between numerically distinct concrete individuals provided they were connected by a chain of mushing-together relations, whereas others, like Bradley, denied the possibility of any relation at all obtaining between them. Their Humpty Dumptyism commits them to countenancing only one true substance.

James's Humpty Dumpty Intuition applies across the board to all concrete relations, not just temporal ones. James enlists Bradley as an ally in this regard, because Bradley agrees that "immediate feeling possesses a native wholeness which conceptual treatment analyzes into a many, *but can't unite*" (*SPP* 52; my italics). Paradoxes of the Zenoian and Bradleyian sort "arise from the vain attempt to reconvert the manifold into which our conception has resolved things, back into the continuum out of which it came" (*SPP* 51). "You can't *confine* content" puts this succinctly (*MEN* 84). We fall into these paradoxes because our conceptualizing intellect commits us to "No discrimination without separation; no separation without absolute 'independence' and thereupon impossibility of union" (*MEN* 113). Things that are "logically distinct nevertheless [do] diffuse . . . you can't pen reality in . . . its nature is to spread, and *affect*, and . . . this applies to relations as well as to terms, so that it is impossible to call them absolutely external to each other" (*MEN* 120–1).

What support can be given for the Humpty Dumpty Intuition's prohibition against the possibility of an immediate relation between discrete, numerically distinct individuals? It is not plausible to claim it to be an obvious, self-evident truth, since there are many of a Humean mentality who reject it. Nor, as has already been shown, can it find support from the way we *ordinarily* perceive the world. Only by appeal to what is vouchsafed by backyard mystical experiences of the mushing together of things can it be supported, for these experiences are supposed to be revelatory of the true nature of reality. Furthermore, since each of the a priori arguments against the possibility of a discrete relation will be seen to have a premise that is supported by the Humpty Dumpty Intuition, these mystical revelations give needed indirect support to these arguments.

III. From Promiscuity to Panpsychism

With the Humpty Dumpty Intuition clearly in mind, we can see how James went from promiscuity to panpsychism and from that to spiritualism. The general schema of his argument for panpsychism from his Humpty Dumpty Intuition is as follows.

1. A relation can immediately obtain between concrete relata only if they are nontransitively identical with each other (are identical but not that identical). the Humpty Dumpty Intuition

2. Only in the wondrously mysterious medium of consciousness can there be such a relation of nontransitive identity – an identity that is not an identity. some kind of truth

3. Therefore, every concrete individual that is a relatum in an immediate relation, which would include every concrete thing, has an inner core of consciousness.

The Humpty Dumpty Intuition, upon which premise 1 is based, is supported by the revelations of backyard mysticism. The best that can be marshaled in support of premise 2 is that we are unable to think of any other medium in which mushing-together relations could occur. That we cannot imagine any alternative does not establish that there isn't any, but in philosophy we must ultimately settle for what we can make intelligible to ourselves after we have made the best effort we can.

It now will be shown how James filled in this general argument from promiscuity with the specific cases of change and causation. James seems to have been born with an innate fear of Zeno, for as early as *The Principles of Psychology* (237) he claims that Zeno's paradoxes show the impossibility of change through a succession of numerically distinct states. In the final two books he argues that the theory of the continuum in modern mathematics fails to neutralize Zeno's challenge, because there cannot be a succession of numerically distinct states even if their ordering is dense or mathematically continuous. The problem is to explain how there can be a transition from an earlier to a later state. Given the Humpty Dumpty Intuition, there is no way to explain this if the states are discrete. Herein it is clear that the Humpty Dumpty Intuition is appealed to in support of a key premise in the Zenoian a priori argument to prove the impossibility of change without immediate successors mushing together.

The only way in which change can be understood is by introspecting what goes on when we intentionally move or change. Thus, he indicts the mathematical physicist's account of change because it "it fails to connect us with the inner life of the flux, or with the real causes that govern its direction. Instead of being interpreters of reality, concepts negate the inwardness of reality altogether" (*PU* 110). The physicist gives us a "knowledge *about* things, as distinguished from living contemplation or sympathetic acquaintance with them... [which] touches only the outer surface of reality" (*PU* 111). The only way to understand change or flux "is either to experience it directly by being a part of reality oneself, or to evoke it in imagination by sympathetically divining someone else's inner life" (*PU* 112). Only in this way can we penetrate to "the inner nature of reality" and understand "what really *makes it go*" (*PU* 112).

The demand to understand change from the "inside" by an act of "intuitive sympathy" is based on James's gut intuitions about what constitutes a rationally satisfying account of reality – a case in point of his own "sentiment of rationality" doctrine according to which philosophers attracted to radically opposed philosophies have different personal predilections about what constitutes an adequate explanation. James has been depicted in the last two chapters as an inside man who wants to penetrate to the conscious inner core of everything, motion included. Thus, motion must be explained by introspecting what goes on in our consciousness when we intentionally move. Not surprisingly, it is found that our action-guiding recipe is not, and conceptually could not be, that of the physicist's description of a traversal of a distance, since it fails to specify an initial and final doing and thereby fails to satisfy a conceptual requirement for being a recipe. This is the point that James really is making when he asserts that the runner "perceives nothing, while running, of the mathematician's homogeneous time and space, of the infinitely numerous succession of cuts in both, or of their order" (*PU* 114). By placing yourself "at the point of view of the thing's interior doing ... all these back-looking and conflicting conceptions lie harmoniously in your hand" (*PU* 117). He interprets Zeno's dichotomy paradox of the runner as demanding that the "number of points to be occupied ... be *enumerated* in succession" (*SPP* 82; my italics). This converting of a motion into an intentional action clearly underlies James's claim that the "continuous process to be traversed . . . is a *task* – not only for our philosophic imagination, but for any real agent who might try physically to compass the entire performance" (*SPP* 88).

Given James's Humpty Dumpty type sentiment of rationality, the only way to explain change is by promiscuous succession. James, however, avoids this transcendental form of argumentation and instead engages in some fake Jack Horner type phenomenology. When we introspect our mind we find that motion is a type of flowing sludge. The only case in which we are experientially acquainted with such change is in our own consciousness. It is not that our awareness of our own consciousness when we perform an action of moving gives us a paradigm case or even a case that is seminal in the order of concept acquisition. It gives us the only case of motion that we can imagine, every case of motion having to be understood in these agency terms. And this is panpsychism!

James's argument is perspicuously rendered as a special case of the general from-promiscuity-to-panpsychism argument.

4. Change requires promiscuous succession. Humpty Dumpty Intuition

5. Promiscuous succession can occur only in consciousness. some kind of truth

6. Therefore, all change involves an inner core of consciousness.

If change is a nonpromiscuous succession, Zeno wins. There is change, and the only way it is possible, given the impossibility of non-promiscuous succession, is by promiscuous succession.

The case of causation is yet another special instance of the general from-promiscuity-to-panpsychism argument. The only way in which causation can be understood is by introspection of what goes on in our consciousness when we intentionally move.

What we feel is that a previous field of 'consciousness,' containing (in the midst of its complexity) the idea of a *result*, developes gradually into another field in which that result either appears as accomplished, or else is prevented by obstacles against which we still feel ourselves to press. . . . It seems to me that in such a continuously developing experiential series our concrete perception of causality is found in operation. If the word have any meaning at all it must mean which there we live through. (*SPP* 106)

What we observe in these personal cases is "the essential process of creation" and "where we predicate activities elsewhere . . . we have a

right to suppose aught different in kind from this" (*SPP* 108). Because
we take our personal experiences "as the type of what actual causation
is, we should have to ascribe to cases of causation outside of our own
life, to physical cases also, an inwardly experiential nature" (*SPP* 109).
And this is panpsychism!

IV. From Promiscuity to Ineffability

The a priori arguments of Zeno and Bradley for the impossibility
of discrete concrete relations also show that reality is ineffable. Before presenting James's best argument for this, it is necessary, so as
to avoid confusion, to set aside two very bad reasons James gives for
reality being ineffable. The first is based on the impossibility of any
description capturing the full richness and determinateness of reality. "Conceptual knowledge is forever inadequate to the fullness of
the reality to be known" (*SPP* 45). The second is based on the failure of concepts to be qualitatively isomorphic with their instantiators.
One version of this claim is the indictment against conceptual representations for failing to produce what they represent. Activity and
causation, for example, are said to be incomprehensible, because "the
conceptual scheme yields nothing like them" (*SPP* 48). The physicist's
space-time diagram of a motion is deficient because it fails to "*reproduce
it*" (*SPP* 47). It doesn't leap off the blackboard and run around the
room.

Another version of the lack-of-qualitative-isomorphism objection is
that necessarily concepts are discrete (there is no "coming and going"
in the Platonic heaven) and the percepts or concrete individuals they
represent mush together and thus they fail to be qualitatively identical
with these concreta.

The conceptual scheme, consisting as it does of discontinuous terms, can only
cover the perceptual flux in spots and incompletely. The one is no full measure
of the other, essential features of the flux escaping whenever we put concepts
in its place. (*SPP* 46)

Plainly, this ground for the charge of ineffability rests on a self-
predication howler that would have done Plato proud. It is required
that concepts or words be autological (apply to themselves) if they are
to be adequate representations of reality. Because concepts of a qualitatively continuous reality are themselves discrete, they fail to meet this

requirement. By this reasoning it could be shown that the concepts of the morning star and evening star fail to be coreferential since they are not identical with each other.

James has a third, and far more interesting, argument for ineffability that is based on both the discreteness of concepts and the Humpty Dumpty Intuition. He begins by granting Hegel's premise that every concrete thing "must in some sort be its own other," and then adds that "When conceptually . . . treated, they of course cannot be their own others" (*PU* 53). No element of our active life can "be treated as a . . . stable grammatical subject, but that whatever *is* has the *durcheinander* character, meaning by that that when you say it is anything, it obliges you also to say not only that it is more and other than that thing, but that it *is not* that thing, both the is and the *is not* implying at bottom only that our grammatical forms, condemned as they are to staticality and alternation, are inadequate, if we use them as literal substitutes for the reality" (*MEN* 123).

Promiscuous relations violate the law of identity, because each of the concrete relata in an immediate relation fails to be strictly identical with itself in virtue of being identical, but not *that* identical, with the other relatum. "To act on anything means to get into it somehow; but that would mean to get out of one's self and be one's other, which for intellectualism is self-contradictory" (*PU* 115). The reason that a conceptual system must satisfy the law of identity is that the purpose of a concept is to be discriminatory by partitioning the world up into those individuals that are and those that are not instances of it. This entails that any instance of a concept cannot enter into promiscuous relations, since then it would fall on both sides of the partitioning. The reason for this is that the concrete individual which is an instance of concept *F* would also fail to be an instance of *F* because it merges with one of its spatio-temporal neighbors that has a property incompatible with being *F*. But it is just this that is necessarily the case with concrete individuals. Therefore, it is conceptually impossible that concepts apply to them and thus they are absolutely ineffable. This argument, when explicitly mounted, looks like this.

7. Necessarily, every concrete individual is promiscuously related to its others. Humpty Dumpty Intuition

8. Necessarily, concepts can apply only to individuals that are not promiscuously related to their others. law of identity

9. Therefore, concepts do not apply to concrete individuals, that is, they are ineffable.

This argument uses conceptually-based reasons to show the limitations of concepts. That concepts can neutralize other concepts is one of their great practical functions. This answers also the charge that it is self-contradictory to use concepts to undermine the credit of conception in general. The best way to show that a knife won't cut is to try to cut with it. (*SPP* 60)

If we are to penetrate to the inner essence of reality we must learn "to think in nonconceptualized terms" (*PU* 131). James's task, like that of the traditional mystic, is to "deafen [us] to talk" (*PU* 131), and he accomplishes this, not by following the traditional mystical way of meditation and asceticism, but rather by contemplating the koans supplied by the arguments of Zeno, Green, Bradley, McTaggart, Taylor, and Royce to show the contradictory nature of our ordinary conceptual scheme.

When we have learned the trick of jettisoning all concepts we shall be able to sympathetically intuit the mushing together of spatiotemporal neighbors. Will we have reverted, thereby, back to "baby's first sensation" of the big, blooming, buzzing confusion, which also is a conceptless sensing? And what is the connection between the mushing-together experience and the experience of a widespread unification, such as is reported by pluralistic and monistic mystics? In answer to the first question, the backyard mystical experience of ordinary things as mushing together differs from baby's first sensation in that the former is a richer and more sophisticated experience in which the subject experiences ordinary individuals *as* mushing together, and thus appears not to be completely devoid of concepts. Only someone who had formerly applied concepts to these ordinary individuals could experience them *as* ceasing to satisfy these concepts in virtue of their entering into promiscuous relations. If I am right, there is the employment of a second-order concept in a backyard mystical experience, namely the concept of an individual that formerly was conceptualized in a certain way no longer being conceptualizable in that way.

The answer to the second question is to be found by an examination of James's 1910 "A Suggestion about Mysticism." It begins with the mushing together account of our perception of time. "The present field as a whole came continuously out of its predecessor and will melt into its successor as continuously again" (*EP* 158). The sort of mushing-together relations that we become aware of in backyard mystical experiences become vastly expanded in the more traditional type of mystical experience. Herein the threshold of ordinary sensory awareness is lowered and there is a "very sudden and incomprehensible enlargement of the conscious field" (*EP* 159). We become conscious of a unification of reality in which "the sense of *relation* will be greatly enhanced." It is not just that our ordinary field of consciousness is vastly expanded, for there is nothing especially mystical about a wide-angle lens view – a mystic isn't someone with especially good peripheral vision – but rather that we experience a richer complex of things as mushing together. The experience is more than just a unifying experience: It is an experience of unification, of the melting together of things that formerly were taken to be discrete (*EP* 159). Traditional mystical experiences of a widespread unification, therefore, differ from backyard mystical experiences only in regard to the extent of the unification. But the fusing and merging together never realizes, for James, that of complete union and that is why the identity of a thing with its "other" is not transitive. Accordingly, James calls himself a "pluralistic mystic," and thereby aligns himself with the traditional theistic mystics who claimed to experience their becoming identical with God but not *that* identical.

V. From Panpsychism to Spiritualism

The Humpty Dumpty Intuition entails not only *panpsychism* but also *spiritualism* or *idealism* – that every concrete individual is nothing but consciousness, has only properties of a conscious sort. This is demonstrated by the following from-panpsychism-to-spiritualism argument.

10. A concrete individual can have a property of a physical sort only if it stands in certain immediate nomic relations to other concrete individuals. James's doctrine of Pure Experience

11. It is impossible for a concrete individual to stand in an immediate relation to another individual that it doesn't promiscuously mush together with. The Humpty Dumpty Intuition

2. Only in the wondrously mysterious medium of consciousness can there be such a promiscuous mushing-together relation. some kind of a truth

12. Every property of a concrete individual is of either a physical or conscious sort. some kind of truth

13. The only properties possessed by a concrete individual are conscious ones. from 10, 11, 2, and 12

3. Every concrete individual has an inner core of consciousness and thus has some properties of a conscious sort. stylistic variation of the conclusion of the from-promiscuity-to-panpsychism argument

14. Every concrete individual has properties of a conscious sort. from 3

15. Every concrete individual has properties of a conscious sort and only such properties. from 13 and 14

Although the scholastic look of this argument would horrify James, all of its premises are ones that James accepts or is committed to accepting. Premise 10 rests on the first tenet of James's doctrine of Pure Experience, which was expounded in Chapter 7, according to which no piece of pure experience, no concrete individual in other words, counts as mental or physical *simpliciter* but only as it is related to earlier and later events. Some of these relations, of course, will be nonmediated. It will count as physical when its relations to these temporally surrounding events obey causal laws of science. I am not sure how to argue for premise 12, and it is the only premise that can't be traced directly to something that James wrote.

VI. A Big Aporia

There is a big aporia that is conveniently overlooked in my exposition of how James's doctrine of the specious present became superseded by the Humpty Dumpty Intuition. It is due to his oft-repeated claim that our experience of change is pulsational, and must be if we are to escape the clutches of Zeno. This creates a big aporia, since there is a seeming contradiction between the pulsational and the Humpty Dumpty accounts of our experience of change. An effort will be made to neutralize this aporia by Poo-bah-izing James's apparently inconsistent claims.

There are many passages in which James claims that our experience of time's flow is pulsational:

we tell it off in pulses. We say 'now! now! now!' or we count 'more! more! more!' as we feel it bud. This composition out of units of duration is called the law of time's discrete flow. (585; see also *PU* 129 and *SPP* 88 for more of the same)

That "Time itself comes in drops" (*PU* 104) is not only purported to be phenomenologically vouchsafed but also supported by neurophysiological facts concerning the thresholds for perceptual awareness (*PU* 104). Furthermore, only if change is pulsational can we escape Zeno's paradoxes.

Either we must stomach logical contradiction, therefore, or we must admit that the limit is reached in these successive cases by finite and perceptible units of approach – drops, buds, steps, or whatever we please to term them, of change, coming wholly when they do come, or coming not at all. (*SPP* 93–4)

We should be suspicious of any phenomenological support for a claim that also is supported by a priori arguments, for the phenomenology invariably turns out to be of the faked Jack Horner variety. Our expectations are not disappointed in this case. James's phenomenologically based claim that "Sensibly, motion comes in drops, waves or pulses" (*PU* 107) flies in the face of ordinary experience. I do not see the rising arm as a discrete succession of droplet type things, as I might if I were watching a motion picture of the rising on an out-of-whack projector. *Pace* James, we need not, and usually do not, experience a bottle emptying drop by drop (*PU* 103–4). It is not uncommon to see a bottle of Chivas Regal decanting in this manner, but not when it is a bottle of Bankers Club vodka. It just pours out! James is right that our experience is pulsational when we count or reiterate the word "Now," but this hardly is typical of our ordinary experiences of change.

How is the aporia to be resolved? One obvious way, which even has some textual support, is to make a distinction between the *act* of experiencing and the *content* of the experience and hold the former alone to be pulsational, the latter being of the mushing-together sort. Immediately after formulating the "law of time's *discrete flow*," James adds that "The discreteness is, however, merely due to the fact that our successive acts of *recognition* or *apperception* of *what* it is are discrete. The sensation is as continuous as any sensation can be" (585). This act-content distinction seems to inform his claims that whereas "things are discrete and discontinuous . . . their comings and goings and contrasts no more break the flow of the thought that thinks them than they break the time and space in which they lie" (*PU* 233) and there cannot be found "in the thought any parts . . . corresponding to the object's parts. Time parts are not such parts" (*PU* 269). If James means to be making this act-content distinction, we must understand his ambiguous claim that our "acquaintance with reality grows literally by buds or drops of perception" (*SPP* 80) as applying only to the perceptual acts, not their phenomenological contents. Via this distinction we can escape having to countenance James's Jack Horner pulsational phenomenological account. This way of interpreting James's pulsational theory of passage makes him an anticipator of Whitehead's doctrine that there is a becoming of continuity, but not a continuity of becoming, in which what becomes is some content.

Unfortunately, James cannot consistently accept this way of applying the act-content distinction to the passage of time, since it has the pulsational manner in which our acts of perception pass constitute the real nature of temporal passage rather than their phenomenological contents, which supposedly reveal a promiscuous type of passage. The most holy of holy philosophical truths for James is that reality is just what it experientially appears to be. "'The insuperability of sensation' would be a short expression of my thesis" (*SPP* 45).

The act-content distinction left us with a *succession of numerically distinct* acts of perception, but this clashes with James's Humpty Dumpty Intuition. It would appear that we have the following choice: We can agree with James that only a pulsational succession of distinct events can avoid Zeno's paradoxes and thereby give up the Humpty Dumpty Intuition or we can hold onto this intuition and reject James's demand that change is to be understood in terms of a pulsational succession. Given how central the Humpty Dumpty Intuition is to James's overall philosophy, he would do better to withdraw his pulsational account of change.

The apparent inconsistency between James's pulsational and Humpty Dumpty accounts of change can be eliminated if we Poobah-ize them with suitable "*qua*"-clause restrictions. *Qua* promethean agent, change is pulsational, the reason being that such an agent requires an action-guiding recipe that presents him with a discrete succession of actions having a first and last member. But, *qua* backyard mystic, his response to Zeno is to promiscuize change. Thus, Zeno's paradoxes challenge both the promethean agent and the backyard mystic, and each has his own separate response. The unresolved problem with this ontological relativism solution to the aporia is that it raises an even bigger aporia, the really big aporia, that James's ontological relativism clashes with the absolute, nonrelativized reality claims made by both the religious and backyard mystic, which is to be an important topic of the next chapter.

11

An Attempt at a One World Interpretation of James

As this book has progressed a number of aporias have been shown to arise out of James's text, and promissory notes were issued for their resolutions, with this being the chapter in which they are to be paid in full. If I do not make good on them, as well I might not, I could be accused of being a philosophical tease for letting the tension build throughout the book with the promise of relief in this chapter, and then when it gets time to deliver nothing happens: No one wants to be called a "teaser," philosophical or otherwise.

Before I undertake this most difficult constructive task, it will be helpful to give a brief summary of these aporias. The biggest aporia, of which the others are special cases, is to find a way to unify James's many selves and the many worlds toward which their interests are directed. James's deep need to have a philosophy that he could live by precludes any self-unification that is not rooted in a metaphysical unification of the many worlds. The need for a metaphysical unification is especially pressing for James, since there were apparent clashes between the things that he said from the perspectives of these different selves, especially the mystical and promethean selves. These are the deepest and most seemingly intractable aporias. In order to bring them into bold relief a brief recap will be given of the account of James's mysticism in the previous two chapters.

James's religious mysticism based on the I–Thou experience involved a partial union with the inner consciousness of other beings, starting with his fellow human beings and extending all the way to a supernatural but finite God. Even nature itself was fair game for the I–Thou experience, if one could only learn to adopt a personal stance toward it. The upshot of this nature mysticism is panpsychism. Like nature mysticism, James's "backyard mysticism" is directed at nature and manages to see it in a radically different way than the promethean agent does; the individuals that the latter sharply separates by applying concepts to them are perceived as mushing together into promiscuous relations, though not to the extent that they cease to have any identity of their own. The upshot of this brand of mysticism was not just panpsychism, since only in consciousness could such promiscuous mushing occur, but spiritualism as well.

There are striking similarities between James's religious and backyard mysticism. Both involve conceptless, and thereby ineffable, experiences of unification that are obtainable only by a passive self. This requires that one's promethean self be held in abeyance, which occasions the first of the clashes between James's promethean and mystical selves. Far more troublesome is that each type of mystical experience is taken by their subjects to be a cognitive revelation of the true nature of reality. The absolute, nonrelativized reality claims based on these experiences clash with the *universal* doctrine of ontological relativism, which requires that all reality-claims be relativized to the perspective of some world or self. Furthermore, because promethean reality claims employ concepts, they hold there to be discrete relations between neighbors, in contrast to the reality claims based on backyard and nature mysticism that promiscuize these relations. Both reality claims cannot be true, unless they are Poo-bah-ized, but this exactly what the nonrelativized reality claims of the mystics will not allow. The mystic would reject any attempt to neutralize the contentful clash between mystical and promethean reality claims by applying restrictive "*qua*"-clauses to them. Not only are mystically-based reality claims incompatible with concept-based ones, the Humpty Dumpy Intuition that is supported by mysticism claims that these concept-based claims could not be true.

But there does not seem to be unity among James's religious and backyard mystics. First, unlike the case of a religious I–Thou experience, there is no talk about the subject of a backyard mystical experience becoming unified with what is experienced, only of a unification among the contents of the experience. Second, whereas the I–Thou experience is of another person, the object of a backyard mystical experience is impersonal.

These differences, however, might not be as great as they seem. A backyard mystical experience does achieve some unification of the subject with nature, since it shows that nature is of a piece with what we discover when we enter into our own consciousness through introspection. Furthermore, the apparent object of a backyard mystical experience is not completely impersonal since it is of a piece with the consciousness of the subject. Thus, a backyard mystical experience of the mushing together of ordinary things bestows on them a personality that is akin to the subject's.

Before considering how to unify James's promethean and mystical selves, along with their separate worlds, the more general problem of unifying his many worlds and selves will be considered. Initially, only quests for unification that can be directly located in James's text will be considered. They will be found to be inadequate, both individually and collectively. This will be followed by attempts to find a unification that is Jamesian in spirit, though it goes well beyond the text, having only a tenuous or even ambiguous relation to it. Here interpretation fades into what-James-ought-to-have-said-but-didn't.

I. James's Quests for Unification

James's ontological relativism was central to his promethean philosophy, for it held that what is real (actual, existent) is relative to the passing interests of an agent. For each of James's many selves there is a world toward which its distinctive desires and interests are directed. As a person's interests change so will the world that is taken to be actual. Immediately after introducing this plethora of worlds ontologically on all fours with each other, James raises the question of what unifies them into a universe, it being up to the philosopher to find an answer. He never gives any explicit answer so it is left to the interpreter to draw one out of the text and thereby complete what James himself described as the "incomplete arch" in his philosophy.

Chapter 7 presented a promethean solution to the unification problem that consisted in each of the many worlds being a possible target for a promethean agent's interest, thereby gaining unification by their common relation to this agent. This enables James's many selves to achieve a first-I'm-this-and-then-I'm-that sort of unification but leaves him a Poo-bah type temporal schizophrenic. It appears as if James's quest to have it all cannot have the one thing that James most wants – to be a truly unified self. Emerson beautifully expressed the agony wrought by this taking turns solution as it applies to the mystical and promethean selves, termed the "soul" and "understanding," respectively.

> The worst feature of this double consciousness is, that the two lives, of the understanding and of the soul, which we lead, really show very little relation to each other; never meet and measure each other; one prevails now, all buzz and din; and the other prevails then, all infinitude and paradise; and, with the progress of life, the two discover no greater disposition to reconcile themselves.

Lowell epitomized Emerson as "a Plotinus-Montaigne." James, certainly, hoped to do better than Emerson in this regard. Unfortunately, his ontological relativism failed to unify his many selves, because it had no way of resolving the clashes between his promethean and mystical selves in regard to whether reality is relative to the interests of an agent and whether concepts should be employed, which really is the question of whether one should take an active or passive stance toward the world.

As James matured as a philosopher he sought a deeper type of unification than the very tenuous one supplied by his Poo-bahistic ontological relativism. One indication of this is a subtle shift in terminology. Whereas he formerly spoke of different worlds in *The Principles of Psychology*, he speaks twelve years later in *The Varieties of Religious Experiences* of "other dimensions of existence from the sensible" one (*VRE* 406). We are said, furthermore, to "enter into wider cosmic relations" when we have mystical experiences rather than experiencing a different world (*VRE* 407). Mystical experiences "open out the possibility of other orders of truth" (*VRE* 335) and are "windows through which the mind looks out upon a more extensive and inclusive world" (*VRE* 339). This shift in terminology from "worlds" to a "wider world" and different "dimensions" of a single world does not in itself achieve any unification, since it leaves undetermined just how these different dimensions, such as those revealed through sense and mystical experiences, are related. In fact, it is misleading to use "dimensional" talk at all, since whatever has a position in any one dimension of an ordinary dimensional or coordinate system has a position in every other dimension of the system, but it is unclear how a mystical or supernatural reality or entity could have a position in every dimension, including those of space and time, of some higher-order dimensional coordinate system.

Fortunately, James's quest for unification went deeper than a mere shift in terminology, and an obscurantist one at that. It took many different forms with no one of them achieving a complete unification of all of the worlds, thus raising the question of whether in conjunction they do the trick. Some of the forms it took were: 1. instrumentalism; 2. working hypotheses; 3. concept empiricism; and 4. trans-world causation. Solutions 1. and 3. both attempt to show that there is a world that is seminal or basic in some sense, all the other worlds being dependent upon it in this respect. The order of dependency might be the familiar ones from the history of philosophy consisting of existence or knowledge, what Aristotle called the orders of nature and experience.

1. James's ontological relativism was quite content to countenance a sharp clash between the common-sense world of sensible objects and the world of theoretical entities of science, due to the latter being devoid of all of the features that are of human importance. James no longer is willing to meet the threat of bifurcationism by applying his ontological relativism to the common-sense and scientific worlds. Instead he finds a way of unifying them through an instrumentalistic reduction of the latter to the former. An extreme, activistic form of his instrumentalism, similar to Dewey's, is that "physics is the science of the ways of taking hold of bodies and pushing them" (*P* 30). Scientific entities "should not be held for literally true. It is *as if* they existed; but in reality they are like co-ordinates or logarithms, only artificial short-cuts for taking us from one part to another of experience's flux" (*P* 92). By instrumentalizing theoretical entities, James goes quite a way to neutralizing the bifurcation between man and nature.

That the common-sense world of sensible objects is more basic in the order of being than that of the theoretical entities of science in that the latter are reducible to the former, being only instrumental constructs out of them, does not show that the ontological contents of *all* worlds are thus reducible to sensible objects. Worlds comprised of abstract entities immediately come to mind. It will be up to James's concept empiricism to complete the task begun by scientific instrumentalism by showing that the ontological contents of all these other worlds are also in some way instrumental constructs out of ordinary empirical objects.

2. There is, however, another respect in which 1. does not go far enough in its unifying efforts. Its exclusive concern with ontological reduction of theoretical to empirical objects leaves untouched the apparent clash between the scientist and the moral agent over the status of determinism. It is here that James can press into service his weak, working hypothesis version of the will-to-believe. For scientists to ply their trade successfully they need not actually believe that determinism is true. They need to adopt determinism as a working hypothesis, and they have an ample will-to-believe type justification for doing so, since there is extensive evidence from the history of science that doing so aids the progress of science. But, in contrast, promethean moral agents must have sweating-with-conviction belief that they have contra-causal freedom of the will if they are to derive the benefit from their belief of becoming more effective moral agents.

If this application of the believing and working hypothesis versions of the will-to-believe doctrine succeeds in neutralizing the apparent clash in beliefs between the scientist and the moral agent over determinism, it could neutralize the apparent clash in beliefs between the mystic and the moral agent over the nature of reality, especially whether it even has an intrinsic nature. Plainly, the mystics will not realize the salvific consequence of their belief that their experiences reveal the true nature of reality if they take it to be only a working hypothesis. But our pragmatic selves, in contrast, can adopt as a working hypothesis that reality is carved up into numerically distinct individuals.

So far so good for the strategy of reconciliation through having only one of the two apparently conflicting propositions be reduced to a working hypothesis. But it breaks down with the clash between the *moral agents'* belief in the reality of this carved up world with the denial of this by mystics. For in this case neither of the two parties can go with the working hypothesis version of their belief. We needn't repeat why the mystic cannot. The reason why moral agents cannot is, as James never tires of stressing, that, unless they actually believe that the world has a constitution that answers back to their deepest feelings and needs, they would have no incentive to live the morally strenuous life.

3. It was seen that 1's scientific instrumentalism did not go far enough, for it did not show how worlds other than that composed of the theoretical entities of science could be reduced to the world of sensible objects. James's concept empiricism generalizes the instrumentalistic account of scientific concepts as devices for leading us from one experience to another to all concepts.

Different universes of thought thus arise, with specific sorts of relation among their ingredients. The world of common-sense 'things'; the world of material tasks to be done; the mathematical world of pure forms; the world of ethical propositions; the worlds of logic, of music, etc. – all abstracted and generalized from long-forgotten perceptual instances from which they have as it were flowered out – return and merge themselves again in the particulars of our present and future perception. (*SPP* 33–4)

James did not consistently adhere to this concept empiricism. Several passages were given in Chapter 1, where James seemed to endorse Platonic realism about universals. There also are passages where he goes back on his scientific instrumentalism. Ostwald's reduction of the "hypersensible entities, the corpuscles and vibrations" of science to our sensations, "seems too economical to be all-sufficient. Profusion, not economy, may after all be reality's key-note" (*P* 93).

The problem with concept empiricism is that it achieves only an epistemological, not an ontological, reduction of everything to sensory experience. The denizens of James's supernatural worlds, such as God or the enveloping mother-sea-of-consciousness, do not seem to be ontologically reducible to perceptual experience, since they lack sensory qualities and are not occupants of space. The same holds for abstract entities.

4. This solution finds unification of the worlds through trans-world causal interaction, in particular between the everyday sensory world and the supernatural world that contains the More – the object of mystical experiences. In religious experiences "spiritual energy flows in and produces effects, either psychological or material, within the phenomenal world" (*VRE* 382). "The conscious person is continuous with a wider self through which saving experiences come" (*VRE* 405). James made sure to emphasize that the causal influence also went from

the lower selves to the higher supernatural being(s). Such interaction shows that the clash between the active promethean self and passive mystical one has been made to appear more formidable than it really is. Even promethean selves must be permitted to sleep, for they won't amount to much as promethean agents if they don't. Similarly, they shouldn't be denied some mystical R and R if it should enable them to return to the war zone better equipped to do battle with the forces of evil. For James, mystical emotions and beliefs are valuable and should be cultivated, not just for their own sake, but also for their instrumental value in inducing morally desirable behavior. James even claimed that for a mystical experience to be veridical or objective its "fruits must be good for Life" (*VRE* 318). In general, the authenticity or worth of any experience or emotion depends on its having a beneficial upshot in the work-a-day world of the moral agent, thus the reason for his intense condemnation of the overly sentimental Russian lady crying her eyes out at the theater while her footman was freezing outside, as seen in Chapter 4 in this volume.

The R and R way of reconciling the promethean and mystical selves fails, however, to neutralize the clash between these selves over ontological relativism and the Humpty Dumpty Intuition. In showing a *causal* interaction, and a beneficial one at that, between the promethean and mystical selves nothing is done to resolve the *intellectual* clash between their rival beliefs.

I must conclude that the unification problem fails to be solved by 1.–4., even when they are agglomerated. I now will seek a solution that is Jamesian in spirit, although it cannot be squarely located in the text.

II. Some Jamesian Style Solutions

At the base of all the aporias is the clash between the pragmatist's ontological relativism and the nonrelativized reality claims made by the mystic. To find a Jamesian style solution we will have to follow the lead of the old Hollywood serials. At the end of last week's episode we saw the Lone Ranger hurtling off a 2000 foot cliff in a burning wagon but now we see that, thank God, it was only Tonto. They spliced the film! "Splicing the film" in James's case requires altering his text, in particular his ontological relativism and/or his mysticism, so that it wasn't James but only Royce, thank God, who was tied hand and foot and thrown into the giant garbage compactor. The aim is to give a one-world interpretation of James that will be textually motivated and Jamesian in spirit, in spite of the need for some "splicing." In a one-world interpretation there will be no need to relativize different types of claims, especially reality claims, to an agent at a time so as to avoid contradiction. There is only one world and all the claims we want to make are unrestrictedly made *quoad* this world. Thus, the type of claims made from the perspectives of common sense, the moral agent, the scientist, and the mystic will be mutually compatible.

With respect to the logical clash between ontological relativism and the nonrelativized mystical reality claims it is clear that one of the two claims must be altered or spliced out so that it will not have been James who was thrown into the giant garbage compactor. One way to secure consistency is to eliminate both ontological relativism and the absolute reality claims of the mystics, but this would violate James's conservative principle for belief revision and, moreover, would render his philosophy completely unrecognizable. Thus we are left with the choice of giving up either ontological relativism or the unrestricted reality claims of the mystic.

Let us first consider giving up the latter. There are four ways in which this can be accomplished. In the first way, the cognitivity of the mystical experiences upon which these unrestricted reality claims are based is denied, thereby rendering these claims false. This violates too much the letter and spirit of James's philosophy. Second, these reality claims could be treated as working hypotheses. But this would undercut the salvific consequences of mystical experience. Third, the claims could be downgraded to targets for a will-to-believe option that involves real belief. Unfortunately, this move does not avoid a clash with the doctrine of ontological relativism. The reason is that, according to this doctrine, the mystic's nonrelativized reality claims fail to qualify as propositions, and only a proposition can be a target of a will-to-believe option (or even a working hypothesis). A reality-claim is triadic: __ is real for person __ at time __. But mystics fail to specify the values for these blank spaces, thereby leaving us with an incomplete proposition, a mere propositional function. Fourth, relativize the mystic's reality claims to a perspective or world, namely that of the mystic. This solution, like the one that denies the truth of these claims, would be rejected by the mystic and James out of hand. Furthermore, by

Poo-bah-izing mystical reality claims, along with all other reality claims, it leaves us temporal schizophrenics of taking-turns sort.

This brings us to the second and better way of splicing the text to achieve consistency, in which James's ontological relativism is to be given up or modified. The basic idea is to Poo-bah-ize Poo-bah-ism by restricting it to certain worlds, namely pragmatic ones in which concepts are employed as teleological instruments to gain control over objects, which includes the worlds of the moral agent and the scientist. This restriction can be motivated by showing that the unrestricted version of Poo-bahism is self-refuting. For it claims that *all* reality claims are world-relative, but it is itself a universal doctrine that is not relativized to any world, thereby constituting a counter-example to itself. Because Poo-bahism no longer purports to hold for all reality claims, it is compatible with the mystic's nonrelativized reality claims. The latter claims, to be sure, entail that Poo-bahism is false in the actual world but not that it is false in every world, such as pragmatic worlds. It just happens to be a contingent fact, if mystical reality claims are true, that the actual world is not a pragmatic world. In granting that pragmatic worlds are *possible* worlds, the mystic or mystically inclined metaphysician can no longer employ a priori arguments to show the impossibility of concepts being true of reality. But this is no great loss, because these arguments are quite bogus. There is no reason why a mystic has to be muddle-headed. Furthermore, the mystic can no longer claim that her Humpty Dumpty Intuition is a necessary truth, since, if it were, no pragmatic world would be a possible world.

It should be noted that the proposition that ontological relativism is true in pragmatic worlds is true in every world, even nonpragmatic ones, just as the proposition that Socrates is snub-nosed in the actual world is true in every possible world in which he exists, including those in which he is not snub-nosed. More generally, if a proposition p is true in a possible world W, then the proposition that p is true in W is true in every possible world, even ones in which p is false. In asserting nonrelativized reality claims the mystic is committed to reality not being world-relative in the actual world, but this is consistent with her admitting that reality is world-relative in certain other possible worlds, namely pragmatic or promethean ones.

What is the textual support for this world-restricted interpretation of ontological relativism? Just after James claims that reality is relative to a person at a time in the chapter "The Perception of Reality" he adds that "This is the only sense which the word ever has in the mouths of *practical* men" (*PP* 924; my italics). Herein there is an apparent restriction of ontological relativism to the world or perspective of the practical person or moral agent. For it is an expression of the practical self or moral agent bent on maximizing desire–satisfaction. The moral agent is aided in this endeavor by believing ontological relativism, since it enables her to give primary importance to different worlds or perspectives as her interests and desires change, thereby facilitating her endeavor to maximize desire–satisfaction. Plainly, the mystic's world is not one of these practical worlds.

There is a worry that the conjunction of the version of ontological relativism that is restricted to practical worlds with the acceptance of the nonrestricted reality claims of mystics will undercut the seriousness with which promethean agents pursue their quest to have it all. What effect will it have on promethean agents to realize that their worlds, the ones that they are up to their necks in via their practical activities, are real only in relation to their passing interests but that the world of the mystic is real *simpliciter*? Might they feel that their practical reality is an ontological booby prize and thus not worth taking seriously, thereby undermining their effectiveness in their quest to have it all?

There is no simple answer to these questions, since human psychology is highly variable in these matters. Some people get depressed more easily than others. The challenge to the promethean moral agent posed by the conjunction of ontological relativism and mysticism certainly is far less than that posed by either determinism or bifurcationism, as previously seen in Chapters 3 and 8, respectively. Many would be inclined to agree with James that their acceptance of determinism or bifurcationism would undermine their incentive to lead the morally strenuous life, but far fewer would find that the acceptance of the conjunction of nonrelativized mystical reality claims and the restricted version of ontological relativism does. There are a lot of mystics of all different persuasions, from pluralistic to monistic, who accept the unreality or illusoriness of the sensible world within which the moral agent operates but nevertheless are uncompromising in their dedication to the cause of fighting worldly evils. No moral holidays for them.

Although the restriction of ontological relativism goes some way toward a one-world interpretation of James, making it possible to assert

everything we want to say *quoad* the actual world, it does not solve
the general problem of unification, since it does not find a way of
metaphysically unifying the many worlds, thereby leaving James and
those of like psychological complexity a temporalized Poo-bah type
schizophrenic. To unify James's many selves requires metaphysically
unifying the many worlds toward which their interests are directed, in
particular the mystical world and the practical worlds comprised of a
multiplicity of numerically distinct empirical objects in space and time.
The practical self is puzzled by the reality claims of mystics, and not just
the extreme acosmic ones that deny *en toto* the reality of the sensible
world. Even those of the backyard mystics that deny the applicability
of concepts, any concepts, to reality are perplexing; for, if reality is not
as we conceptualize it in our promethean phases, why is it that our
concepts do such a good job in helping us to succeed in our worldly
endeavors. This is analogous to the acosmic mystic having to explain
why the allegedly illusory sensible world appears so substantial and
real. There is the story of the Indian rashi who, after completing a
lecture on the unreality of the sensible world, is on his way home and
has to climb a tree to escape a raging elephant; and, when asked why
he did so, since the elephant is unreal, said that it was only his unreal
self escaping from an unreal elephant.

   The intelligent reader should have realized all along that I was
playing the tease throughout the book in issuing promissory notes
to find a way, on James's behalf, to unify James's many worlds and
selves, especially the promethean and mystical ones. I certainly am
not going to succeed where all of the great mystical traditions and
mystically influenced metaphysicians have failed miserably, for they
have been forced to leave it an ultimate mystery as to why there should
be any world other than the mystical one. Metaphorical talk about
emanations out of the Eternal One or its overflowing like a fountain
so as to yield a multiplicity of changing objects is no help. James is
in the same basic fix as are these past mystics and mystically-inclined
metaphysicians. One of our many selves, the mystical one, craves unity,
self-containment, the safety and peace that comes from abiding in the
present. But our promethean self is always running ahead of itself
into the future, living on the dangerous edge of things, risking failure
and facing its inevitable death. What James's quest to have it all most
wants is to be both of these selves *at the same time*. What we really want

is to be both a Sartrian *In-Itself* that self-sufficiently abides in its total completeness within the present and a *For-Itself* that is always running ahead of itself into the future so as to complete itself. We want to be God, in other words. Not surprisingly, this is forever beyond our grasp. To be human is to accept the unresolvable tension between wanting to be both at the same time. The best we can hope for is a taking-turns solution of the first-I'm-this-and-then-I'm-that sort. One does not solve this problem. One can only bear witness to it. And no one has done so with more passion, honesty and brilliance than William James.

Before concluding this book, two underlying assumptions that have guided the discussion throughout should be made explicit so that they can be critically assessed. The first is that there is something pernicious about being a divided self of the temporal schizophrenic sort and the second that a contradiction in our web of beliefs is pernicious and to be avoided at all costs. Each will be discussed in turn.

According to the first assumption it is bad to be a Poo-bah type temporal schizophrenic who successively adopts different perspectives that clash with each other unless their claims are world- or perspective-restricted: Now I'm a backyard mystic having conceptless intuitions of the essential nature of reality as a flowing sludge devoid of any discrete, numerically distinct individuals, everything being its own Hegelian other. But in two hours I will adopt the scientific perspective and think of the world as conceptually carved up into subatomic particles behaving in a rigidly deterministic way that precludes free will; but after that I'll be leading the morally strenuous life and believe in the reality of undetermined spiritual acts of causation in a nonbifurcated world, and so on and so on. But, really, what's so bad about this? There is good empirical evidence that there is nothing wrong with being a Poo-bah type divided character. I love to do philosophy, teach, hang out with my wife, children and grandchildren, work out, do home remodeling projects, shoot the breeze with my colleagues and students, fish, play the piano, etc., but why should I require that there is some integral unity between these different ways of being in the world? James's hipsterism, his wild passion to have it all, to grab for all the gusto he can, qualifies him to wear a button saying "Kiss me. I'm a Divided Self" as he leads the parade up Fifth Avenue on I-Am-a-Divided-Self-And-I-Love-It Day.

Unfortunately, there is one problem that might completely mar the joy of the day, and James will be the first one to raise it. Our absolutistic metaphysical doctrine, based on the Humpty Dumpty Intuition, claims that concepts cannot apply to reality and thereby charges our various pragmatically based perspectives, including that of the moral agent, with having an erroneous view of the way things are. Won't this queer things for these perspectives, since it does not give these perspectives or propensities any "object whatever to press against. A philosophy whose principle is so incommensurate with our most intimate powers as to deny them all relevancy in universal affairs, as to annihilate their motives at one blow, will be even more unpopular than pessimism"? (*PP* 940) Recall in this connection James's dilemma of determinism argument to show that a belief in determinism leads to an undesirable sort of pessimistic passivity. Why take the conceptually carved-up workaday world seriously if it isn't the way things really are? This is the problem that has plagued acosmic mystics throughout the ages. All that can be said is that this has not sapped most mystics' incentive and energy to lead the morally strenuous life. Realizing that the practical world in which we are so passionately involved is not fully real might be just the counterbalancing force that is needed to keep us from drowning in this world and, surprisingly, make us more effective promethean beings.

The promethean spirit of James's philosophy coupled with his mad quest to have it all should have led him to question the sanctity of the law of noncontradiction, that no exceptions will be allowed to it no matter what. But he did not. He was committed to this law throughout his career. In his very early essay "The Sentiment of Rationality," James speculates that the reason why we cannot abide a contradiction is "as natural and invincible as that which makes us exchange a hard high stool for an arm-chair or prefer traveling by railroad to riding in a springless cart" (*EP* 33).

Maybe James was too timid in showing such excessive obeisance to the law of noncontradiction and not going all the way with his promethean humanism, which holds that "Our nouns and adjectives are all humanized heirlooms, and in the theories we build them into, the inner order and arrangement is wholly dictated by human considerations, *intellectual consistency being one of them*" (*P* 122; my italics). It was argued in Chapter 5 that the law of noncontradiction really functions as an instrumental rule in James's theory of belief acceptance, admitting of an exception when desire–satisfaction can be maximized by believing a contradiction. If it be asked why believe one contradiction rather than any other, the reply of the rule-instrumental pragmatist is that the pragmatic benefits of such beliefs in regard to maximizing desire–satisfaction varies with the contradiction. Thus, it might be pragmatically desirable to believe the conjunction of ontological relativism and the absolute reality claims of mystics but not to believe that the Chrysler Building is taller than itself. The last of prometheus's worries should be having to countenance a contradiction. Better that than being forever bound to the rocky peak on Caucasus or, in James's case, keeping the doors and windows shut against the full richness of experience.

Things could be done to make it easier to live with the radical promethean solution. Certainly, we wouldn't want actively or occurrently to believe incompatible propositions at one and the same time. We could create a pill that would keep us from actively remembering one of our former beliefs, allowing it to remain dormant in the purely dispositional state. When we are in our mystical moods and are actively or occurrently believing that reality in itself is just the way we are experiencing it to be, we could pop a pill that would prevent us from actively recalling that in our earlier promethean phases we believed in ontological relativism.

Even if we were up to performing such an elaborate juggling act with our beliefs, there are, in my opinion, as well as in James's, fatal flaws in the radical promethean solution. First, James thought that a person's philosophy should be something that she lives by, something that actively guides her in her quest for self-realization. A metaethical theory, for example, should serve as a guide for a person in making first-order ethical choices. This desideratum would be violated by a utilitarian who, on the one hand, promulgated a metaethical theory requiring us always to act so as to maximize utility, and, on the other hand, required us to make our first-order ethical choices on the basis of what principles of virtue or justice require, since by doing so we maximize utility in the long run. Analogously, James's universal thesis of ontological relativism should guide us in making first-order reality claims so that we build into them the required "*qua*"-clause restriction. But in the radical Promethean solution, one is supposed to believe ontological relativism yet not make use of it when making their first-order mystically based reality claims.

Second, James's commitment to intellectual integrity would not have permitted him to be a pill popper, no matter how much it would maximize desire–satisfaction. There is an intrinsic value to being an intellectually integrated self who does not engage in self-deception. Here is yet another instance in which he has deep deontological intuitions that clash with his official casuistic rule requiring us always to act so as to maximize desire–satisfaction over desire–dissatisfaction.

The radical promethean solution based on allowing special exceptions to the law of noncontradiction, therefore, requires some splicing of the text. It squares with James's hipsterism, his quest to have it all, but clashes with his intellectual scruples. In my opinion, James would do better to go all the way with his hipsterism and learn to live happily with the conflicts and tensions, even contradictions, between the different perspectives of his many selves. And, if it should be pointed out to him that he is irrational, he could flash his "I've given up noncontradiction and I love it!" button.

Bibliography of Works Cited

Works by James

All works by James, except for his letters, are contained in *The Works of William James*, edited by Frederick H. Burkhardt, Fredson Bowers, and Ignas Skrupskelis, Cambridge, MA: Harvard University Press, 1975–1988. The original publication date appears in parentheses. These volumes are listed in the chronological order of their original publication and will be referred to in the body of the book by the abbreviated name listed before the name of the volume. Quotations are given without alteration, unless otherwise noted.

PP   *The Principles of Psychology*, 1981 (1890)
PBC   *Psychology: Briefer Course*, 1984 (1892)
WB   *The Will to Believe and Other Essays in Popular Philosophy*, 1979 (1897)
TT   *Talks to Teachers on Psychology, and to Students on Some of Life's Ideals*, 1983 (1899)
VRE   *The Varieties of Religious Experience*, 1985 (1902)
ERE   *Essays in Radical Empiricism*, 1976 (1912)
P   *Pragmatism*, 1975 (1907)
MT   *The Meaning of Truth*, 1975 (1909)
PU   *A Pluralistic Universe*, 1977 (1909)
SPP   *Some Problems of Philosophy*, 1979 (1911)
EP   *Essays in Philosophy*, 1978

ERM   *Essays in Religion and Morality,* 1982
EPS   *Essays in Psychology,* 1983
EPR   *Essays in Psychical Research,* 1986
ECR   *Essays, Comments, and Reviews,* 1987
ML   *Manuscript Lectures,* 1988
MEN   *Manuscript Essays and Notes,* 1988
LWJ   *The Letters of William James.* Edited by Henry James in two
      volumes. Boston: Atlantic Monthly Press, 1920
CWJ   *The Correspondence of William James,* Vol. 1–4, Edited by Ignas
      Skrupskelis and Elizabeth Berkeley. Charlottesville:
      University Press, 1992

Suggested Further Readings

The best secondary source to begin with is Ralph Barton Perry's master-piece, *The Thought and Character of William James* (Nashville: Vanderbilt University Press, 1996). It gives an insightful account of the connection between the man and his philosophy, which is especially important for understanding James. The best overall account of James's philosophy and psychology is in Gerald E. Myers, *William James: His Life and Thought* (New Haven: Yale University Press, 1986). Another fine critical exposition is found in Ellen Kappy Suckiel, *The Pragmatic Philosophy of William James* (Notre Dame: University of Notre Dame Press, 1982). *The Cambridge Companion to William James*, edited by R. A. Putnam (Cambridge: Cambridge University Press, 1997), contains stimulating, thought-provoking essays by the leading James interpreters. The following two books do a good job of bringing out James's mysticism, which is ignored by most commentators: Eugene Fontinell, *Self, God, and Immortality: A Jamesian Investigation* (Philadelphia: Temple University Press, 1986); and Henry S. Levinson, *The Religious Investigations of William James* (Chapel Hill: The University of North Carolina Press, 1981). T. L. S. Sprigge's *American Truth and British Reality* (Chicago: Open Court, 1993) gives an in-depth account of James's philosophy by contrasting it with that of his arch philosophical enemy, F. H. Bradley. Russell B. Goodman's *Wittgenstein and William James* (New York: Cambridge University Press, 2002) is a fascinating account of the influence that James's *The Principles of Psychology* exerted upon the later Wittgenstein.

Index